the
sum
of
you

six forces
that make you
who you are

Alan Graham

Hodder Education
338 Euston Road, London NW1 3BH.

Hodder Education is an Hachette UK company

First published in UK 2011 by Hodder Education

This edition published 2011.

British Library Cataloguing in Publication Data: a catalogue record for this title is available from the British Library.

10 9 8 7 6 5 4 3 2 1

www.hoddereducation.co.uk

Typeset by Cenveo Publisher Services.

Printed in Great Britain by CPI Antony Rowe, Chippenham and Eastbourne.

Contents

Introduction

The sum of you

This is a book about numbers. But it is also a book about people and personality. They are more closely bound together than you might think.

For many people, their first interest in mathematics arises from a practical *need*: if you work on the questions and problems that crop up in your everyday life, you will discover mathematical methods and ideas that really help to answer many of your everyday problems. Alternatively, you may be interested in asking deeper and more abstract questions simply because you are curious about them. But, whatever your area of interest or your particular personality type, everyone asks questions that mathematics can help to answer.

This book explores the sorts of questions – both practical and curious – that many ordinary people are asking. It also enquires into the motivations and curiosities of a selection of mathematicians throughout history – after all, it was such human reflections and questions that gave rise to the various areas of mathematics in the first place. And if you look inside your own mind and consider what makes you curious about the world, you may find that these and similar questions represent the core of the person you are.

You may not be surprised to learn that your personality and personal interests will strongly affect which mathematical ideas you will be attracted to. It is this idea of knowing your core personality, and the mathematical ideas that connect to it, that is the starting point of this book.

So, before you read a word of mathematics, you are asked to begin by mapping your personality profile, using the following quiz.

The personality quiz

Here is a personality quiz for you to try.

When you have finished, carry on reading and all will be explained.

   (a) Look at each of the 40 statements. If the statement is true for you, enter '1' in the *shaded square* on the right. Otherwise leave all the squares blank.

	Personality quiz statements	A	B	C	D	E	F
1	I get cross about people dropping litter.					▦	
2	I enjoy taking photographs.		▦				
3	I enjoy meeting new people from different backgrounds.	▦					
4	I am fascinated by the lives of people in the past.	▦					
5	I like to explore the world of my imagination.	▦					
6	I'm interested in finding out how mechanical things work.	▦					
7	I sometimes look at clouds and trees and try to form shapes in them.		▦				
8	I enjoy debate and argument.						▦
9	When doing the lottery, I would feel I have to use the same numbers every time.			▦			
10	I have grown plants (in the ground or a pot or window box).					▦	
11	I am able to converse in a second language.	▦					
12	I enjoy white-knuckle rides at fairgrounds.				▦		
13	I occasionally paint, draw or knit for fun.		▦				
14	I'd prefer to live in a society that values justice higher than mercy.						▦
15	When gambling, a 'near miss' would make me think that if I keep playing I will win.			▦			
16	I prefer to walk across a busy road than to go 50 metres to a pedestrian crossing.				▦		
17	I prefer to trust reason rather than feelings.				▦		
18	I tend to drive faster than average.			▦			
19	I'm more interested in truth than winning arguments.						▦
20	I often cook by following a recipe.				▦		
21	I enjoy changing my appearance.		▦	▦			
22	I have tested the pH of my soil.				▦	▦	
23	I believe in fate.			▦			
24	I try hard to save energy in my home.					▦	
25	Often, in an idle moment, I doodle with a pencil.		▦				
26	I find it interesting to consider where people's religious beliefs come from.						▦

	Personality quiz statements	A	B	C	D	E	F
27	The search for an answer is often more important to me than the answer itself.						▓
28	I prefer to plan carefully rather than to improvise.				▓		
29	I have taken an evening class to learn something new.	▓					
30	My close friends think of me as a logical person.				▓		▓
31	I care a lot about the welfare of wildlife.					▓	
32	I care a lot about the effects on the planet of global warming.					▓	
33	I enjoy watching TV programmes on science and technology.				▓		
34	I try not to be a noisy person.					▓	
35	I often like to defy convention.	▓	▓				
36	I sometimes look at a word and wonder where it came from.						▓
37	I am a superstitious person.			▓			
38	When making judgements I try to look for evidence rather than going on a hunch.				▓		
39	I can imagine myself living happily in another country.	▓					
40	I enjoy going to galleries or sculpture parks.		▓				
	Total						

(b) Add up the numbers in each of the six columns, A to F, and write the totals at the bottom.

The six columns that you have just totted up refer to the following six personalities:

A = explorer
B = artist
C = gambler
D = scientist
E = environmentalist
F = philosopher

As you will shortly discover, the 30 chapters of this book have been organized under these same six headings. The categories do not represent six different people – they are six facets of human nature that exist in us all, to a greater or lesser degree.

You may be thinking, 'I never paint or sketch. I don't even own a spade! How can I be all these people?' But you don't need to paint to be able to see with an artist's eye and appreciate the beauty of forms and harmonies. You don't need to toil in the fields in order to be interested in how the natural world works and concerned about the health of our planet. By being a thoughtful, sensitive, curious human being, you are all of these people at the same time.

As you read this book, you should see how the big ideas of mathematics inform our ability to perform these life roles successfully. You should also get an insight into the nature of mathematics and so begin to see how and why mathematical ideas developed in the first place.

Just as you have many faces and moods, so too has mathematics. When it comes to calculating percentages and working out best buys, the mathematical mood is practical, with an emphasis on utility. But when you start to use mathematics to explore questions of pattern and structure, it is so much more. There is no limit to your curiosity, so mathematical ideas can let you soar like an eagle and explore the full range of your personality and imagination. Enjoy the view!

The six personalities

In this section you can find out more about the six facets of personality by reading about six interesting characters who embodied their qualities.

Explorer (Captain James Cook, 1728–79)

For most of us, our sense of cultural and national identity would have been very different had the earliest humans not made their migration 'out of Africa'. The impulse to explore is not simply the preserve of the fearless few but, over many millennia, has led to the mass movement of people as a whole. It is hard to imagine the bravery of these ordinary people as they walked, rowed and sailed across thousands of miles to seek a better life. Nevertheless, today when we say 'explorer', we think of the good and the great – men like Sir Francis Drake, Ferdinand Magellan, Vasco Da Gama, Christopher Columbus, for example. Yet it should be remembered that these adventurers were often motivated less by the desire to discover new lands for the common good than by a drive to plunder gold, silver, spices and slaves, impose their religion on the wider world and increase their own power and prestige.

Despite these misgivings, however, the many advances achieved in navigation, commerce, transport and cultural life owe much to the questing spirit of the human explorer. Take the case of James Cook, born in Marton in Yorkshire in 1728. At the age of 18 years, bored of shop work, he travelled to the port of Whitby to join the merchant navy as an apprentice. As part of his apprenticeship, Cook worked hard at his studies of algebra, geometry, trigonometry, navigation and astronomy – all skills that he would need later as captain of his own ships.

During the 1760s, Cook mapped the mouth of the St Lawrence River as well as the jagged coastline of Newfoundland. In 1766 he travelled to the Pacific ocean to observe and plot the path of Venus across the Sun. Between 1768 and 1779 he made three historic expeditions to take in Australia and to circumnavigate New Zealand (thereby proving that it was a separate land mass from Australia). In his journals, he and his accompanying scientists meticulously recorded a wealth of valuable scientific information. For example, in order to create accurate navigational charts of large areas of the Pacific, they made careful measurements of latitude and longitude. Although there was a well-understood method for measuring latitude at the time (a quadrant was used to measure the angle of the Sun or a star above the horizon), longitude was more difficult to measure. Based on his knowledge of navigation, Cook was able to make accurate measurements of longitude and advance human understanding of it, thereby making ocean travel safer and more reliable.

Cook was able to identify correctly the historical relationships among all the peoples in the Pacific, despite their being separated by thousands of miles of ocean. He and his travelling scientists collected more than 3,000 plant species, as well as making over 200 botanical drawings.

Artist (Leonardo da Vinci, 1452–1519)

Leonardo was born in the Tuscan town of Vinci. As the illegitimate son of a wealthy legal notary, he took his name not from his father but from the town of his birth – da Vinci means 'of Vinci'. He received a short education in Latin, geometry and mathematics but did not appear to excel academically.

At the age of fourteen, he was apprenticed to the artist known as Verrocchio and it was here that he learned about chemistry, metalworking, plaster casting, leather working and carpentry as well as drawing, painting, sculpting and modelling. Early in his apprenticeship, Leonardo worked with Verrocchio on a painting of the baptism of Christ. The story goes that his painting of an angel holding Jesus's robe was so superior to his master's efforts that Verrocchio set down his brush and never painted again. Of course, such stories are often apocryphal but in Leonardo's case, anything is possible!

Leonardo is perhaps best known today for two particular paintings – the *Mona Lisa* and the *Last Supper* – and his iconic drawing known as the *Vitruvian Man* (also known as the *Canon of Proportions* or simply *Proportions of Man*). This depiction of a man with arms and legs reaching out to touch the circumference of a circle was based on the writings of an ancient Roman architect, Vitruvius, who was fascinated by the connections between human and geometric proportion.

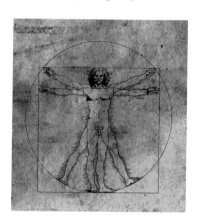

● **Figure 0.1** *Vitruvian Man*, Leonardo da Vinci.

There is no doubt that, as an artist, da Vinci was a genius. However, his talents didn't end there. Amongst his many achievements, he was also an outstanding musician, scientist, engineer, inventor, cartographer and mathematician. A question often asked is whether this sort of genius is born or made. The evidence of art history would suggest that Leonardo worked at his genius by developing his understanding in these diverse fields. For example, he made a close study of anatomy, coming close to achieving a full understanding of the circulation of blood. He also studied how rocks were formed, how drapery fell and he explored the mysteries of perspective, light and shadow. It is clear that this knowledge would have contributed to the brilliance of his paintings. What is less obvious is how painting was linked to his many other studies.

For example, he made highly sophisticated designs for several aircraft, a submarine and even an armoured car.

Da Vinci constantly tried to explain what he observed. Fortunately he wrote down and sketched in his notebooks many of his observations, some of which still exist. His systematic approach to experimentation and observation helped to lay the foundation for the modern (scientific) approach to human understanding of how the world works and how we perceive it.

Gambler (Nick the Greek, 1883–1966)

While there are a few professional gamblers able to make a decent living from their chosen profession, everyone else has to be resigned to the fact that gambling is really a mug's game. What keeps the professionals in business is that most of us refuse to admit the full extent of our losses, remembering only the occasions when our 'skill and expertise' at selecting an unknowable random number actually paid off. It seems that being good at gambling requires two key attributes. First, you need to understand the laws of probability and be able to apply that knowledge to situations where dice, coins and cards are generating those unknowable random outcomes. Second, you need to have nerves of steel, yet know when to quit.

One of the most celebrated professional gamblers and high rollers of the 20th century was Nicholas Andreas Dandolos, better known as 'Nick the Greek'. Born on the Greek island of Crete, Nick spent his adult years in the cities of Chicago and Montreal. From his late teens he was bankrolled with a generous allowance from his wealthy parents. He cut his gambler's milk teeth betting on horse races but his fame in gambling circles derived from his capacity to 'win big' and then, inevitably, lose it all again with impunity the following day.

During 1951 he took part in a sideshow event – a marathon two-player poker match held in public view, which was the forerunner to the modern-day World Series of Poker. His opponent, Johnny Moss, was 24 years his junior. After about five months of gruelling play, stopping only to eat and to sleep, the exhausted Nick finally left the table some $2.4 million down with the immortal words, 'Mr. Moss, I have to let you go.'

While attending a physics symposium, Albert Einstein stopped off in Las Vegas. He was met at the airport by Nick, who took Einstein around the Vegas casinos. Believing that his gambling friends may be neither familiar with, nor particularly impressed by the Nobel Prize-winning scientist, Nick is said to have introduced Einstein as 'little Al from Princeton', adding that he 'controlled a lot of the numbers action around Jersey'.

It is estimated that Nick won and lost over $500 million in his lifetime. He donated over $20 million (about $450 million in today's money) to educational and charitable organizations. In 1979, 13 years after his death, Nick and Johnny Moss were the first two players inducted into the Poker Hall of Fame. Despite his considerable wealth throughout most of his life, Nick was far from materialistic. According to a friend, on his death, the entire collection of his personal possessions could have been fitted into a shoebox.

Scientist (Florence Nightingale, 1820–1910)

Most people are familiar with the story of Florence Nightingale's crusade against the contagious diseases that were rife in the Scutari hospital during the Crimean War. A major problem for her was to convince the authorities that they needed to make fundamental changes in essential medical facilities, basic hygiene and the diet of soldiers in hospital. She had two main weapons at her disposal. First, she came from a wealthy upper-class family which moved in the highest echelons of Victorian society. So when she was denied the basic supplies and food that were needed, she could turn for support to influential friends like the then Secretary at War, Sidney Herbert. Second, she had her own private means and sometimes resorted to by-passing the military bureaucracy by purchasing the supplies she needed out of her own pocket.

Florence Nightingale's other great strength was that she was interested in, and keen to exploit, statistical information. Indeed, she became a formidable and respected statistician, pioneering a number of original and imaginative measures and forms of graphical representation. She managed, successfully, to unleash on a sceptical, male military world an array of well-researched and clearly presented statistics which changed attitudes and encouraged the institution of fundamental reforms.

Her 'data figures' showed mortality patterns clearly, demonstrating that when measures were taken to improve hygiene, mortality rates fell rapidly. In defiance of the military authorities, Florence Nightingale published her data and analyses. Not content with relegating the statistical sections of her reports to dusty shelves, she printed these off separately and circulated them to every Member of Parliament. It was the intuitive simplicity of the calculations and graphical representations that she herself devised – as well, of course, as her political shrewdness and rhetorical capabilities – that brought the needless deaths of wounded soldiers to the public consciousness.

Most of the accounts of her life and work confirm that Florence Nightingale cared passionately about the plight of others – particularly those too poor or sick to be able to fend for themselves. She took the view that the ruling classes of Victorian England (both in the military hierarchy and in government) were either unwilling or unable to see the truth about conditions in Scutari and elsewhere, unless presented with irrefutable evidence. Her main contribution to science was as a statistician and here she pioneered two key developments in scientific thinking. First, she needed data that she could trust. The data had to be accurate, comprehensive and comparable between hospitals and between regions. This resulted in her long-running campaign to standardize hospital record-keeping. Second, she was aware that most decision-makers were statistically illiterate and so tables of figures, however accurately compiled, were simply not winning over their hearts and minds. This led her to devise innovative diagrammatic and graphical representations of her data that demonstrated the underlying patterns in ways that no one could ignore.

Environmentalist (Sir David Attenborough, 1926–)

In this book, the word 'environmentalist' refers to a wide range of human endeavours. Amongst others, it takes in the farmer who has a practical and personal concern for crops, animals and the land, the biologist who makes a scientific study of the natural world, and the ecologist who is concerned with the relationships of living organisms to each other and their surroundings. Of all the species that play their part in this delicately balanced set of relationships, it is that pesky, upright-walking, consciousness-possessing mammal, homo sapiens, who has the greatest capacity to mess it up. It is tempting to suggest that the whole purpose of the life of any thinking person should be to try to come to terms with the relationship between themselves and the natural world around them. There is no better role model for such a thinking person than Sir David Attenborough.

Best known for his television documentaries on natural history, David Attenborough is a much loved and highly respected British broadcaster, writer and naturalist. As a child in Leicester, England, he filled his personal 'museum' with his collection of stones, fossils and animal skeletons. A particularly prized piece was given to him by one of his sisters – a chunk of amber containing several tiny prehistoric creatures. Fifty years later, this artefact became the centrepiece of his television programme *The Amber Time Machine*.

In 1945 Attenborough won a scholarship to Cambridge, where he studied geology and zoology and obtained a degree in Natural Sciences. After a spell in the navy, he joined the BBC in 1952 as the producer of a range of programmes including the quiz show *Animal, Vegetable and Mineral* and a series about folk music called *Song Hunter*. Having been told that his teeth were too big for him to play a role in front of camera, Attenborough remained behind the glass until 1954. When producing the programme *Zoo Quest*, his presenter Jack Lester was taken ill. At the last moment, Attenborough had to step into his shoes and the rest, as they say, is natural history.

In his early days of broadcasting, in keeping with the ethos of most television broadcasting at the time, Attenborough's natural history programmes were largely factual and were rarely used as vehicles for his own opinion. However, he was becoming increasingly aware of the mutual dependency between any one animal and the millions of other species of animals and plants around it. The implications were that, if you wanted to save a rhinoceros, you needed to save the environment in which it lived. Although he has always claimed to be 'not in politics', he has become an important campaigner for science and the promotion of environmental issues. In more recent times, he has argued that really unpopular political decisions can be taken only if the electorate is convinced of the value of the environment and that is what natural history television programmes should be for.

Inspired by Attenborough's blend of passion, wisdom and scientific knowledge, subsequent generations around the world are coming around to his view that an understanding of the natural world, and what's in it, is not only a source of great curiosity and fulfilment but also, in the long run, essential to our future survival.

Philosopher (Plato, c.428–348 BCE)

Exact details of Plato's birth are shady but it is believed that he was born to an aristocratic family in Athens between 429 and 423 BCE. He excelled in several fields, but particularly in philosophy and mathematics. His teacher and mentor was Socrates; Plato, in turn, was teacher to Aristotle. Together, these three great thinkers helped to lay the foundations of Western philosophy and science.

Plato is best known for his so-called Socratic dialogues – a collection of 36 dialogues (spoken conversational exchanges) and 13 letters, which have been used over many centuries to teach philosophy, logic, ethics and mathematics. In keeping with his ideas on beauty and goodness, Plato's name is associated with the idea of perfection in two modern usages. First, 'platonic love' refers to a relationship in which a 'beautiful' other person inspires one's mind and the soul and directs attention to spiritual rather than carnal thoughts. Second, in mathematics, the five 'platonic solids' are the five polyhedral shapes that have the property that all their faces are the same (these are the tetrahedron, cube, octahedron, dodecahedron and icosahedron).

As well as being a deep thinker about abstract ideas, Plato had much practical wisdom to offer about many aspects of human existence. Here are just a few of his gems.

On education:
- If women are expected to do the same work as men, we must teach them the same things.
- Ignorance is the root and the stem of every evil.
- Never discourage anyone … who continually makes progress, no matter how slow.

On laws and government:
- Laws are partly formed for the sake of good men, in order to instruct them how they may live on friendly terms with one another, and partly for the sake of those who refuse to be instructed, whose spirit cannot be subdued, or softened, or hindered from plunging into evil.

- The price good men pay for indifference to public affairs is to be ruled by evil men.

On argumentation:

- The partisan, when he is engaged in a dispute, cares nothing about the rights of the question, but is anxious only to convince his hearers of his own assertions.
- Wise men speak because they have something to say; fools because they have to say something.

On kindness:

- Be kind, for everyone you meet is fighting a hard battle.

On play:

- You can discover more about a person in an hour of play than in a year of conversation.

Debriefing the personality quiz
Exploring the six personalities

The **Explorer** personality is represented by questions 3, 4, 5, 6, 11, 29, 35, 39.

Typically, explorers are gregarious, interested in people from different backgrounds and from different ages in history. They are also willing to explore the world of their own imagination – something that will support a mathematical curiosity about numbers.

The **Artist** personality is scored on questions 2, 5, 7, 13, 21, 25, 35, 40.

Artists are not afraid to let their imagination run free and are generally willing to make the time to create a beautiful object. They tend to notice and indeed to seek out underlying patterns in the world around them. It is this interest in pattern that they share with the mathematician.

The **Gambler** can be identified with questions 9, 12, 15, 16, 18, 21, 23, 37.

These questions rate gamblers according to two characteristics. First they are risk-takers – perhaps the sort of person willing to eat those sausages from the back of the fridge, long after their sell-by date. Second, gamblers are prone to being superstitious and take a rather fatalistic view of life. The downside of this is that they may be susceptible to wheeler-dealers and conmen, which may put them at a disadvantage when it comes to gambling – an area where their intuitions may let them down. They should find that engaging with some basic ideas of probability will help them to challenge some of their faulty intuitions.

The **Scientist** personality is linked to questions 6, 17, 20, 22, 28, 30, 33, 38.

Scientists tend to be logical and methodical – they try to base their judgements on the evidence and are willing to take the trouble to design an experiment rather than jumping too quickly to a conclusion. When it comes to interpreting their evidence, scientists will take a particular interest in statistical ideas.

The **Environmentalist** personality is based on questions 1, 10, 11, 22, 24, 31, 32, 34.

Environmentalists can be characterized as 'issues' people, who express concern for plants, animals and the planet, but they are also prepared to put their ideas into practice in their everyday life. Like the artist, the environmentalist is intrigued by the beauty of the natural world and will look to a range of mathematical ideas to help understand and protect it.

Finally, the **Philosopher** personality is picked up in questions 8, 14, 17, 19, 26, 27, 30, 36.

Philosophers are interested in ideas and beliefs. They enjoy debate and will take the time to discuss some of the big existential questions such as 'Who are we?', 'Where do we come from?' and 'What's it all about?'. These are the sorts of questions that are well supported by mathematics in terms of its use of logic and its careful use of language.

How did you get on?

Clearly there is no single 'correct' personality type. We all have different interests and values and these are reflected in the patterns shown up in our personality profiles. Inevitably, our personalities are not set in stone, as our life view is affected by our health, our age, and the responsibilities we have to others (for example, to children and elderly parents). In putting together the quiz, I invited the participation of 27 friends and family members – 16 female and 11 male. I should say at the outset that 27 is too small a sample on which to form anything more than tentative conclusions. Also, the patterns that resulted may say more about the idiosyncratic views of my particular

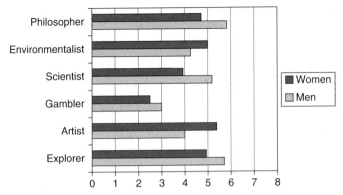

● Figure 0.2 Average score of each on each score for men and women.

friends and family than about the population as a whole. Nevertheless, a number of interesting features did emerge.

In some cases there were definite similarities between certain members of the same family (for example, my brother and I came up with almost identical charts). With other families this matching was less marked. There were some interesting comparisons by gender. The chart (Figure 0.2) shows the average score on each personality for men and for women. Based on my small, personal sample, the men emerged more strongly in four of the six categories, with a particular emphasis on philosopher and scientist, while the women showed up as artists.

Focusing on some particular statements in the quiz, the top score (24/27) was for number 3 (I enjoy meeting people from different backgrounds), closely followed by numbers 19 and 39 (both scoring 23/27).

The lowest score (4/27) was for statement 22 (whether they had tested the pH of their soil), closely followed by number 15 (When gambling, a 'near miss' would make me think that if I keep playing I will win), which scored 6/27.

Although the men and women were similar in many of their answers, there were also interesting differences. The women doodled much more than the men (94% compared with 27%) and they cared a lot more about global warming (94% compared with 55%). They were also more inclined to believe in fate (63% compared with 27%). A much higher proportion of men admitted to driving faster than average (64% compared with 13%). The men were also more inclined to believe that they could live happily in another country

(82% compared with 38%) and they were far more likely to dash across that busy road (73% compared with 31%). Another factor that showed up some differences was the age of the respondents; for example, the younger ones tended to show a greater interest in environmental matters.

Follow-up conversations with the respondents about the answers they had given raised interesting points. For example, statement 23 (I believe in fate) revealed that there are differing views about what we mean by fate. For some it was a sequence of predestined events that was inevitable and unchangeable (i.e. 'just meant to be'), whereas for others it was little more than a goal that they aspired to achieve.

There were a few surprises too. For a start, it is impressive how many of the respondents believed that their close friends think of them as being a logical person (22 out of 27).

Another statement that raised a smile was number 19 (I'm more interested in truth than winning arguments), which 23 of the 27 respondents agreed with. Well, all I can say is that I know these people and I just wish that this were even slightly true!

What do these personalities have to do with mathematics?

For many people, the idea of reading a book about mathematics would be a rather daunting prospect. One way of making your entry into the mathematical world more attractive to you is to focus on the aspects of mathematics that best match your interests. This is where these six personalities come in. For example, Shula took the personality quiz and found that she scored highly as an artist. With this in mind, she may be particularly interested in Chapters 6–10 (Part 2 of the book). Liddy's enthusiasm for different cultures gave her a score of 8 as an explorer, so she may find lots to interest her in the first five chapters (Part 1).

Of course it would be a mistake to feel that you are trapped by your personality profile. Andre's score of 3 in the artist questions made him feel that here was an area that he wanted to find out more about. He had a different motivation from Shula to work on Chapters 6–10 and so explore these relatively uncharted waters.

The explorer
Discovering my world

The explorer is curious about the world around him and actively tries to make sense of it. The first human explorer – our earliest ancestor – was operating largely in survival mode, trying to be a successful predator while at the same time avoiding being someone else's prey. But he has always possessed a drive to do things better and more efficiently. It is the questing spirit in all of us that first led the explorer to try to quantify his world.

It is likely that our early explorer's attempts to think mathematically were in response to grappling with questions such as 'how many' and 'how much'. Over the next five chapters you will learn about the evidence of archeology – animal bones some 30,000 years old that bear scratch marks suggesting a tally of some sort. This leads to questions about how and why counting developed into the form we know it today. But is it only humans who can count? You will find out about the prodigious counting skills of a chimpanzee called Ayumu, in a research institute in Japan, and discover whether the German horse, Clever Hans, really could calculate square roots.

Our early explorer of mathematical ideas was driven not just by questions of practical utility. He was fascinated by the patterns he observed in numbers and sought to find names to describe their properties – for example, square, triangular and prime numbers. Through considering questions about the Earth and its place in the wider universe, he found that he needed to extend his number system to accommodate very large and very small numbers. These big ideas also provided the platform for him to wrestle with ideas of infinity and religion. It was his response to these sorts of questions of both utility and curiosity that led our explorer, over many millennia, to lay down the foundations of mathematics as we know it today.

Chapter 1 • **Where numbers come from**, starts some 30,000 years ago and considers what sorts of questions might have first caused the early explorer to think that counting could be useful to him. A related and fascinating question is whether counting is a skill that only humans possess.

Chapter 2 • **Writing numbers: numbers through the ages**, looks at some of the ways in which numbers have been written down throughout history and shows why having a symbol for zero is so important.

Chapter 3 • **Calculating with numbers**, describes some of the ways that were devised to speed up calculations, including a mechanical device called a soroban and the invention of logarithms.

Chapter 4 • **Special numbers: introducing primes**, sees our explorer hang up his walking boots and explore the numbers in his imagination. Here he is concerned less with counting physical objects than with looking at the abstract patterns that can be formed by different sets of numbers. A key idea here is the prime numbers – a particular set of whole numbers that have been described as the building blocks of mathematics.

Chapter 5 • **Beyond our imagination**, sees our explorer thinking on a cosmic scale to look at the properties of the Earth and the universe that contains it. This causes him to wonder what sense he can make of a world in which time, space and numbers go on for ever.

Chapter 1
Where numbers come from

Music is the pleasure the human mind experiences from counting without being aware that it is counting.

G. Wilhelm Leibniz (German philosopher, mathematician and political adviser, 1646–1716)

Counting

It is interesting to speculate about where and how mathematical activity first began. At some point in pre-history, the early human explorer began to develop counting skills but, of course, with no written records we just don't know what form this may have taken or whether he had words for the numbers he used. Anthropologists have tried to get a handle on this question by working with isolated tribes whose lifestyles have not changed much over the last 20,000 years or so and investigating their number skills. For example, studies of the Pirahà people from the Amazonian rainforests of Brazil suggest that they have just three words for numbers – 'one', 'two' and 'many'. A popular linguistic theory suggests that we can only understand things that we have a language for – put simply, language is understanding. If true, this would imply that the Pirahà people's understanding of numbers above 2 or 3 would not be strong. Indeed, studies have shown this to be the case – when asked to copy numbers of objects, they could do so accurately up to three, but for four or more objects tended to make mistakes. Of course, this raises a further question: do the Pirahà have a limited understanding of number because they don't have a language for larger numbers, or is it the reverse? Does their language not include these words because they don't need them? These are murky waters! And, to be fair to the Piraha people, they are able to whistle their language when hunting in the jungle, which is more than most of us can do when on safari in our local supermarket.

Early counting

The earliest examples of counting are likely to have arisen from the need to keep track of possessions, of which livestock would have been an important component. Evidence from East Asia and Africa suggests that the first domestication of animals began about 15 000 years ago, with the dog. It took another 5 000 years for sheep and goats to become domesticated, shortly followed by pigs and cows. But it was only as recently as 4000 BCE, a mere 6 000 years ago, that the horse was first tamed by humans. As their acquisition of livestock expanded, early humans needed to keep these valuable possessions secure. This made counting a necessity, but not necessarily counting in the form that we know it today.

For example, imagine that you wished to round up all your sheep and place them safely in a pen overnight. How would you know next morning that they were all still there, without having counted them? A solution, and the one that was probably used by our earliest ancestors, was to create some sort of tally – perhaps by cutting notches on a stick or placing pebbles into a pot, where one notch or one pebble corresponded to a sheep. The following morning, as the sheep are led out of the pen, you simply check the passage of each sheep against your tally. If one is missing, then you know you can forget your plans for a leisurely swim that morning – you've got a job on!

● **Figure 1.1** A tally stick.

The earliest known counting stick dates back to around 35 000 BCE. It is known as the Lebombo counting stick as it was found in the Lebombo cave in South Africa. 29 notches were made in all, carved on a baboon's leg bone, but we can't be sure of their purpose – perhaps they were a count of some collection of prized possessions or marked the passing of time (maybe the number of days from one full moon to the next).

The earliest evidence of the use of numbers in Europe is a wolf bone discovered in what today we call the Czech Republic. It has 57 marks cut in 11 groups of five with two on the side. There has been much speculation as to why these tallies were made. One possibility is that it was some sort of lunar record made over a period of two months. But the truth is that we just don't know.

As already suggested, our knowledge about the early use of number derives from the evidence of artefacts that have survived to modern times. Fortunately, animal bones are highly durable; we can only speculate about other artefacts that have not survived. Come forward to 3000 BCE and to the settlements of a variety of people in Mesopotamia – a huge region occupied by modern-day Iraq, eastern Syria, south-eastern Turkey and south-west Iran. The reason we know about their mathematical understanding is that, remarkably, many thousands of inscribed clay tablets survived from that time. These tablets reveal a society rich in commerce and highly knowledgeable about astronomy. We are also able to deduce the form of their number system, which used the sexagesimal system (with a base of 60, rather than the 10 used in our decimal system today).

Counting today

In today's world, counting is the very first formal mathematical skill that most children learn. But what are they actually doing when counting out their toys or sweets? An analysis of successful counting reveals that it is a slightly more complicated procedure than might at first appear. In order to be able to count accurately, you need to have mastery of the following three key skills:

(1) knowing the names of the numbers and being able to recite them in the correct sequence;
(2) being able to identify each element in your set of counting objects once and only once;

(3) the skill known as one-to-one correspondence – being able to match each object in turn with your recitation of the numbers in sequence. You only need to observe a three-year-old trying to count fairly unsuccessfully to discover that one-to-one correspondence is even trickier than it sounds.

Which of the three counting skills listed above did our ancestors need when using the tally stick approach to counting?

Solution
They required skills (2) and (3) but not skill (1). So, if asked how many sheep were in the pen, they might have replied, 'All of them!', rather than, say, 'All 18 of them'. In other words, they could say whether or not all the sheep were present but would not know exactly how many there were.

There are still occasions today where full-blown counting with numbers is abandoned in favour of tallying. One example is when strings of prayer beads or rosaries are used to enable the faithful to recite prayers without omission. Another is when cricket umpires keep track of the number of balls bowled from each end of the wicket. After six balls are bowled from one end, the umpire calls 'over', the fielders move round and the next six balls are bowled from the other end. As you may imagine, after a long day in the 'field', the mind of the umpire can start to play tricks ('Now, was that the fourth ball or the fifth ball. . . ? Hmm, . . . not sure!'). In practice, most cricket umpires 'count' by placing six pebbles into one hand and, as each ball is bowled, transferring one pebble to the other hand. No explicit counting is involved – it's a question of moving another and another until all are transferred, at which point they know that the 'over' is over. Of course, they have to remember whether it is 'left hand to right hand' or the other way around but, hey, these are highly trained operatives!

Can animals count?

Humans are not the only species capable of counting. Many animals have a good awareness of 'more than' and 'less than'. For example, when one pride of lions hears the roaring of a neighbouring pride, they are able to make a judgement about the relative sizes of each pride and respond appropriately. If the other pride outnumbers them by more than three to one, they remain silent; otherwise, they roar back. Animals with large litters also know when one is missing. But it isn't clear whether these are examples of counting or of something else.

There is evidence that chimpanzees possess remarkable spatial awareness. In an experiment carried out in the Primate Research Institute in Kyoto, Japan, a chimpanzee called Ayumu was shown the numbers 1 to 8, randomly placed on a touch-sensitive screen. These numbers were visible for just under a second, after which they changed to small white squares. To gain his reward, Ayumu was required to touch the squares in the sequence 1 to 8 corresponding to the original positions of the numbers. Researchers were impressed to discover that Ayumu could perform this task as well as a small sample of Japanese children. But things took a remarkable turn in the next phase of the experiment. The time that the numbers were visible was progressively reduced – first 0.65 seconds, then 0.43 seconds, then 0.21 seconds and finally a mere 0.09 seconds (note that the average duration of an eye blink is between 0.3 and 0.4 seconds). Astonishingly, while the children's scores fell away considerably with these shorter times, Ayumu's performance remained at nearly the same level. What this suggested was that Ayumu had a prodigious photographic memory and spatial awareness, far surpassing anything that humans could manage.

Clever Hans, the mathematical horse

One of the most famous non-human mammals to demonstrate skills with number was the horse known as Clever Hans. His performances took place in Germany over several years, starting from around 1890. As well as being able to tell the time and name people in the audience, it seemed that Hans could perform amazing feats in mental arithmetic. His master, Wilhelm Von Osten, would invite mathematical questions

● **Figure 1.2** Clever Hans and his master Wilhelm Von Osten.

from the audience – perhaps a simple calculation such as, 'What is 4 added to 3?' Hans would then tap his hoof seven times. Later he progressed to tackling problems involving square roots and fractions!

So how did Hans manage to do it? It wasn't until 1907 that researcher Oskar Pfungst was able to work it out. Pfungst applied a series of carefully controlled tests, including putting blinkers on the horse so that he could not see his master. He discovered that the horse could only answer correctly when Von Osten himself knew the answer to the question. Eventually the full story emerged. By making a number of slight, involuntary body movements, Von Osten was cueing the horse when to start and when to stop tapping. Interestingly, not even Von Osten was aware that he was doing this!

Why is mathematics abstract?

People sometimes criticize mathematics by saying things like, 'The trouble with mathematics is that it is abstract'. Well, that's a bit like saying, 'The trouble with rain is that it is wet' or 'The trouble with knives is that they are sharp'. A feature of problems that crop up in the real world is that they are often highly complex. Mathematical solutions involve stripping away the complicating detail from everyday problems and applying mathematical tools to simplified 'models' of reality, a process known as modelling. Although modelling involves a loss of contextual detail, it provides many benefits, not least enabling known mathematical procedures to be brought to bear when solving problems.

A child's first exposure to this idea of abstraction occurs when learning about numbers. A great leap forward in our awareness of numbers is what is often referred to as grasping the 'threeness of three'. This means realizing that any set that contains three objects (whether it is three sheep, three pebbles, three jelly babies, etc.) has the same basic property – threeness. (Clearly, the same principle applies to the 'fourness of four', the 'sevenness of seven' and so on.) Understanding this abstract property of numbers allows us to give numbers a life of their own, removed from, and independent of, the particular set of objects that created them. And isolating numbers from any context provides the starting point from which abstract mathematical skills can really develop, enabling us to investigate patterns and properties of various subsets of numbers (even, odd, square, prime and so on). We can develop and apply a range of manipulative skills such as basic arithmetic (add, subtract, multiply and divide) as well as more advanced arithmetic (raising to a power, finding the square root, taking logarithms, and so on). Many of these number patterns and skills of arithmetic will be explored over the next few chapters.

The explorer invents numbers

In the 21st century, we often hear that overused phrase, 'Safety is our number one priority'. A similar philosophy would have defined the life of our earliest human explorer, but he may have substituted the word 'survival' for 'safety'. Where human activity is stripped down to little more than eating and avoiding being eaten, mathematical needs are fairly basic. Nonetheless, particularly where hunting, foraging and protecting his livestock were concerned, the earliest human must have explored his world needing to know about size (how big. . . ?) and quantity (how many. . . ? and how much. . . ?). It was from these most primitive of questions that the skills and language of counting and number first emerged.

Something for you to try

1 *Suppose you wish to count the number of children playing in a school playground. Which of the three counting skills listed in the 'Counting today' section would present difficulties in this situation?*
2 *Have a guess as to how Clever Hans was able to 'name' people in the audience.*

Solutions
1 *When counting large numbers of things (or children!) that are moving around, skill number 2 (being able to identify each element in your set of counting objects once and only once) would be difficult.*
2 *Apparently Hans spelt out their names one letter at a time, tapping his hoof to indicate each letter's position in the alphabet; impressive, but a snip compared with calculating square roots, which Hans could do at a canter!*

Chapter 2
Writing numbers: numbers through the ages

'Data! Data! Data!' he cried impatiently.
'I can't make bricks without clay.'

From *The Adventure of the Copper Beeches*,
a Sherlock Holmes story by Sir Arthur Conan Doyle,
first published in 1892

Fives and tens

Bearing in mind the basic design of a human hand, it shouldn't be too surprising that most number systems throughout history and around the world are based on tens and fives. As mentioned in Chapter 1, early examples of tallies were simply sets of short straight lines scratched (or cut as notches) on a hard surface.

Although less popular these days, tallies are still used. The commonest arrangement is in groups of five (drawn as four vertical lines and one diagonal), sometimes referred to as the five-barred gate. It can be thought of as holding aloft the four fingers with the thumb lying across them, indicating a count of all five fingers.

● **Figure 2.1** A tally of five.

The word *numeral* refers to how a number is written. The earliest systems of numerals were largely based on tallies. For example, the Egyptian number hieroglyphs (introduced around 3400 BCE) used single vertical strokes up to nine and then separate symbols for ten, 100,

1	10	100	1000

● **Figure 2.2** Egyptian symbols for 1, 10, 100 and 1000.

1000, and so on. The meanings of the symbols shown in Figure 2.2 are:

1 is a single stroke.
10 is a hobble for cattle.
100 is a coil of rope.
1000 is a lotus plant.

The usual ordering of the hieroglyphs was in descending order of magnitude, reading from right to left. An example showing the hieroglyphs for the number 1235 is shown in Figure 2.3.

● **Figure 2.3** Reading from the right: 1235.

Roman numerals

One of the few ancient number systems still recognized today is the Roman system. Roman numerals can be found on clock faces, in the credits of films and TV programmes to indicate their year of release, as page numbers in prefaces to books and in the names of kings and queens (for example, Elizabeth I, Louis XIV, and so on). The most common of the Roman numerals are:

Roman	I	V	X	L	C	D	M
Conventional	1	5	10	50	100	500	1000

A feature of the Roman numeral system is that the position of each symbol affects the overall value of the number. Where a lower-valued numeral immediately precedes a higher-valued one, the lower is subtracted from the higher. The reverse is true when the lower-valued numeral comes immediately after the higher-valued one. Thus:

IV is 4, whereas VI is 6
IX is 9, whereas XI is 11
XDII is 492, whereas DXII is 512

and so on.

One weakness of the Roman system of numerals is that it is not a convenient notation for performing calculations. For example, try adding DXXIV and XCVIII (i.e. 524+98). Now try multiplying them! A second drawback, and one shared by most of the early number systems, is that it doesn't include a symbol for zero.

Zero – a big fuss about nothing?

Suppose you were to place three pebbles into the hand of an ancient Roman or Egyptian mathematician and ask them how many pebbles they were holding. They would correctly tell you the number, 3. But had you then removed all three pebbles and asked how many they were holding, those mathematicians would have been stumped. Their answer would have been something like, 'I cannot say because I cannot count them'. The notion of zero as an abstraction is a relatively recent one, emerging only slowly in the modern world around 1500 years ago. Traditionally, the function of numbers was for counting and if there were no objects present, then counting could not take place. Yet zero was actually a very important invention for two reasons. First, as an extension of the counting numbers, it paved the way for a systematic development of negative numbers, fractions and decimal fractions. Second, it enabled the invention of a highly efficient and unambiguous way of writing down numbers. Before the invention of zero, it was unclear, except by context, whether a 3 followed by a 7 meant 3 tens and 7 units (37), or 3 hundreds and 7 units (307) or 3 hundreds and 7 tens (370), or something else! But with zero as a place-holder, these ambiguities disappeared.

The Hindu-Arabic system

Particularly over the past 50 years, with the rapid international growth of computers and calculators, the Hindu-Arabic system of numerals has become standard throughout most of the world. The Hindu-Arabic numerals are:

0 1 2 3 4 5 6 7 8 9

This system of numerals has evolved over time and represents a fusion of two systems. It began in the Indus valley of India over 2,000 years ago and was adopted and adapted in the Middle East some six or seven hundred years later, at which point the zero was included.

The character chosen to depict each number is based on the number of angles each numeral contains. This is not clearly evident in the printed numbers above, but the straight-line versions in Figure 2.4 show the angles more clearly. In the second line, the angles in the first five numerals have been marked with a dot). Clearly, the symbol for zero, having no straight lines, contains no angles.

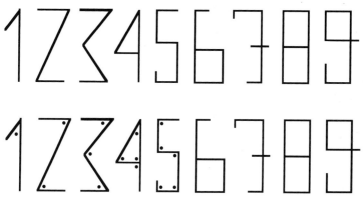

● **Figure 2.4** Straight-line versions of Hindu-Arabic numerals, showing how each one has its own number of angles.

If you write down a large four-digit number like 3072, you can only appreciate its value by being aware of the place value of each digit. Reading from left to right (in the order written) the place value of each digit in turn is thousands, hundreds, tens and units. So this number represents 3 lots of 1000, zero lots of 100, 7 lots of 10 and 2 lots of 1.

Confirming place value with a calculator
The previous statement may appear obvious, but sometimes a thing can be so obvious that you fail to see it! You can convince yourself that this all comes to 3072 by keying the calculation into a scientific calculator. (This won't work on a basic four function calculator because it performs the calculations in a different order.)

Using a scientific calculator, press:

$$3 \times 1000 + 0 \times 100 + 7 \times 10 + 2 \times 1 =$$

Confirm that you get the expected answer of 3072.

Counting numbers, whole numbers, integers

There is often a fair degree of 'terminological inexactitude' surrounding these three types of numbers: counting numbers, whole numbers and integers.

As you have already seen, the *counting numbers* are the numbers we count with: 1, 2, 3, 4, and so on. Let's keep these counting numbers and throw zero into the mix; we now have the *whole numbers*, which are: 0, 1, 2, 3, 4, and so on. Finally, keep the whole numbers and add all the negative whole numbers to get what are known as the *integers*. These three sets of numbers are illustrated pictorially as follows:

Counting numbers:

        ●   ●   ●   ●
        1   2   3   4 ...

Whole numbers:

      ○   ●   ●   ●   ●
      0   1   2   3   4 ...

Integers:

... ● ● ● ○ ● ● ● ●
   −3 −2 −1 0 1 2 3 4 ...

Just as ancient civilizations puzzled over the concept of zero, they struggled even more with the idea of negative numbers. Clearly it is hard to make sense of a negative number of objects, but the notion of negativity is useful when trying to quantify a debt (the earliest use of negative numbers has been linked to societies where ownership was a feature of their social organization). For example, if A has no chickens, then his assets, chicken-wise, are zero. If A then borrows three chickens from B, and consumes them, he still has no chickens in his possession but his chicken assets have fallen to −3.

Parts of a whole: fractions

If you start with any two integers, by adding, subtracting or multiplying them you will always end up with another integer. Mathematically, this idea is expressed by saying that the set of integers is *closed* to the operations of addition, subtraction and multiplication. However, the same property does not hold with division (i.e. sharing). When things don't share exactly this creates non-integers known as fractions.

In modern notation, a fraction is represented by two numbers separated by an oblique or horizontal line. The top number, or *numerator*, is the number of items to be shared, while the bottom number, or *denominator*, is the number of shares. So, for example, if three loaves are to be shared equally among 5 people, the fraction that each person will receive is written as $^3/_5$.

The ancient Egyptians based their notation for fractions on the idea of a mouth biting the whole into a certain number of parts. Thus the fraction $^1/_3$ was depicted

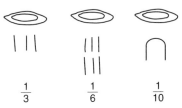

● **Figure 2.5** Egyptian fractions: the mouth at the top denotes a fraction.

by a mouth below which were three vertical lines; $^1/_6$ was a mouth with six vertical lines below, and so on.

While the Egyptian notation was creative, it did have one drawback – the depictions were restricted to fractions that had a numerator of 1; such fractions are called *unit fractions*. So how did the Egyptians depict a non-unit fraction like, say, $^3/_5$? You might think that they would write this as $^1/_5 + ^1/_5 + ^1/_5$, but in fact they had a strict rule for displaying any non-unit fraction: they were not permitted to use the same unit fraction more than once. But with a little investigation, you will discover that the fraction $^3/_5$ can be constructed by adding the unit fractions $^1/_2$ and $^1/_{10}$. (You can check for yourself that $^1/_2 + ^1/_{10} = ^3/_5$.) So, the ancient Egyptian depiction of the fraction $^3/_5$ was as shown here.

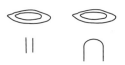

● **Figure 2.6** The Egyptian fraction $^3/_5$.

Decimal fractions

In the modern world, fractions are increasingly being replaced by decimal fractions, largely because they are more convenient and more machine-friendly. It was shown earlier in the chapter that place value describes the positional property of numbers (thousands, hundreds, tens and units). You will notice that each step to the right involves a division by 10. When dealing with integers, the right-most position is units. But these can be further subdivided into smaller bits. Keeping going with the 'divide by ten' pattern, this gives tenths ($^1/_{10}$), hundredths ($^1/_{100}$), thousandths ($^1/_{1000}$) and so on.

The decimal point is simply a marker to show where the units end and the tenths begin – in other words, it separates the whole number part from the fractional part. The decimal fraction for $^3/_5$ is:

0.6

Calculating with fractions is distinctly dull. However, as you will see in Chapter 3, once decimal notation has been fully understood, calculating with decimal fractions becomes a snip.

The explorer invents numerals

There was little point in our explorer making a count of the key items in his world if he was unable to remember afterwards how many there were or could not communicate this information to others around him. For this reason, having some form of written number notation became a necessity and so numerals were invented. When he needed to count well beyond the number of his fingers and thumbs, a more systematic and efficient notation was required than simply carving or scratching a series of lines. Such a system needed two features; first it needed to have the capability of keeping a record of 'how many'; but also it had to allow the manipulation of numbers of all sizes so that calculations could be carried out. It took many, many centuries for these features to evolve into the system we use today, which is based on the number ten and makes efficient use of place value by the strategic inclusion of that all-important zero.

1 *What number is represented by the set of Egyptian hieroglyphs below?*

2 *What fractions are represented by these Egyptian fraction hieroglyphs?*

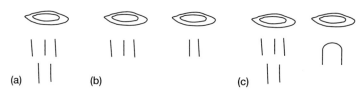

(a)   (b)   (c)

3 *If the number zero is removed from the set of whole numbers, what set of numbers are you left with?*

Solutions

1 The number 3247.
2 (a) $^1/_5$, (b) $^1/_3 + \frac{1}{2} = \,^5/_6$, (c) $^1/_5 + \,^1/_{10} = \,^3/_{10}$.
3 The counting numbers.

Chapter 3
Calculating with numbers

Ludwig van Beethoven had never mastered the elements of arithmetic beyond addition and subtraction. A thirteen-year-old boy whom he had befriended tried unsuccessfully to teach him simple multiplication and division.

Jan Ehrenwald

Why calculate?

Arithmetic, or performing calculations, is an essential feature of solving problems in our daily lives. These problems might crop up in a practical context (when shopping, budgeting for a family, paying tax, taking out a loan, pursuing a hobby, cooking or planning a garden, and so on) or in the course of exercising a general curiosity about the world ('I wonder why this works', 'Why is it shaped like that?', 'How can I pack this more efficiently?', and so on).

We have the choice of carrying out calculations with great precision, with answers given to many figures (perhaps using a computer or calculator), or keeping them rough and ready (maybe, as tradition demands, done on the 'back of an envelope') and therefore very approximate. The degree of precision you use will depend on two factors – the reliability of your input data and the precision requirements of the answer.

Calculating sensibly

Some may argue that there is no need to learn arithmetical skills these days since we can just leave it to the calculator and computer. However, this presents a dangerous scenario. For a start, all that a machine can do is perform a calculation – it requires the wisdom of the human to know which calculation to do and how to interpret the answer. Second, while these machines rarely break down, they are highly susceptible to human keying-in errors. Without basic estimating and checking skills, how would we know whether or not the answer 'seems about right'? Here are just some of the many examples where a failure to make sensible estimates or to check arithmetical procedures has had dire consequences.

- There are a number of documented cases where calculations of drug dosages have contained a misplaced decimal place. A drug that is ten times too weak is useless, but administer a drug that is ten times too strong and the consequences could be fatal.
- In 1998, the $125 million Climate Orbiter spaceship set off for Mars. Its trajectory was based on calculations compiled by a team of Lockheed Martin engineers. Unfortunately, while NASA operated with metric units, the Lockheed Martin team used Imperial units. The result: the Orbiter gradually went 60 miles off course before being obliterated in the Martian atmosphere.
- According to a *New Scientist* report published on 4 April 2001, a misplaced minus sign contained in the command software caused a jet fighter's control system to flip the aircraft on its back when it crossed the equator.
- Back in 1870, researcher Dr E. von Wolf published a finding that spinach had ten times more iron than other green leafy vegetables. This result came about from a misplaced decimal place (the iron levels of spinach are actually on a par with similar vegetables).

Developing the fourth example above, 1929 saw the arrival of the first Popeye strip cartoon, followed four years later by the first Popeye animated cartoon. The recurring theme was that eating lots of spinach gave Popeye big muscles, thereby enabling him to 'save his goyl' from the clutches of that dastardly Bluto. In 1937 a team of German scientists discovered the mistake, announcing that spinach had just one tenth the level of iron previously claimed.

However, this correction failed to percolate through to the general public, many of whom still encouraged their children to eat up their spinach and get big muscles like Popeye!

The need to calculate

It is easy to imagine how the 'four rules' of add, subtract, multiply and divide came into being. As our human explorer began travelling to ever more distant lands, his desire to exchange and barter for goods expanded. In the early stages of trading, all parties needed to agree on rates of exchange for goods; later these were replaced by an exchange system based on money, for which more complicated calculations were required.

Exchange rates

A relatively recent example of how exchange rates developed is the fur trade in North America, which began in the early 17th century. From the outset of trade, and until as late as 1820, the beaver pelt was the basic unit of currency. In 1820, a North American trapper could exchange one beaver skin for:

a kettle, or
1 pound of shot, or
5 pounds of sugar, or
12 buttons, or
20 fishhooks.

Six beaver pelts were worth a blanket, while 10–12 beaver pelts were required for a gun.
By the 1830s, dollars and cents had taken over as the main unit of currency. This enabled more subtle and complex exchanges to take place, as well as bringing a need for correspondingly more demanding calculations.

Calculating devices

Simple calculations can be performed mentally but as societies became more sophisticated the need arose for methods that were quicker and more accurate. The earliest calculating device was the counting frame or what, today, we refer to as the abacus. The earliest known abacus appeared around 2400 BCE in Babylonia and, over subsequent centuries, similar devices appeared in Egypt, Iran, Greece, China, India, Japan and elsewhere.

The Japanese abacus, called a *soroban* (literally, a 'counting tray'), was imported to Japan from China around 1600. Despite the availability of cheap, efficient modern electronic calculators, the soroban is still used in Japanese primary schools to help lay the foundations of children's mathematical development.

The layout of the soroban is based on tens and so matches the way that numbers are organized throughout most parts of the world. Reading from right to left, the columns represent the units (1s), 10s, 100s, 1000s and so on. Each column consists of one heavenly bead (worth 5) placed above the horizontal bar and four earthly beads (each worth 1) below it. The 'off' position is where the beads are pushed *away from* the bar; a number is entered by pushing the appropriate beads *towards* the bar.

● Figure 3.1
A soroban – the Japanese abacus.

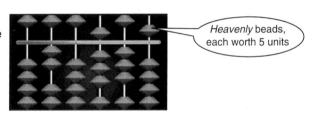

Heavenly beads, each worth 5 units

For example, in the soroban shown in figure 3.1:
- the right-hand column (the 1s) shows one heavenly bead in the 'on' position and all the earthly beads in the 'off' position, so this signifies $5 + 0 = 5$;
- the second from right-hand column (the 10s) shows the heavenly bead in the 'off' position, and three earthly beads in the 'on' position so this signifies 30;
- and so on.

See if you can carry on reading the soroban in the figure to identify the number represented. The answer is 20 835.

Of course, the soroban is more than just a means of representing numbers visually. It is principally an excellent aid to calculation. It should be fairly obvious how it can be used for addition and subtraction. There are also standard methods for performing multiplication and division, and indeed it can handle more complicated calculations such as finding square roots and cube roots. Japanese children use the soroban in primary school but at some point they are encouraged to put it away and use the 'virtual soroban' of their imagination.

Logarithms

John Napier (1550–1617) was born just outside the city of Edinburgh. He achieved considerable expertise in many fields, including mathematics, military invention, agriculture, astronomy and religion. He is best known today for his work on logarithms and how these can be used to speed up calculations, particularly the arduous operations of multiplication and division. By no means were all of Napier's needs for calculation based on questions of astronomy. One of his main interests was chronography, which involved making complicated calculations from information gleaned from the Book of Revelation to predict the date of the Apocalypse (he believed that the end of the world would occur in either 1688 or 1700).

The slide rule

Napier's principle of using logarithms of numbers to aid calculations lies at the heart of a neat device known as a slide rule. Slide rules were commonly used in secondary schools up until the 1970s. They were superseded by the electronic calculator.

● **Figure 3.2** A slide rule.

You don't need to have spent much time performing different calculations using just pencil and paper to realize that addition and subtraction are easier operations to perform than multiplication and division. The secret of Napier's invention is that, by turning numbers into logarithms, you can reduce multiplications to additions and divisions to subtractions. Here is a very simple illustration, based on the calculation 100 × 1000.

Calculation: 100 × 1000
Step 1: Rewrite the numbers as powers of 10. $10^2 \times 10^3$
Step 2: For multiplication, add the powers. $10^2 \times 10^3 = 10^5$
Step 3: Return the answer to a conventional number. $10^5 = 100\ 000$

Now let's try the same idea using more awkward numbers: finding 38 × 237.

Calculation: 38 × 237
Step 1: Rewrite the numbers as powers of 10. $10^{1.5798} \times 10^{2.3747}$
Step 2: For multiplication, add the powers. $10^{1.5798} \times 10^{2.3747} =$
        $10^{1.5798+2.3747} = 10^{3.9545}$
Step 3: Return the answer to a conventional number. $10^{3.9545} = 9005$

There are three points worth noting here:

(a) The first step where the numbers are turned into powers of ten is called 'finding the logarithm'. Since these numbers are expressed as powers of ten, this is referred to as finding a logarithm to base 10. For example, we say that the logarithm, to base 10, of 38 is 1.5798. This is written as: $\log_{10} 38 = 1.5798$. For those readers old enough to remember using a book of logarithm tables in school, this step involved looking up the numbers 38 and 237 in this book.

(b) The third step returns the power of ten to a conventional number. This is the reverse of finding the logarithm and is known as finding the antilogarithm (again, traditionally done using tables). Thus, $\text{antilog}_{10} 3.9545 = 9005$.

(c) The method is not perfectly precise. So, if you key 38 × 237 into a calculator, you'll find that the answer is 9006, not 9005. In general, the greater the number of decimal places used when finding the logarithms, the greater the precision of the result.

The need for calculation

It is a truism that travel broadens the mind. You only have to observe the different bath taps, toilet facilities and light switches in a foreign hotel to experience the sudden awareness that there are other ways of designing these objects. In societies of the past, where people tended to remain within their close communities and saw few visitors from outside, there was little need to develop their language or to consider whether there might be alternative ways of doing things. But our explorer changed all that; through barter and trade with other communities he found that he needed to improve his skills of counting, measuring and calculating. Making mistakes became ever more costly and all of these factors sowed the seeds for developing calculating aids like the soroban and the use of logarithms to speed things up.

Something for you to try

1 *Below are two soroban numbers before and after an addition has been performed. Identify each of the two numbers and deduce the calculation that was performed.*
   (a) Before.
   (b) After.

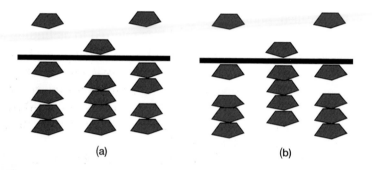

(a)   (b)

2 *How could the soroban be used to perform money calculations involving pounds and pence, or euros and cents, or dollars and cents?*
3 *Write down the logarithm, to base 10, of the following numbers:*
   10 000, 1 million, 10, 1, 0.01, 0.001

Solutions

1 *The 'before' and 'after' numbers are, respectively, 152 and 191. By subtraction, you can deduce that the added number was 39. So, the sum was: 152 + 39 = 191.*
2 *The position of the decimal point is arbitrary on a soroban. So, to enter money calculations to two decimal places using pounds, euros, dollars, etc, simply define the right-most column to be 0.01, its adjacent column to be 0.1 and the third column from the right to be units.*
3 *10 000 = 10^4, so $\log_{10} 10\,000 = \log_{10} 10^4 = 4$.*
   1 million = 10^6, so $\log_{10} 1$ million $= \log_{10} 10^6 = 6$.
   10 = 10^1, so $\log_{10} 10 = \log_{10} 10^1 = 1$.
   1 = 10^0, so $\log_{10} 1 = \log_{10} 10^0 = 0$.
   0.01 = 10^{-2}, so $\log_{10} 0.01 = \log_{10} 10^{-2} = -2$.
   0.001 = 10^{-3}, so $\log_{10} 0.001 = \log_{10} 10^{-3} = -3$.

Chapter 4
Special numbers: introducing primes

Prime numbers are what is left when you have taken all the patterns away.

From Mark Haddon, *The Curious Incident of the Dog in the Night-Time*, 2003

Curious

Haven't you often marvelled at how ontogeny so often recapitulates phylogeny? Not often? Then you are probably not alone, as these are rather esoteric terms! But the phrase 'ontogeny recapitulates phylogeny', which was first used in the 19th century by German zoologist Ernst Haeckel, actually encapsulates a very interesting idea

The word *phylogeny* describes how a whole species develops. *Ontogeny* refers to the growth and development of an individual member of that species. The clever-sounding phrase 'ontogeny recapitulates phylogeny' usually refers to how children's learning and development, over just a few short years, often have interesting parallels with the way human understanding has developed over many millennia. This is particularly true in areas such as mathematics, where we often observe in children similar developmental processes to those undergone by past generations when the ideas were first invented. Indeed, many successful teaching programmes in mathematics work so well *because* they recapitulate the development of these ideas by our ancestors.

Even, odd, square, triangular

It was observed in Chapter 1 that, from a learner's perspective, numbers eventually start to take a life of their own, independent of the context in which they were first used. For thousands of years, the human explorer has been curious about the many patterns that numbers possess and has sought to organize them into interesting sets.

So, run your mind back a few thousand years and imagine that you are a number-curious early human with a pile of pebbles or seashells to hand. You pick up eight pebbles and discover that you can arrange them in two equal rows of four. You try the same with six pebbles and again you get two equal rows.

But with 7 pebbles, after two equal rows have been formed, you are left with an 'odd' one. The same thing happens with 5 and 9 and 11 pebbles. What you have observed is a fundamental property of whole numbers – they are either *odd* or *even*. Specifically, numbers like 8 are exactly divisible in two but odd numbers cannot be split in this way.

However, our early explorer did not stop there. With his pile of pebbles, he would have been curious to see what other patterns could be made. For example, 4, 9, or 16 pebbles will make a perfect square. These numbers are part of the set of square numbers (1, 4, 9, 16, 25, . . .).

Some numbers can form triangles – for example 3, 6, 10 and so on. These are part of the set of triangular numbers (1, 3, 6, 10, 15, …).

● **Figure 4.1** Eight pebbles can form two equal (even) rows of 4.

● **Figure 4.2** With seven pebbles there is an 'odd' one over.

● **Figure 4.3** These nine pebbles form a square, showing that 9 is a square number.

● **Figure 4.4** Ten shells form a triangle, showing that 10 is a triangular number

Rectangular and prime

Most whole numbers can be arranged into a rectangular shape. For example, 12 shells can be arranged as four rows of three, three rows of four (as shown here), two rows of six or six rows of two. Whichever way you want to arrange them, 12 is a rectangular number. Since all squares are also rectangles, the set of square numbers belongs to the set of rectangular numbers.

Thinking in terms of its number properties, a feature of any rectangular number is that it can be split up into *factors* – for example, 12 can be arranged as 4×3, 3×4, 6×2, 2×6, 12×1 or 1×12. This particular number can even be split into *three* factors, $2\times2\times3$. (Note: another name for a rectangular number is a composite number – so called because it is composed of two or more factors.)

● **Figure 4.5** Twelve arranged as three rows of four.

But there is one set of whole numbers that cannot be arranged as just described. They include 2, 3, 5, 7, 11 . . . Try as you might, these numbers of pebbles cannot be arranged in a rectangular pattern. All you can do is lay them out in a straight line. These very special numbers are known as prime numbers.

This particular feature of prime numbers – their 'non-rectangularity' – means that they cannot be further factorized. In fact, the usual definition of a prime number is that it is a number with exactly two factors – itself and 1.

● **Figure 4.6** Five shells can only form a line, showing that 5 is a prime number.

So what's the big deal about prime numbers? Prime numbers have occupied a special place in our hearts for the very reason that they cannot be further subdivided (i.e. factorized).

As mentioned earlier, a composite number like 12 can be broken down into its prime factors (2×2×3) but will go no further. So, primes have been considered to be the fundamental building blocks of our entire number system and mathematicians from the earliest times have been intrigued to explore their properties.

Picking out primes

One of the timeless questions of mathematics has been whether it is possible to come up with a formula for identifying prime numbers. Meet Eratosthenes of Cyrene, a mathematician in the 3rd century BCE, who had already made his reputation by calculating, with great precision, the length of the Earth's circumference (for more details of this story, see Chapter 5). He was also interested in prime numbers and wanted to find a systematic way of listing them. He invented a simple 'sieve' for scooping out the composites from the counting numbers, leaving behind just the primes. It works as follows:

(1) Write out the counting numbers in a table (in the example below I have listed the numbers from 2 up to 99).
(2) Start with the 2, leave it untouched and cross out each subsequent number that is divisible by 2.
(3) Identify the next available number, the 3, leave it untouched and cross out each subsequent number that is divisible by 3.
(4) Identify the next available number – note that the 4 has already gone, so this is the 5 – leave the 5 untouched and cross out each subsequent number that is divisible by 5.
(5) Continue in this way until all the composites are eliminated. What remains are the prime numbers (in the shaded boxes in Figure 4.7).

	2	3	4	5	6	7	8	9
10	11	12	13	14	15	16	17	18	19
20	21	22	23	24	25	26	27	28	29
30	31	32	33	34	35	36	37	38	39
40	41	42	43	44	45	46	47	48	49
50	51	52	53	54	55	56	57	58	59
60	61	62	63	64	65	66	67	68	69
70	71	72	73	74	75	76	77	78	79
80	81	82	83	84	85	86	87	88	89
90	91	92	93	94	95	96	97	98	99

● **Figure 4.7** Eratosthenes' sieve for identifying the primes.

Unspeakable numbers

It is hard to overestimate the power that numbers have held throughout history. At various times and in different cultures, certain numbers have been lucky, unlucky, holy, tainted, evil, and so on. One group of mathematicians who took their numbers very seriously were the Pythagoreans (c.525 BCE), a highly secretive Greek order that was devoted to the study of mathematics and religion. They believed that numbers ruled the universe and that numbers were therefore endowed with mystical and spiritual qualities.

Before the full implications of Pythagoras' Theorem had kicked in, the Pythagoreans were comfortable with the idea that all numbers were 'rational' – i.e. that they could be written as a ratio of one whole number divided by another. For example, consider the numbers 5½, 7 and 8.23. These are all rational numbers because:

5½ can be written as $^{11}/_2$
7 can be written as $^7/_1$
8.23 can be written as $^{823}/_{100}$.

However, it is possible to create numbers that do not have this property. For example, calculations involving the lengths of sides of right-angled triangles introduce a new type of number that doesn't follow this pattern.

The Pythagoreans considered the following question: How long is the hypotenuse of a right-angled triangle if the lengths of the shorter sides are both equal to 1? According to Pythagoras' Theorem, the answer is found as follows:

(1) Square and add the two shortest sides, giving $1^2 + 1^2 = 1 + 1 = 2$.
(2) The length of the hypotenuse (the side opposite the right angle) is the square root of the answer, $\sqrt{2}$.

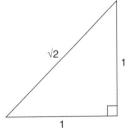

So, the length of this third side must be a number that, when squared, gives the answer 2. But there is no rational

● **Figure 4.8** A right-angled triangle with a hypotenuse of length $\sqrt{2}$.

number that, when squared, gives 2 – so what sort of numerical Frankenstein had they created?

The square root of 2 (written as √2) is an example of what today is called an *irrational* number – its decimal value goes on forever and there is no repeating pattern in the digits. Expressed to 20 decimal places:

$$\sqrt{2} = 1.41421\ 35623\ 73095\ 04880...$$

Most square roots are irrational (for example √3, √5, √6, √7, . . .), so the Pythagoreans had uncovered a whole class of numbers that called into question their notion of the numerical harmony of the universe. So upset were they by these numbers that they were sworn to secrecy about their discovery. The Pythagoreans referred to them (privately, of course) as *alogon*, which means 'unspeakable'. The story goes that a certain Hippasus of Metapontum (born c.500 BCE) was able to demonstrate to the Pythagoreans that the square root of 2 was irrational and therefore that such numbers must exist. Unfortunately he made one fatal error with his proof – he presented it on board a ship at sea and when outnumbered by a group of Pythagoreans. The story goes that he was thrown overboard by the Pythagoreans who didn't like sharing their mathematical secrets. And anyway, nobody likes a smart Alec.

The explorer uncovers prime numbers

Not all exploration involves a long and arduous physical trek in walking boots and carrying a backpack and compass. In this chapter, our explorer has set off on a journey of his imagination, driven only by a desire to uncover patterns in the properties of numbers. Just as the human mind seems drawn to regularities in shape, colour, musical pitch and rhythm, so number patterns hold a fascination for the curious mind. Some of the more obvious number properties include even, odd, square, triangular, cube, and so on. But where do prime numbers fit into this figure? As the narrator remarks in Mark Haddon's *The Curious Incident of the Dog in the Night-Time*, 'prime numbers are what is left when you have taken all the patterns away'. Because prime numbers cannot be further subdivided, they can be thought of as the building blocks of our whole number system and represent one of the really big ideas in mathematics.

1 Can you think of an even, prime number?
2 Why, according to the definition of a prime number given in this chapter, is the number 1 not prime?
3 The number 8 has an even number of prime factors (there are four: 1, 2, 4 and 8). Which set of numbers has an odd number of factors?

Solutions

1 The only even prime is 2.
2 If we define a prime as 'having exactly two factors, itself and 1', the number 1 fails this test as it has only one factor.
3 The number 4 has an odd number of factors (three of them: 1, 2 and 4) as has the number 16 (five of them: 1, 2, 4, 8, 16). The set of numbers with an odd number of factors is the set of square numbers. Why is this so? If you imagine arranging the factors of a number in pairs, the number's square root is counted only once and so is the odd factor over.

Chapter 5
Beyond our imagination

> *The church says the Earth is flat, but*
> *I know that it is round, for I have seen*
> *the shadow on the moon, and I have more*
> *faith in a shadow than in the church.*
> Ferdinand Magellan (Portuguese navigator
> and explorer, 1480–1521)

The Earth is round

According to the popular Gershwin song of the 1930s, 'They all laughed at Christopher Columbus, when he said the world was round.' Of course, the Earth *is* round – or more correctly, it is spherical – and in fact there are very few flat-Earthers (known as *planists*) any more, largely because there is so much evidence to the contrary.

For most people, the mathematics that they learned in school was largely contained within the pages of their textbook. It is important to remember that the impulse for many of the discoveries of mathematics was the curiosity of people with adventurous spirit, thinking about big questions that relate to planet Earth and the universe in which it is located. And the only sensible way for the explorer to test whether his theories were true was to go out and collect evidence. As you will see, these and similar questions prompted the invention of numbers so large that they are truly unimaginable.

Can you think of an experiment that might demonstrate to a flat-Earther that their theory was incorrect? One such experiment is described below.

The Bedford Level experiment

In the summer of 1838, Samuel Rowbotham, then president of the Flat Earth Society, conducted a classic experiment to demonstrate the truth of his society's theory. He chose a 6-mile stretch of a slow-flowing drainage canal that ran in an uninterrupted straight line as part of the old Bedford River in Norfolk. Rowbotham stood in the middle of the river looking through his telescope, which he held 8 inches above the water, to observe a boat with a 5-foot mast rowing away from him. Rowbotham 'observed' that the mast remained in clear view for the full length of its 6-mile journey, thereby demonstrating that the Earth was flat. According to the alternative spherical Earth theory, this could not have occurred. In fact, given the known curvature of the Earth's surface, the top of the mast should have been roughly 11 feet below his line of sight.

Now, from a sphericist's perspective, this was a rather surprising result and, in 1870, a qualified surveyor, Alfred Wallis, decided to repeat the experiment. Avoiding Rowbotham's errors and with a more impartial eye, Wallace came up with a quite different result, demonstrating that the boat's mast did indeed sink out of view.

● **Figure 5.1** The middle pole was higher than the other two.

In another experiment on the same stretch of river, three poles were fixed at equal heights above the water level, along the length of the canal. It was found that, when they were viewed through a theodolite from a sideways perspective, the middle pole was roughly 3 feet higher than the other two, thereby demonstrating the curvature of the Earth.

These demonstrations proved to be the final kiss of death for the theories of the flat-Earthers and in the early 20th century the three-pole experiment was often carried out by schoolchildren to demonstrate this important fact about the shape of our planet.

How big is the Earth?

Here's a question for you to ponder. How would you set about measuring the size of the Earth? In the 21st century, with the benefit of established air routes, global positioning satellites and search engines like Google, this is not such a difficult question. However, go back just over two thousand years to the time of Eratosthenes of Cyrene (whom you met in Chapter 4) and imagine how he might have set about finding the answer.

He came up with the following extremely elegant solution. He selected two towns that were a considerable distance apart, Syene (today known as Aswan) and Alexandria. In Syene, on the day of the summer solstice at midday, he observed that the Sun shone straight down a vertical well, indicating that it was directly overhead. On the same day of the year at exactly the same time, a measurement was taken of the angle of the Sun in Alexandria. This was done by measuring the length of the shadow cast by a tall tower of a known height. The Sun's angle was worked out to be one fiftieth of a complete circle (that's 7.2° in today's terms).

It's worth spelling out some of the background to this method. Unlike Samuel Rowbotham some two thousand years later, the ancient Greeks were aware that the Earth was (almost exactly) spherical – a fact that was central to Eratosthenes' calculation. Also, the two towns he chose were eminently suitable. For one thing, Alexandria lay due north of Syene, which was another essential factor in the calculation. For another, not only did Syene possess a deep well but also at Alexandria there was a very tall column, which was convenient!

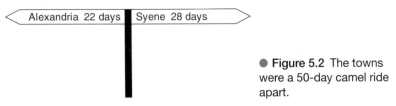

● **Figure 5.2** The towns were a 50-day camel ride apart.

All that remained was for Eratosthenes to work out the distance between the two towns – again not a trivial task. It was known that a camel train would take 50 days to complete this journey. Camel trains typically travel a distance of 100 stadia per day, so the towns were roughly 5000 stadia apart. (Note: a 'stade' was the length of a public stadium.)

From this information, Eratosthenes could calculate that the total circumference of the Earth was $5000 \times 50 = 250\,000$ stadia, which comes to approximately 39 250 km. Bearing in mind the many potential sources of error in his method (the measurement of the angle of the Sun and the distance between Alexandria and Syene, to name just two), this wasn't a bad estimate – the modern Figure is roughly 39 840 km, so his figure represents an error of about 1.4%. (Note that we can only provide an approximate calculation for the circumference of the Earth because our planet is not exactly spherical and the answer rather depends on where you choose to measure it.)

Eratosthenes (276–c.195 BCE)

Eratosthenes was born in Cyrene (in modern-day Libya). He was a Greek mathematician, who excelled in many fields including poetry, astronomy and the theory of music. He also invented the discipline of geography, making several important discoveries including the invention of a system of latitude and longitude and the creation of a map of the world. During his lifetime he was given the nickname 'Beta' (the Greek letter 'B') because he was reckoned to be the second best in the world in almost any field! He was a close friend of Archimedes (famed for his 'Eureka' moment in the bath) and, like Archimedes, made important contributions to mathematics and science.

Infinity

Most of us, at some point in our childhoods, have stared into the night sky and pondered those great unanswerable questions:

Is there an end to the universe?
Will time go on forever?
When did time start?

These and similar questions relate to the infinite and this is where religion and mathematics can become intertwined. There are corresponding questions that apply to numbers. For example, whenever you get to the biggest whole number, there must always be another one (simply add 1!), so you can never get there. The mathematical symbol used to represent infinity is ∞, which is the number 8 on its side. I like to think of it as a racetrack with no beginning and no end.

Infinities crop up everywhere in mathematics. You have already seen in Chapter 4 that a feature of irrational numbers is that they possess an infinite number of decimal places. Other numbers whose decimal expansions go on to infinity include π (the Greek letter, pi) and the mathematical constant e. (The story of π is told in Chapter 7.)

For many children, their first inkling of infinity in the mathematics classroom crops up when they are dividing by fractions:

Let's start by dividing 1 by a half: $1 \div \frac{1}{2} = 2$.
Now make the fraction smaller: $1 \div \frac{1}{20} = 20$.
Make the fraction smaller again: $1 \div \frac{1}{200} = 200$.

The underlying pattern here is that, when dividing by a fraction, the smaller the fractional divisor, the larger the answer. Let's extend this principle. It would appear to follow that, if the divisor is so small that it equals zero, the answer will be infinitely large. Expressed mathematically, this would mean that:

$$1 \div 0 = \infty$$

However, it is not quite as simple as that. In mathematics, division by zero can create problems and absurdities, as the following logical fallacy demonstrates.

A fallacy based on dividing by zero

We know that multiplying any number by zero gives zero, so:

$0 \times 1 = 0$ and $0 \times 2 = 0$.
Therefore, $0 \times 1 = 0 \times 2$.
Dividing both sides by zero: $\frac{0}{0} \times 1 = \frac{0}{0} \times 2$.
Cancelling the zeros: $1 = 2$.

Now clearly 1 does not equal 2, so there must be a fallacy in this argument. It is fallacious because of the division by zero. For reasons that should now be apparent, the operation 'division by zero' is to be avoided in mathematics. However it is valid to state that, when dividing 1 (or any positive number) by a fraction, *the answer will approach infinity as the fraction approaches zero*.

Really big numbers

The mystery of infinity has been a source of intense speculation and exploration for many thousands of years. One civilization that has always had a passion for very large numbers is India. It was largely the desire to explore beyond the 'calculable' physical world that led early Indian mathematicians to discover the place value system and so gain a better mathematical understanding of the idea of infinity. Their word *asankhyeya* means, literally, 'a number that is impossible to count'. More poetically, it is described as 'the sum of all the drops of rain which, in 10 000 years, would fall each day on all the worlds'.

A question I like to ask children is, 'What is the largest number of objects that you can think of?' Some come up with the number of seconds you've been alive or the number of insects on earth or perhaps the number of stars in the sky. Others say the number of grains of sand on the shore or in the Sahara desert. To get really large numbers, however, you need to reduce your counting objects to the size of atoms. For example, a 70 kg human body would contain approximately 7×10^{27} atoms. That is, 7 followed by 27 zeros:

7 000 000 000 000 000 000 000 000 000

Even larger is the number of atoms in the observable universe, which is of the order of 1 followed by 80 zeros. In order to communicate the very large and the very small, a different format for writing down numbers is required. Scientists use a form known as *scientific notation*, which is explained in Chapter 16.

The word *googol* is the large number 10^{100}, or 1 followed by one hundred zeros. The term was coined in 1938 by the nine-year-old nephew of American mathematician Edward Kasner. Counting at a rate of two numbers per second, it would take you approximately 10^{90} centuries to get to the end of a googol!

Back in 1997 the pioneers of a little-known search engine called BackRub decided that it needed a new name. Eventually, after considerable discussion, they went with Google, which was a play on the word 'googol'. This choice reflected the seemingly infinite number of items of information that was appearing on the web.

In more recent times, as mathematical fields have become ever more diverse and computing power has increased exponentially, mathematicians have come up with even larger numbers than a googol. A googolplex is 10 raised to the power of a googol. Don't try this at home, but if you were to write down a googolplex in conventional notation, you would need more paper than could be contained within the entire known universe!

Some big questions

It seems to be a defining characteristic of humankind to want to ask fundamental questions about space, time, the Earth and the universe. Now clearly, it isn't too hard to make up out of your head a theory about how the world works. Whether or not your theory is true will depend on how well it is supported by the facts. We can presume that it was the impulse to test his theories (rather than simply accept them at face value) that drove our explorer to get out there and collect relevant evidence. In this chapter, the explorer has asked questions about the size and shape of planet Earth and tried to find ways of measuring it. He has contemplated the notion of infinity and considered how it might be accommodated into his wider understanding of the number system.

Something for you to try

1 *Based on information available today, what evidence is there that the Earth is spherical?*

2 *What is the largest number that a scientific calculator is capable of handling?*

3 *The factorial of the number 5 is $5 \times 4 \times 3 \times 2 \times 1$, which comes to 120. It is written 5! (i.e. 5 followed by an exclamation mark). Factorials are normally applied only to positive whole numbers. What is the largest factorial that a scientific calculator is capable of handling?*

4 *A quadrillion is 10^{15}. Which of the following numbers are equal to a quadrillion?:*
a million billion, a billion million, a thousand million million, a thousand trillion.

Solutions

1 There is plenty of evidence in today's world that the Earth's surface is curved. For example:

Look carefully at the horizon and you will see that it is slightly curved – try taking a digital photo of it and then superimpose a grid on the computer screen to see the curve.

As Magellan observed 500 years ago, on the occasions when you can see the Earth's shadow on the surface of the Moon, you will observe that the shadow is circular.

Photographs of the Earth from space reveal its true spherical shape.

When you observe a ship sailing away from you, it gradually disappears from view – the last thing you see is the tip of its mast. Of course, in past times, this sort of evidence was not always available or accepted.

2 The answer may vary slightly between different models of calculators but they should all be able to handle numbers just less than a googol (my calculator will accept 9.9999999×10^{99}, but gives an error message for anything larger.)

3 The largest factorial that a scientific calculator can handle is 69! which has a value of roughly 1.71×10^{98}. The numerical value of 70! is just larger than a googol and entering this factorial will generate an error message on your calculator.

4 All of them.

Be an explorer

They say that travel broadens the mind. Certainly, an important part of being an explorer is the opportunity that travel provides to learn about other cultures, to come into contact with the questions they are asking and to see the sorts of answers that people from different backgrounds come up with. Living in the 21st century means being part of an increasingly multi-cultural community, and so you don't need to travel far to find people whose backgrounds are very different from yours. We can 'broaden our minds' without having to make very much effort. Along with an awareness of these other 'ways of seeing' will come ideas that stimulate and inform your mathematical understanding. For example, what do you know about the mathematical structures in Islamic art, Russian peasant multiplication, body counting systems from Africa and elsewhere, the Chinese board game *Pong hau k'l*, the mathematics of drumming, Celtic knots. . . ?

The artist
Exploring patterns

The visual artist is fascinated by pattern and colour, by texture and perspective, by light and shadow. We may never know what inspired the artist to paint images on the walls of his cave in the Haute Garonne region of France some 32 000 years ago. Since many of these caves were not inhabited at the time (indeed, many of them were well off the beaten track) we can only suppose that his work had some ceremonial or religious purpose. But whatever the impulse for these paintings, it would seem that the artist's drive to find within him some sort of artistic expression has a very long history.

However, you don't need to be skilled in painting or drawing, in music or in pottery to be able to see the world in an artistic way and appreciate the beauty of forms and harmonies. The artist is a close observer of patterns, always trying to describe them and identify their general properties. Indeed, many of the big ideas of mathematics came about as a result of questions posed by the artist and these two ways of seeing the world are closely bound together.

Chapter 6 • **Symmetry**, looks at issues to do with the balance inherent in objects such as the human face and raises the question of how our perception of beauty might be linked to ideas of symmetry.

Chapter 7 • **Drawing circles: the story of pi**, explores a central property of all circles, namely that they all possess the same shape, and looks at what is so special about circles that makes them all look the same. This is a question that has fascinated the artist for thousands of years and led to the discovery of a remarkable number, pi.

Chapter 8 • **Keeping in proportion: the golden rectangle**, takes further what is meant by the phrase 'the same shape', looking at ideas of proportion, scale factor, aspect ratio and the so-called 'golden' ratio, a shape that artists have found to be so perfect that they referred to it also as the divine proportion.

Chapter 9 • **Harmonizing: mathematics and musical scales**, turns the spotlight on musical patterns, looking at some of the big ideas that help us to connect mathematics with music. In particular, it considers how the work of Pythagoras has helped musicians to tune their instruments.

Chapter 10 • **Maintaining perspective**, considers a question that has bothered artists for centuries – how to transform a three-dimensional image onto a two-dimensional canvas while plausibly maintaining perspective.

Chapter 6
Symmetry

Symmetry is what we see at a glance.
Blaise Pascal (French mathematician, 1623–62)

Balance

When an artist creates a work of art, a central feature of what he is trying to achieve concerns the balance of his composition. This refers to how its shapes, colours, lines, textures, and other elements are arranged. A key part of what the artist sees when trying to achieve balance is to do with the management of symmetry. A pattern is symmetrical if there is at least one way in which it can be moved (for example, reflected, rotated or translated) without the pattern being changed. This chapter looks particularly at reflective and rotational symmetry.

I can remember, as a child, sitting on the edge of the bath and watching my dad shave. Looking into the mirror, at the reflection of his face, I suddenly realized that the person there looked different from my dad in real life! Many other thoughts tumbled out – for example, that the one person in the family who didn't really know what my dad looked like was my dad himself. I also began to wonder what *I* actually looked like.

● **Figure 6.1** Tom:
(a) actual and (b) 'mirror'

(a)   (b)

Could this be why most people say, 'I take a terrible photograph'? Compared to the image of themselves that they are used to seeing in the mirror, photographs will always be something of a shock.

● **Figure 6.2** Alice: actual and 'mirror'.

Now compare the two faces of Alice, aged 5 years (Figure 6.2). I find I'm hard pressed to say which is the real Alice and which the 'Alice through the looking glass'. The reason why Alice's looking-glass and actual images are more similar to each other than Tom's (Figure 6.1) is to do with the symmetry of her facial features. As we get older, our faces acquire a number of subtle, 'characterful' changes – for example eyes, eyelids, noses and ears start to move around the face slightly and blemishes appear, all of which result in a reduction in the symmetry of our looks.

Beauty and the brain

Numerous researchers have looked into the question of which characteristics are associated with physical beauty. Two elements stand out. The first is the degree of symmetry of the face, and a good way of checking this is to place side by side an actual photograph and its mirror image. A second marker of facial beauty is the avoidance of extremes. It seems that we are hard-wired to be attracted to physical features that are average – the gap between the eyes, the length of chin, the physical stature, etc. should be neither too large nor too small. A possible explanation for this is that we are programmed to favour features that suggest health and fertility and these are the ones that tend to lie in the middle of the range of human attributes.

Research psychologists Piotr Winkielman of the University of California and Jamin Halberstadt of the University of Otago in New Zealand have suggested that, as we observe each new face, we store its characteristics in our brain and gradually build up a prototype of what constitutes a human face. Our preference for average faces is due to the fact that such faces are closer to this mental prototype. The suggestion is that, because the information from an average face is easier for the brain to process, such an image receives a more positive assessment.

This human preference for the average may be a slightly surprising finding, but if you look at digitally-mastered composite photographs based on dozens of different faces morphed into one, you will see that they always appear beautiful, even though many of the individual faces may be less so. For examples of this phenomenon, have a look at: http://www.faceoftomorrow.com/

It seems that this preference for the average is not restricted to human faces – we have a tendency to favour prototypes of other categories, such as fish, shoes, even patterns of dots on a page, that avoid extreme features or untypical configurations.

Line symmetry

An obvious branch of mathematics where ideas of symmetry are important is geometry. Have a look at the geometry of the face below. I ensured its symmetry by constructing it using the following steps:
- slicing it in half vertically (and disposing of the left half);
- duplicating the right half and creating its mirror image;
- joining the left and right halves together.

The vertical mirror line has the property that what is on one side is an exact reflection of what is on the other. In mathematics, this mirror line is called the *line of symmetry*. The human face possesses what is known as *line symmetry* (also called *reflective symmetry* or *mirror symmetry*), the line in question being the vertical line, shown in the drawing, that runs equidistant between the eyes and ears and splits the forehead, nose, mouth and chin.

Different geometric shapes have different numbers of lines of reflective symmetry. The triangle drawings in Figure 6.4 show that an isosceles triangle has only one line of symmetry, whereas an equilateral triangle has three.

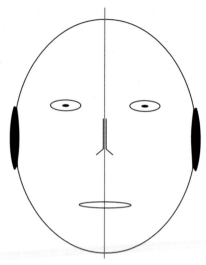

● **Figure 6.3** A symmetrical face.

● **Figure 6.4** Lines of symmetry of (a) an isosceles triangle and (b) an equilateral triangle.

(a)

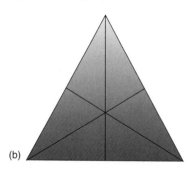

(b)

Most objects that are considered to be beautiful possess line symmetry. My personal top five beautiful physical objects (excluding human forms) would probably include a guitar, an apple, a violin, a flower and a vase (my wife is a sculptor so I really have to include this one!). All of these objects possess line symmetry. Try making your own top five list and check them for line symmetry. It would be surprising if any of them lack this property.

Rotational symmetry

You are probably familiar with the type of early learning sorting toy where the child needs to 'post' a number of different 3-D shapes through the hole of a matching shape into a container. Not only do young children find the toy absorbing and entertaining but also the activity lays firm foundations for their mathematical thinking. When sorting, the child is starting to engage with some of the following ideas, either consciously or unconsciously:

● **Figure 6.5** Child's sorting toy.

(a) All the 3-D shapes share an important property – they are all prisms. (In Figure 6.5, the four shapes on the right are a rectangular prism (or cuboid), two triangular prisms and a star shaped prism.)
(b) All shapes are posted by matching the shape of the hole with the shape of the prism's end face.
(c) Some shapes are easier to post than others – and there must be a reason for this!
(d) To give a coherent explanation for point (c) above, it is necessary to understand something about rotational symmetry. A shape possesses rotational symmetry when, if you turn it around, it looks the same. (Of course, if you rotate it through a full turn it will look the same, but this doesn't count, as every shape has this property!).

A shape that does not have rotational symmetry is said to have rotational symmetry of order 1 (i.e. there is only one position in which it looks the same).

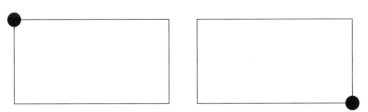

● **Figure 6.6** A rectangle has rotational symmetry of order 2.

Figure 6.6 shows how a rectangle rotated through 180° will look the same. It is said to have rotational symmetry of order 2. (The blob is there to indicate the rectangle's orientation.)

A square rotated through 90° will look the same, which means that a square has rotational symmetry of order 4.

Using the tool of rotational symmetry, it is now possible to explain why some shapes are more difficult for a child to post than others.

Look at the five shapes below, which represent the cross-sections of five of the usual sorting shapes. Using the idea of rotational symmetry, can you decide which would be the easiest and which the hardest for a child to post?

● Figure 6.7

Solution
From right to left the five shapes have rotational symmetries of the following orders: square = 4, triangle = 3, circle = infinite, octagon = 8, five-pointed star = 5.
In general, the higher the order of rotational symmetry, the more viable orientations there are posting the shape. So the easiest shape to post should be the prism with a circular cross-section (i.e. a cylinder) and the hardest one will be the triangular prism.

Symmetry and creativity

Symmetry is a central feature of design, whether you are looking at Islamic patterns at the Alhambra in Granada, Spain, or at wallpaper designs by William Morris. There are many artists, such as the Dutch artist Maurits Escher (1898–1972), for whom all the symmetries mentioned in this chapter are central to their work. Playing with symmetry, even if subconsciously, is also a feature of musical composition. The simplest type of musical harmony, of playing the tune 'a third up' (this corresponds to a musical interval of four semitones), is often a useful starting point for harmonizing in singing and this is an application of *translation* symmetry to the melody.

An outstanding exponent of musical harmony was Johann Sebastian Bach (1685–1750) and this is clearly evident in many of his greatest works, including his masterpiece, the *Mass in B minor*. Rhythmic symmetries are also to be found in his *Goldberg Variations*. Below is an example of a simple translation taken from Bach's *Concerto for Two Violins in D minor*. Look at the melody in the first two bars of the piece (Figure 6.8). Bars 14 and 15 (Figure 6.9) are identical but now the melody has been raised by a musical interval of one fifth (which corresponds to an upward shift of seven semitones).

● **Figure 6.8** The first two bars of Bach's *Concerto for Two Violins in D minor.*

● **Figure 6.9** Bars 14 and 15 of the same piece.

● **Figure 6.10** The composer's name, created by Scott Kim, the Inversions Gallery (http://www.scottkim.com/inversions).

In Figure 6.10, the name J. S. Bach has been cleverly constructed by exploiting its visual symmetry. Try to explain how this was achieved, using the language of symmetries.

Solution
The image has been achieved using reflective symmetry about a vertical mirror line passing between the letters 'b' and 'a'.

The artist plays with symmetry

Artists do not always adhere strictly to the rules of symmetry. Nonetheless, in all art forms, some aspects of symmetry (what the visual artist might refer to as 'balance')

are key to the composition of any work. This feature can be found in great paintings such as Leonardo Da Vinci's *Last Supper* (painted between 1495 and 1498) and is the starting point for many artistic creations, even if the artist goes on to break or challenge the underlying symmetries to provoke a particular effect. In music the artist plays with symmetries to develop melodic harmonies as well as to explore variations on a theme.

A footnote on symmetry in mathematics
Beyond geometry, symmetry is important in several branches of higher mathematics, including *group theory*. Within these topics, ideas of symmetry are normally explored algebraically rather than with figures but, in general, symmetry refers to something that does not change as a result of a set of transformations.

Something for you to try

1 *If you write down in sequence the letters of the alphabet, in capital letters, what is the first one that possesses rotational symmetry of order 2?*

2 *What are the next two items in the following sequence?*

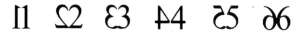

Solutions

1 *The first (capital) letter of the alphabet that possesses rotational symmetry of order 2 is H.*

2 *The next two items in the sequence are shown below – the sequence is of the counting numbers, attached to their mirror images, using a vertical line of symmetry.*

Chapter 7

Drawing circles: the story of pi

The history of pi is a quaint little mirror of the history of man.

Petr Beckmann

Seeing circles

From ancient times, spherical and circular shapes have dominated the artist's life. Not only have they become woven into his arts and crafts, but also he has needed to grasp their fundamental properties in order to function effectively in the practical everyday world. He sees circles every day in the form of wheels, coins, rings, eyes and buttons. When he throws a pebble into a pool he observes a series of perfect, concentric, circular ripples spreading out from where it landed. As a child, he will have gazed in wonder at the Sun and the Moon. When it snows, he rolls two snowballs to make a snowman based on spherical shapes. From birth the artist has been bombarded with powerful two- and three-dimensional images based on circular shapes – fruits, balls, pots and pans, cups, spectacles . . .

Clearly, circles and spheres are firmly established in the artist's consciousness. They are part of his toolkit of basic shapes and as such represent important building blocks of his work. But to understand the nature of circularity more fully, he needs to explore further the properties of circles . . .

The same shape

Of all the two-dimensional shapes we see around us, the two most fundamental are the circle and the square. There is a good reason for this: circles and squares share a special property enjoyed by no other shape – which is that all

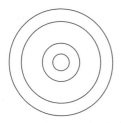

● **Figure 7.1** Concentric circles: all *circles* have the same shape.

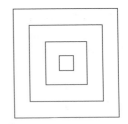

● **Figure 7.2** Concentric squares: all *squares* have the same shape.

circles are identical in shape to each other, as are all squares. What this means is that any one circle is simply a scaled-up or scaled-down version of any other circle. And the same property holds for squares. The mathematical term for 'the same shape' is *similarity*. So, we can say that 'all circles are similar' and 'all squares are similar'.

Contrast this with rectangles, which come in many different shapes – long and thin, short and fat and so on. No matter how you scale the first rectangle in Figure 7.3, or turn it around, it will never have the same shape as either of the other two. So it is not the case that all rectangles are mathematically similar.

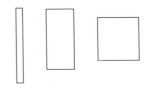

● **Figure 7.3** Rectangles can take many different shapes.

This property of the similarity of circles is one reason why humans have long been fascinated by them. Its study goes back beyond recorded history – the invention of the wheel is based on the discovery of fundamental properties of a circle. And, as you will see in this chapter, circles and their properties are inextricably bound up with that most famous of all mathematical numbers, π.

The crossing

Imagine that two ants are sitting side by side on the rim of a teacup and both want to cross to the other side. Ant A, being more adventurous, decides to take the direct route along the conveniently placed lolly stick. Ant B has a poor head for heights and chooses the scenic route around the

cup's rim. Assuming that both ants walk at the same speed, if ant A takes 10 seconds to get to the other side, how long would you expect ant B to complete his longer journey?

● **Figure 7.4**

I've asked a number of friends this question and their estimates were all somewhere between 12 and 18 seconds. Let's now strip the problem down to its bare, mathematical essentials.

From above (as in Figure 7.4), you can see that the rim of the teacup is a circle. The journey along the lolly stick represents the circle's diameter. The 'scenic' route around the rim represents half of the circumference of this circle. In order to make your guess about the duration of ant B's journey, you need to make an intuitive comparison of these two distances. Let's suppose that you guessed, say, 15 seconds – this suggests your intuition is telling you that the semi-circular path is 1.5 times the length of the diameter. Put another way, this would mean that you would estimate the complete circumference to be three times (because $1.5 \times 2 = 3$) the length of the diameter. Three times? But is that exactly three or is three just an approximation. . . ?

Properties of pi

The point of this ants' story is to reveal a rather amazing fact about circles, which is that, regardless of the size of the circle, the ratio of the circumference to the diameter is always the same. It is a number slightly larger than 3, and this number is known as pi (written π). The reason why this ratio is fixed is that all circles have the same 'shape', which ensures that all proportional relationships are maintained.

In fact, the true value of pi is roughly 3.14 or approximately $^{22}/_{7}$. But these numbers are only approximations. For many centuries, one of the fascinations for mathematicians about the numerical value of pi has been to try to find its exact value. However, its mystery remains because we now know that its value can never be pinned down exactly. Writing it out to the first fifty places of decimals, we get:

$$\pi = 3.14159265358979323846264338327950288419716939937510\ldots$$

As noted in Chapter 5, the exact value of pi is an infinitely long decimal number in which the decimal digits contain no systematic repetitions. Note that if you use the well-known school classroom estimate for pi of $^{22}/_{7}$, and divide these numbers out, you get a number whose decimal part is infinitely long but *does* contain a repetition – the decimal part repeats every six digits, thus:

$$22 \div 7 = 3.142857\textbf{142857}142857\textbf{142857}\ldots$$

Another important fact about pi is that it is an *irrational* number, an idea you were introduced to in Chapter 4. In order to understand what this means, let's look at the idea of a *rational* number. A rational number is one that can be expressed as the ratio of two whole numbers (note that *ratio*nal contains the word *ratio*). So you can deduce, for a start, that all fractions are rational, since by definition they are the ratio of two whole numbers – for example $^{3}/_{4}$ is rational. But also $4^{2}/_{3}$ must be rational because it can be written as $^{14}/_{3}$, which satisfies the condition of being the ratio of two whole numbers. Next, what about decimal numbers like 3.14 or 5.128? Well, these too are rational because they can be written as the ratio of two whole numbers ($^{314}/_{100}$ and $^{5128}/_{1000}$, respectively). So all conventional fractions and decimals are rational numbers. Irrational numbers are the ones left over, and that includes the 'unspeakable' square root of 2 (written $\sqrt{2}$) and the quirky numbers like π.

Squaring the circle

We use the phrase 'squaring the circle' when something is so hard to achieve that it is actually impossible. The origins of the expression can be traced to the following problem proposed by ancient geometers.

Using only compasses and a straight edge, can you construct a square with the same area as a given circle by using only a finite number of steps?

For example, suppose that the circle in Figure 7.5 has a radius of 1 cm. Knowing that the area of any circle is equal to π times the square of the radius (this is a standard area formula), the area of the circle is therefore equal to $π × 1^2$ square centimetres, which simplifies to π cm².

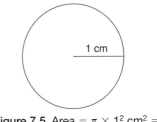

● **Figure 7.5** Area $= π × 1^2$ cm² $=$ π cm².

Squaring the circle means trying to construct a square with exactly the same area as the circle. It turns out that this is impossible to do, for the reason that there is no way to calculate the length of side of this square exactly. The explanation is based on understanding the idea of a square root. You might know that the positive square root of 9 is equal to 3. (Note that there is a second, negative, square root of 9, which is –3, but let's not get into that here!) The reason that the square root of 9 equals 3 is because when you reverse the operation and find the square of 3, the answer equals 9. Similarly, the square root of 100 equals 10 because ten squared (i.e. 10^2) = 100. In general, the square root of some unknown number, say, x is $\sqrt{x}$, because $\sqrt{x} × \sqrt{x} = x$.

In the problem here, we are trying to construct a square of area equal to π cm². Such a square will need to have sides whose length, when squared, gives the required area of π cm². So, what number, when squared, gives π? Using the argument above, the answer is the square root of π, which we write as $\sqrt{π}$. So this square would require sides of $\sqrt{π}$ cm long. And, take it from me, it is impossible to construct a square of side length $\sqrt{π}$ cm, whether you are using a straight edge or compasses or can lay your hands on a copy of the *Big Book of Magic Constructions*!

The world had to wait until 1882 for convincing proof that the construction was impossible. It came from the Lindemann-Weierstrass theorem which proved that π is a transcendental number – i.e. its value cannot result from the solution to any polynomial equation with rational coefficients. (Note that polynomial families of equations include linear, quadratic, cubic, quartic equations, and so on.)

Anyway, the moral of this story is, don't waste your time attempting to square the circle. Better minds than yours and mine have tried and failed and now there is proof, courtesy of Messrs Lindemann and Weierstrass, that shows it is an impossibility!

Calculating pi

One of the entertainments (in some cases, 'obsessions' might be a better word) of mathematicians over many centuries has been to find ways of calculating the value of pi as accurately as possible. The Babylonians were happy to use the approximation of $3\frac{1}{8}$, which is slightly less accurate than our school classroom approximation of $3\frac{1}{7}$. The early Greek mathematicians did not work with π as a number but rather as the abstract concept of the ratio of the circumference of a circle to its diameter. However, the Greek mathematician Archimedes (c.287–12 BCE) was greatly interested in trying to pin down its numerical value more closely. He did so by using a quite brilliant idea based on constructing a pair of regular polygons, one touching the inside and the other touching the outside of the circle.

Archimedes (c.287–c.212 BCE)

Archimedes of Syracuse was a Greek mathematician, scientist, inventor and astronomer who is considered one of the leading thinkers of ancient times. His many mathematical discoveries include a method (referred to as the method of exhaustion) to calculate the area under the arc of a parabola and a remarkably accurate approximation of pi (described here). He devised formulas for calculating the volumes of surfaces of revolution and a clever system for expressing very large numbers.

Archimedes was born in the seaport city of Syracuse, Sicily, but details of his early life are obscure. Details of his death, however, are well documented. According to the Greek historian, Plutarch, he was in Syracuse during the second Punic war when the Roman soldiers had lain siege to the city. After the city was captured, Archimedes was commanded to come to meet the Roman commander, General Marcellus. But Archimedes, busily working on a mathematical diagram, said that he would come when he had completed it, at which point the enraged soldier drew a sword and killed him. Marcellus was greatly displeased that the greatest mind of the time had been dispatched before he had been able to tap into the wisdom it contained.

Archimedes' first attempt at estimating the value of pi might have been to start with very simple regular polygons, such as the two squares in Figure 7.6. His reasoning was that the circumference of the circle must be greater than the perimeter of the inner square but less than the perimeter of the outer square. Here he was making use of the idea of 'bounds' – i.e. that the value you require is contained somewhere in the interval between a 'lower bound' and an 'upper bound'.

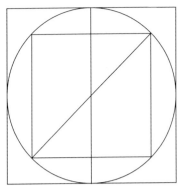

● **Figure 7.6** Two squares, one inside and one outside a circle.

Based on approximating the circumference of the circle to the inner square, Archimedes' method estimates the value of π to be roughly 2.83 (or, more precisely, $2 \times \sqrt{2}$). Using the outer square, it gives an upper bound of 4. So it follows that the true value of π must lie between 2.83 and 4, which is an interval of about 1.17 units wide.

In fact, Archimedes' first attempt was based on using regular hexagons (polygons with six sides) rather than squares. As you can see in Figure 7.7, compared with the squares, these polygons are closer in shape to the circle and so one might expect them to provide a more accurate estimate. Archimedes' estimate of the value of π based on the inner hexagon was 3 and, based on the outer one, 3.46, giving an interval of width 0.46 – clearly much narrower than that produced by the squares.

However, in order to make his estimate more accurate, Archimedes could see that he needed to construct polygons with a larger number of sides. Ingeniously, he found a way of building

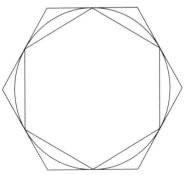

● **Figure 7.7** Two regular hexagons, one inside and one outside the circle.

up his calculations based on doubling the number of sides each time. Using this approach, he could find the lower and upper bounds of his estimates of π for 6, 12, 24, 48 and finally 96 sides. His final calculation, based on 96-sided polygons, gave lower and upper bounds, respectively, of $3^{10}/_{71}$ and $3^1/_7$. Note that the Greeks didn't have the benefits of decimal notation so these comparisons had to be based on fractions. Using decimal notation, this gives a lower bound of 3.1408 and an upper bound of 3.1429, which is an interval of just 0.0021.

In Figure 7.8, the two vertical bars show the intervals between the lower and upper bounds of the estimates of π, based on using Archimedes' method. The longer bar represents the results based on using 6-sided polygons and the extremely short second bar represents the results based on using 96-sided polygons. The horizontal line shows the position of the 'true' value of π (roughly 3.1416). The Figure illustrates how much more accurate is

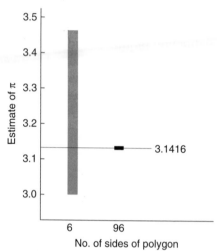

● **Figure 7.8** Interval estimates of pi based on Archimedes' method.

the estimate when 96-sided polygons are used rather than polygons with just 6 sides. So Archimedes' calculation managed to pin down the value of pi, correct to about three decimal places. Yet inherent in his method is an awareness that he could never find the exact value of pi but only progressively narrow the interval that contained pi. And indeed, for over two thousand years since the time of Archimedes, enthusiasts have continued his quest to focus ever more closely on an approximation to the true value of pi, while knowing that it can never be attained exactly.

Today, with powerful computers at our disposal, we can do a little better than Archimedes. Fast-forward to

31 December 2009; using a single desktop computer costing less than $3,000, the French mathematician Fabrice Bellard claimed the world record for calculating pi – to a staggering 2.7 trillion places. To put this into context, this number required more than 1000 gigabytes of memory to store it. If you were to recite the number it would take you about 50 thousand years to get to that final 2.7 trillionth decimal place! On his website, he answered the question, 'Why did you do this?' as follows:

> I am not especially interested in the digits of pi, but in the various algorithms involved to do arbitrary-precision arithmetic. Optimizing these algorithms to get good performance is a difficult programming challenge.

Pi is exactly 3

Below is an extract from one episode of the TV cartoon show *The Simpsons*. The scene is a scientific meeting where the speaker (Professor Frink, wearing a white lab coat) is trying vainly to get the attention of the audience (also all wearing white lab coats).

Audience: blah blah blah . . .
Speaker: Uh . . . may I have your attention please?
Audience: blah blah blah . . .
Audience: blah blah blah . . .
Speaker: Pi is exactly 3!
Audience: *GASP*
Speaker: I'm sorry it had to come to that, but I needed to get your attention.
Speaker: Please, pay attention!

It may have struck you that things would be a lot more convenient if π turned out to be exactly 3. In fact, this idea is still circulating in various parts of the world, particularly where the word of scripture is taken literally.

Here is a relevant extract from the Bible (1 Kings 7:23):

> He made the sea of cast metal, circular in shape, measuring ten cubits from rim to rim and five cubits high. It took a line of thirty cubits to measure around it.

So, what we have here is a circular rim with a diameter of 10 cubits and a circumference of 30 cubits. Following the logic of these measurements, this implies a value of $\pi = 3$ (the ratio of circumference to diameter $= {}^{30}/_{10} = 3$).

In April 1998, an entertaining spoof news story circulated on the Internet claiming that 'responding to pressure from religious groups, Alabama's state legislature redefined the value of π from 3.14159 to 3 in order to bring it into line with Biblical precepts'. The parody, written as an April Fool's joke by Mark Boslough, was taken seriously and reported widely around the world. However, it did reflect a real event that had taken place one hundred years earlier; in Indiana in 1897, a law was indeed passed redefining, on religious grounds, the value of π to be equal to 3. The bill was subsequently killed in the State Senate.

The artist discovers that all circles are the same

For many visual artists, a major technical challenge is how to represent the three-dimensional world on a two-dimensional canvas or sheet of paper. Not only must the artist maintain the underlying proportional relationships involved but also shapes must be redefined – blocks become rectangles (or parallelograms) and spherical shapes become circles. He becomes intrigued by the simple perfection of circles – what is it about them that makes them so special? His conclusion? It is that, regardless of their size, all circles have the same shape or, to put it another way, all circles are mathematically similar. This implies that if you were to take any two linear measures from a circle (say, circumference and diameter) and divide one by the other, then regardless of the size of the circle, the answer will always be a constant. The numerical value of this constant, when circumference is divided by diameter, turns out to have a value just greater than 3. The journey to pinning down its exact numerical value has already lasted several thousand years and is proving to be a much more interesting adventure than anyone could ever have predicted.

1 *Here are three standard approximations to pi: $3^1/_8$, $3^1/_7$, $^{355}/_{113}$. Which of these is the closest approximation?*

2 *True or false?:*
   (a) *Circles are the only one-sided shape with an area.*
   (b) *A straight line is a circle with an infinite area.*
   (c) *A circle is the locus of a point equidistant from another central point.*
   (d) *Comparing the areas contained by all 2-D shapes with the same perimeter, the circle is the one with the greatest area.*

3 *There are many mnemonics for pi in a variety of languages (the digits are represented by the number of letters in each word). For example, the following statement is a mnemonic for pi to 20 decimal places:*
   How I wish I could enumerate Pi easily, since all these horrible mnemonics prevent recalling any of pi's sequence more simply. [3.14159265358979323846]
   Try creating your own mnemonic for pi.

Solutions

1 *Expressed to six decimal places, the three approximations give, respectively, 3.142859, 3.125000 and 3.141593. The third one ($^{355}/_{113}$) is therefore much the closest estimate.*

2 *All of these statements about circles are true.*

3 *Here is a French one:* Que j'aime à faire apprendre ce nombre utile aux sages. *It gives 11 digits and can be roughly translated as 'Me, I like to teach a number useful to wise men.'*

Chapter 8
Keeping in proportion: the golden rectangle

The good, of course, is always beautiful,
and the beautiful never lacks proportion.

Plato (Greek philosopher, c.427–347 BCE)

Getting it to scale

Figure 8.1 is the sort of drawing we may all have done as children. (Alternatively, it may be a highly valuable work 'in the primitive style' by a 21st-century artist!) There are times when we may wish to play about with the relative scale of the drawing's component parts for an artistic effect. But if your aim is to depict objects as they appear in everyday life (realism), then it is important to get the scale of the figure correct. This applies particularly to depictions of the human form and buildings, where the eye of the beholder can quickly spot elements that are out of proportion.

The artist's 'key measure'

The artist holds up his pencil in front of him as he surveys the scene that he is about to draw. But what exactly is he doing? The chances are that he is performing some rough-and-ready measuring procedure.

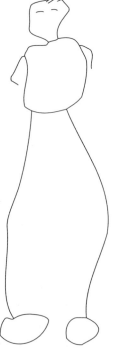

● **Figure 8.1** A typical child's drawing.

● **Figure 8.2** Banyalbufar, Majorca.

For example, look at the photograph of a lovely Majorcan village (Figure 8.2). Alongside, on the left, is the end of the artist's pencil with a metal band and eraser at the bottom; this part of the pencil can be used as a measuring tool to ensure that a drawing is to the correct scale. As you can see, the length to the top of the metal band corresponds roughly to the height of the nearby door.

Using this length as the basic unit, the height from the ground to the window above the door is roughly two units, as is the height from the ground to the top of the gable of the house on the right. Artists often refer to such a basic unit as their *key measure*. Based on numerous rough-and-ready measures provided by their key measure, they will start a drawing or painting by trying to fix the locations of the various landmarks and marking them onto their paper or canvas.

Proportion

When a drawing is 'out of proportion' (like the child's drawing in Figure 8.1), it is usually obvious where the problem lies – the nose is too long, the legs too short, the tree too wide and so on. In order to develop the skill of drawing things to the correct scale, the artist needs to gain a better understanding of the idea of proportion.

So, to get to grips with the key principles underlying proportion, let's strip the figure down to something much simpler – a right-angled triangle. It is shown opposite with *vertices* (this means its corners) marked A, B and C. The lengths of the three sides are:

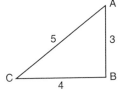

● **Figure 8.3** Right-angled triangle.

AB = 3 units, BC = 4 units and AC = 5 units.

Now I'm going to construct a larger right-angled triangle *with the same shape* as the one in Figure 8.3. Note that, for the shape to be maintained, the three angles of the triangle must not change – only the lengths of the sides. I will attempt to do this in two ways, one of which gives the correct result while the other doesn't.

Method 1

- Increase the length of each side by 2 units.
- The original triangle had dimensions 3, 4 and 5 cm. Adding two units to the length of each side gives the following dimensions: AB = 5 units, BC = 6 units and AC = 7 units.

I've tried to construct this triangle, as shown in Figure 8.4. (Note that, to maintain the shape of the original triangle, the angle at B is a right angle.) However, as you can see, I am unable to do it: with the two shorter sides (AB and BC) in place, the longer third side won't stretch all the way from point C to point A. There's a gap!

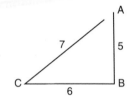

● **Figure 8.4** Result of trying to enlarge the triangle, using method 1.

Let's now move to the second method.

Method 2

Increase the length of each side by 50%.
This gives the following dimensions:
AB = 4.5 units, BC = 6 units and AC = 7.5 units.
I've constructed this triangle, as shown in Figure 8.5, and as you can see, method 2 is a success! The three angles at A, B and C are the same as in the original triangle and, overall, it has maintained the same shape.

Method 2 reveals the big idea that underlies proportion. Two shapes are 'in proportion' provided the ratios of corresponding lengths are the same. In this example, a 50% increase is equivalent to multiplying by a *scale factor* of 1.5.

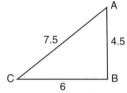

● **Figure 8.5** The triangle enlarged, using method 2.

Scale factor

The idea of a scale factor is a very useful one.

Suppose that a tax of 15% is applied to a wide range of goods. This means that prices rise to 115% of what they were previously. In other words, they increase by a factor of $^{115}/_{100}$ – which simplifies to a scale factor of 1.15. Similarly, a rise of 50% means an increase to 150% of what it was previously. This corresponds to an increase by a factor of $^{150}/_{100}$; i.e. a scale factor of 1.5.

The same principle applies to proportional reductions. A price cut of 30% means a decrease to 70% of what it was previously. This corresponds to a decrease by a factor of $^{70}/_{100}$; i.e. a scale factor of 0.7.

To take an everyday example, imagine you are standing beside a photograph of yourself and that the length of your actual arm is four times the length of your arm in the photograph. So the scale factor is 4. In Figure 8.6, the reason why the person and his photograph are in proportion is that this scale factor of 4 is maintained for any measure you choose to make – the person's leg length, the gap between their eyes, their overall height, and so on will all be four times that of the corresponding feature in the 'photograph'.

● **Figure 8.6** Scale factor 4: a person four times the size of his 'photograph'.

Aspect ratio

One common rectangular shape that has changed noticeably over the past 60 years is what we fondly refer to as 'the box' – i.e. our television screens. When TV sets first appeared in people's living rooms in the 1950s, their shapes were much more 'square' than they are today. TV/cinema screens and also photographic images are all basically rectangles. Their shapes are defined by a number known as the *aspect ratio*, which is calculated by dividing the longer side by the shorter. Note that this measure says nothing about the *size* of the rectangular shape in question but only about its shape.

The rectangular shapes in Figure 8.7 show some of the screen aspect ratios that have been used at various times on TV and in cinemas. The 4:3 ratio (i.e. 1.33:1) represents the screen shapes adopted during the first 50 years of television. Indeed, this ratio was the shape first used in the early days of cinema – the story goes that when Thomas Edison was asked by his engineer what shape of screen he wanted, Edison replied, 'about like this' and formed his fingers in the approximate shape of a 4 by 3 rectangle.

4:3

16:9

2.2:1

2.35:1

● **Figure 8.7** Popular TV and cinema screen ratios.

When digital television arrived in the UK in 2001, the screen shape was elongated to a ratio of 1.78:1, or 16:9 as it is more commonly known. Cinemas have used a range of ratios but in recent years have consistently offered 'wider' screens than domestic television – 2.2:1 (Panavision) and 2.39:1 (Cinemascope) are popular today.

The golden rectangle

Ideas of ratio and proportion touch a vast range of contexts, including art, music and architecture. To end this chapter, you are invited to explore one very special rectangle called the golden rectangle. The drawing entitled *Golden Window* (Figure 8.8) has been created by the artist in a rectangular frame with proportions deliberately chosen to match the so-called 'golden ratio'.

The golden rectangle, otherwise known as the divine proportion, is a particular rectangular shape that has been known about since the time of the ancient Greeks, two and a half thousand years ago. In fact, it may date back even earlier, to the time when the Egyptians built the pyramids, some four and a half thousand years ago. If you were to find a photograph of the Parthenon and draw a rectangle around the outside, you would find that your rectangle has an aspect ratio that is 'golden'.

But what is so special about the shape of this particular rectangular? In order to explain why it is unique, let's look first at a rectangle that does *not* possess these proportions. The left-hand rectangle in Figure 8.9 is an everyday rectangle possessing no special properties. Mark off a square shape at one end (shaded), cut it off and look at the shape of the rectangle that remains. As you can see, the shape of the remaining rectangle is different from that of the original rectangle.

● **Figure 8.8** The golden or divine rectangle: *Golden Window*, by Sheila Graham.

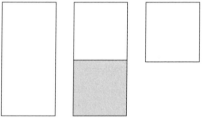

● **Figure 8.9** The remaining rectangle has a different shape from that of the original rectangle.

Try this yourself, starting with rectangles of various shapes and you'll almost certainly find that in no cases will you end up with a rectangle that has the same aspect ratio (i.e. the same shape) as your original.

In fact, there is only one particular rectangular shape where, when a square is cut off from it, you end up with a rectangle that has exactly the same shape as the original. It is the golden rectangle and it is shown in Figure 8.10. Figure (a) shows the original rectangle. In Figure (b), the square is shaded. In Figure (c), the square end has been cut off. In Figure (d), the remaining rectangle has been rotated through 90° to give it the same orientation as the original rectangle. You can see that rectangles (a) and (d) have the same shape.

The fact that only one shape of rectangle possesses this special property sets its particular aspect ratio apart from all others. For centuries, many artists and architects have proportioned

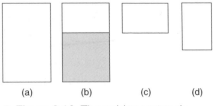

(a)   (b)   (c)   (d)

● **Figure 8.10** The golden rectangle.

their works to approximate to the golden ratio, believing this unique proportion to be aesthetically pleasing. Indeed, some believed that it was such a perfect proportion that it must have a divine provenance, which is why it is often referred to as the divine proportion.

Numerical value of the golden ratio (ϕ)
The value of the golden ratio is 1.6180339887. . . :1 (i.e. roughly 1.618:1)

It is often referred to as φ (the lower-case Greek letter phi).

So what is the exact numerical value of this golden ratio? In fact, written as a decimal, it is another of those numbers that goes on forever – it's an example of an irrational number, just like π and the square root of 2. Its value is approximately 1.618. So, a rectangle whose proportions are fairly close to 'golden' would have dimensions of 8:5 (this gives 1.6:1). A closer approximation again would be the aspect ratio 13:8, which gives 1.625:1.

In Chapters 21 and 22 you will have the opportunity to discover more about the golden ratio and how it crops up in nature.

A mathematical aside on calculating the value of ϕ
You may be wondering how it is possible to calculate the value of ϕ to so many decimal places. The seven steps below explain how an equation for φ can be set up and solved.

1 The large rectangle in Figure 8.10(a) is a golden rectangle, so its dimensions can be marked as ϕ units long and 1 unit wide (this gives the required aspect ratio ϕ:1).

2 In Figure 8.10(b), the shaded square has dimensions 1×1, so the dimensions of the smaller (golden) rectangle above it are $\phi-1 \times 1$.

● **Figure 8.11**

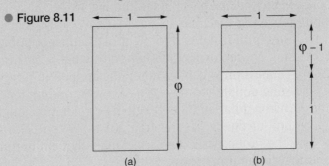

(a)   (b)

3 Consider the golden rectangle in Figure 8.11(a) and the smaller golden rectangle in Figure 8.11(b). As these have the same shape, they must have the same aspect ratio.

4 The aspect ratio of the larger golden rectangle in (a) = $\phi/1$.
The aspect ratio of the smaller golden rectangle in (b) = $1/\phi_{-1}$.
As these rectangles have the same shape, their aspect ratios must be equal, giving:
$\phi/1 = 1/\phi_{-1}$.
This equation can now be solved for ϕ.

5 To simplify, multiply both sides of the equation by $\phi-1$.
This gives: $\phi(\phi-1) = 1$
Multiplying out: $\phi^2-\phi-1 = 0$

6 To solve a quadratic equation like this, apply the 'quadratic formula'; this gives the result: $\phi = {(1+\sqrt{5})}/{2}$

7 With the help of a calculator, this provides the numerical result, $\phi = 1.618033989$.

In fact, this is only an approximation to the value of ϕ. Because it contains the $\sqrt{5}$ component, which is an irrational number, ϕ itself is irrational and its decimal expansion goes on forever.

The artist keeps things in proportion

The artist experiences his surroundings as a cornucopia of relationships, rhythms and patterns. He trains his mind to be observant, ever on the lookout for regularities in all the world's complexity. It seems to be true of all human societies that aesthetic pleasure comes from recognizing and creating aural, visual and rhythmic patterns. Where there are the beginnings of agreement about which patterns are worth attending to and a mutual recognition of the pleasure they bring, then we see the birth of a shared culture.

Mathematics fits into this story in terms of giving the artist greater understanding so that he can achieve his goals more effectively. In this chapter, the big artistic idea has been about achieving 'balance' in an artistic work. Mathematics provides helpful insights into the artist's concept of balance by offering a more explicit definition of what it means. The idea of proportion is central here; it is defined in terms of maintaining equality in the ratio of corresponding lengths. You've also read about a rectangle (the golden rectangle) whose unique shape has inspired artists for centuries. So perfect are the proportions of this rectangle that is often referred to as the divine proportion.

Something for you to try

1   The two triangles here are the same shape (assume that the measurements are in cm).
    (a) Calculate the scale factor by which the larger triangle is bigger than the smaller one.
    (b) Use the scale factor to work out the length of the two unmarked sides of the larger triangle.

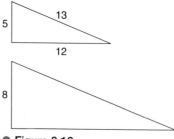

2   The two most common aspect ratios produced by digital

● Figure 8.12

cameras are 3:2 and 4:3. Suppose that you wish to print your photograph and place it in a frame measuring 140 mm × 105 mm. Which of the two aspect ratios better matches the shape of your frame?

Solutions

1 (a) The ratio of corresponding sides of the larger triangle: smaller triangle = 8:5 or 1.6:1. So the scale factor = 1.6.
  (b) The lengths of the two unmarked sides are: bottom side = 12 cm × 1.6 = 19.2 cm; hypotenuse = 13 cm × 1.6 = 20.8 cm.
2   Dividing out the aspect ratios: 3:2 is equivalent to 1.5:1 and 4:3 is equivalent to 1.33:1. The aspect ratio of the frame = 140:105, which divides out to give 1.33:1. So, the aspect ratio of the frame matches the 4:3 photographic ratio.

Chapter 9
Harmonizing: mathematics and musical scales

He who lives in harmony with himself lives in harmony with the universe.
Marcus Aurelius (Roman emperor, 121–180 CE)

Twanging rulers

As a child interested in musical patterns, the artist no doubt twanged a ruler at some point. A twanged ruler is one of the most basic musical instruments you can create and, let's face it, one of life's true simple pleasures.

Something for you to try

Place a ruler so that it overhangs a hard surface such as a table, hold it firmly on the surface and twang the overhanging part. Now vary the length of the overhang and see how the note is affected. Next, find an empty glass bottle and blow across the top to produce a note. Fill the bottle with water until about a quarter full and blow again. Repeat this procedure for different amounts of water in the bottle and see how the note varies accordingly. What general principles apply here?

After a little experimentation, the artist discovered that when the length of vibrating ruler was short, the note was high, and with more length, the note became lower. He also tried blowing across the top of a partly filled bottle and discovered a similar principle – that the shorter the column of air it contained (i.e. the more water there was in the bottle), the higher the note. But why should this be?

The key to what is going on is the idea of frequency of vibration. If you twang a long section of ruler, there is more of it to vibrate and so the frequency of its vibrations will be slower than if the ruler were shorter. It is the vibration frequency that determines the pitch of the note; the faster the vibrations, the higher the note. A similar principle applies to the vibrating column of air in the bottle. A small column of air has less work to do and so can vibrate faster than larger ones; and this in turn produces a high note. There are numerous examples of this principle at work – have a look at the pipes of a church organ and consider which make the low notes and which the high notes. Also, watch a trombonist at work – to make a low note, he pushes out with his arm to lengthen the piping in the instrument and so increase the amount of air it contains.

Measuring notes

When we hear a note, our ear is picking up vibrations in the air. It is the frequency of those vibrations that determines the pitch of the note we hear. Whereas musical notation for pitch is based on using letters like D, E flat, F sharp and so on, a more precise measure favoured by scientists is the frequency of vibration produced by the note. Frequencies are normally measured in hertz (Hz), where one hertz = 1 cycle per second. The note that musicians call middle C (the C note that lies in the middle of the piano keyboard) has a frequency of 256 Hz. The C above middle C has a frequency that is double that of middle C, namely 512 Hz. The C below middle C has a frequency that is half that of middle C, namely 128 Hz.

Now let's imagine that a very professional-looking piano tuner has just expensively tuned the strings of your baby grand piano and you decide to check his work. Whipping out your oscilloscope, you hit the piano key corresponding to middle C and take a reading. You may be surprised to find that, if he has done a good job, the reading will be rather higher than 256 Hz – in fact, it should be somewhere between 261 and 262 Hz. So what's going on? But before explaining this mismatch, let's take a stroll past a blacksmith's forge in the company of our old friend, Pythagoras of Samos.

> *Pythagoras of Samos (c.570–c.495 BCE)*
> Pythagoras was a mathematician, philosopher and religious leader. He was born on the Greek island of Samos, but there are few hard facts to provide reliable details of his life. Many mathematical and scientific

discoveries were attributed to him, including that famous theorem that we all learned at school. In case you need reminding, this states that, 'given a right-angled triangle, then the square on the hypotenuse (the longest side) is equal to the sum of the squares on the other two sides'. The simplest Pythagorean triangle has sides of 3, 4 and 5 units (because $3^2 + 4^2 = 5^2$). Note, by the way, that the corollary of Pythagoras' Theorem is also true – if the sides of a triangle possess this numerical relationship, then it must be right-angled. Thus a $5 \times 12 \times 13$ triangle must be right-angled (because $5^2 + 12^2 = 13^2$) but a $7 \times 15 \times 17$ triangle is not (because $7^2 + 15^2 \neq 17^2$.)

Interestingly, although he is remembered today mostly for this great theorem, Pythagoras was probably better known during his lifetime for his influence on religion. As you read in Chapter 4, it is known that Pythagoras founded a quasi-religious/scientific/mathematical sect known as the Pythagoreans, which was cloaked in mystery and secrecy. However, myth and legend about him were so extensive that it is hard to separate fact from fiction – for example, the story that his father was the god Apollo can be taken with a pinch of salt! Indeed, many of the achievements and accomplishments credited to Pythagoras may have been the work of his fellow sect members.

Pythagoras's anvils

As suggested in our short biography of Pythagoras, there are many urban myths around the precise details of various mathematical discoveries. The stories of Isaac Newton's falling apple and Archimedes' bath-time discoveries are also examples. So the finer points of the following tale may well fall into the same category. According to legend, Pythagoras was walking past a blacksmith's forge one day and noticed that the hammers striking the anvil were producing different notes. On further investigation, he observed that the higher notes were struck by the small hammer and the lower notes by the large hammer. Indeed, this discovery is consistent with what you already know about a twanged ruler and a blown bottle. But Pythagoras is credited with taking the idea further.

Imagine a length of string (such as a guitar string) under tension. You will know that plucking it produces a note. The three key factors that determine the pitch of this note are:

- the gauge (thickness) of the string: lighter-gauge strings produce higher notes;

- the tension of the string: the higher the tension, the higher the note;
- the length of the string – the shorter the string, the higher the note.

Here we are interested in the third of these relationships, so let's assume that the string gauge and tension are fixed. Imagine, then, a single guitar string set to a fixed tension. We can vary the effective length of this string by placing a finger on the keyboard at any point, to shorten it. The aim is to investigate in more detail the relationship between the length of vibrating string and the pitch of note it sounds. By experimenting with different string lengths, Pythagoras discovered that when he shortened the string length by a simple fraction, there was always a harmonious interval between the note produced by the original string and the note produced by the shortened one. For example, halving the string length has the effect of producing the same note as the original one but one octave up. Two thirds of the original length produces a musical interval of a fifth (another very harmonious interval). In general, Pythagoras found that the simpler the fraction by which the original string was subdivided, the more pleasing to the ear was the harmony of the interval produced.

Fretted

On most musical instruments there is a restriction on the total number of notes you can play – for example, a piano has a fixed number of keys, a guitar has a fixed number of frets, and so on. Other instruments, like a fiddle, do not have clearly marked-out notes. There are literally an infinite number of possible notes that could be played on a fiddle and a key skill acquired by fiddlers is learning where to put their fingers to produce the same notes as those generated by their fretted friends.

Pythagorean musical scales

Let's start with a little background information about what is meant by a musical scale. For the sort of music that most people in the developed western world are familiar with, an octave consists of 12 different notes or *semitones*. For example, the twelve semitones in the octave for the key of C are:

C, C#, D, D#, E, F, F#, G, G#, A, A#, B

The scale is completed with the inclusion of a final C at the top end, making 13 notes altogether, thus:

C, C#, D, D#, E, F, F#, G, G#, A, A#, B, C

So the scale of C starts and ends with the keynote, C, where the final C is an octave higher than the starting C. The five notes marked with a sharp (#) correspond to the black notes on a piano keyboard, and the remaining eight notes are white. An issue that has engaged the minds of musicians for many centuries has been how the notes in the scale are to be tuned.

Up until the 18th century, most musical instruments in the western developed world were tuned according to the principles discovered by Pythagoras some 2500 years ago. The idea was to produce the notes within the octave by repeatedly taking intervals of musical fifths. This meant reducing the string lengths repeatedly by a factor of $^2/_3$. The simplest form of Pythagorean tuning is therefore based on this fraction ($^2/_3$) and the principles of this method are described below.

String 1: Start with a string, say of length 1 (the lowest note in the octave, which we tune to middle C).
String 2: The string of length $^1/_2$ (giving a note one octave above, which is the C above middle C) will sound pleasing played together with the string of length 1 and these two string lengths correspond, respectively, to the highest and lowest notes in the octave. All of the intermediate notes are found by repeatedly taking fractions of two thirds ($^2/_3$) and, where necessary, making an adjustment in order to keep the note inside this single octave. For example:
String 3: Take a string length of $^2/_3$, which is a musical fifth above the original note – producing the note named G.
String 4: Take a string length that is $^2/_3$ of the length of string 3. This is $^2/_3 \times {}^2/_3 = {}^4/_9$ of the length of the first string and it produces a note that is a musical fifth above G. This is the note D but unfortunately it lies above the octave. This problem is overcome by dropping it down one octave and we do this by doubling its length from $^4/_9$ to $^8/_9$.

These first four notes are shown on the piano keyboard in Figure 9.1. They are: middle C, D, G and the C above middle C. Figure 9.1 also shows the four string lengths corresponding to the same four notes.

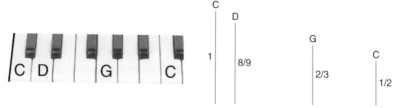

● **Figure 9.1** One octave of a piano keyboard showing the first four notes created (left); and the first four strings: middle C, C above middle C, G and D (right).

The procedure described above can be continued until all 13 strings are in place – i.e. you multiply each new string length by $^2/_3$ and, if the result lies outside the required octave range (i.e. numerically less than $^1/_2$), then double it to bring the fraction back into the required range (i.e. between $^1/_2$ and 1).

Different musical scales
Many different musical scales are used around the world. Most include the notion of an octave, but by no means all divide an octave into twelve different semitones. In Middle Eastern music, for example, which uses *quartertones* (half semitones) rather than semitones, there are more than 300 different scales in use. One very simple and popular scale is the *pentatonic* scale, so called because it consists of just five notes in an octave. An example of the pentatonic scale is the following sequence of black notes on a piano – F# G# A# C# and D#. The sixth and final note of F# completes the pentatonic octave. Many traditional folk songs are written using this scale: for example, 'The Skye Boat Song' and the first few notes of George Gershwin's 'Summertime'.

Equal temperament

Up until around the time of Johann Sebastian Bach (1685–1750) most musical instruments were tuned on the basis of the Pythagorean tuning above. Provided that tunes were played in the musical key to which the instruments of the time were tuned, the results were highly harmonious. However, the reality was that when expressed as ratios, the intervals between adjacent notes were not all equal. This was not a problem provided the musicians were all playing instruments designed for the same key, but as new instruments were developed, composers began to explore a variety of keys, where the simple fractional relationships between the notes started to break down and it all began to sound discordant.

The problem was solved by the invention of a new type of tuning which guaranteed the same interval between adjacent semitones. Rather than moving from one frequency to another using the scale factor of a simple fraction, a more formal mathematical approach was used. In order to ensure that all the semitone intervals were exactly equal, the factor chosen to move from the frequency of one note in the octave to the next higher semitone was the twelfth root of a half – written as $^{12}\sqrt{(0.5)}$ – which has a numerical value of approximately 0.9439. For obvious reasons, this new tuning became known as *equal temperament*.

The choice of 12 in this calculation is because there are 12 distinct notes in a scale. If you wished to create an equally tempered pentatonic scale consisting of five distinct notes, the required factor would be $^{5}\sqrt{(0.5)}$, which has a numerical value of approximately 0.8706.

Something for you to try

To help you understand the pattern of equal temperament, *try the following calculator exercises. (Note that most calculators allow you to use an automatic constant for calculations like these where the same operation is repeated – check your calculator manual if you aren't sure how to do this.)*

The equally-tempered pentatonic scale
Enter the following sequence in your calculator: 1 × 0.8706 × 0.8706 × 0.8706 × 0.8706 × 0.8706. The result should be close to 0.5.

The equally-tempered twelve-note scale
Enter the following sequence in your calculator: 1 × 0.9439 × 0.9439 × 0.9439 × 0.9439 × 0.9439 × 0.9439 × 0.9439 × 0.9439 × 0.9439 × 0.9439 × 0. 9439. As before, the result should be close to 0.5.

Bach was thrilled with the invention of this 'well-tempered' tuning and revelled in the new-found opportunity to write keyboard pieces for any key – something that musicians take for granted today. To celebrate the opportunities that were now available to him, he composed a set of preludes and a second set of fugues, systematically working through every possible key, both major and minor. If you do the calculation (2 × 12 × 2), you can work out that this makes a total of 48 pieces and these are known as Bach's *48 Preludes and Fugues for 'The Well-Tempered Clavier (German: Das Wohltemperierte Clavier)'.*

The artist tunes in to musical patterns

Almost certainly, the early human musician used his voice to create melodies and learned to beat with his hands and with sticks to create rhythmic patterns. Over the millennia, his musical tastes gradually matured into something more sophisticated. He began to experiment by creating new musical instruments. This required making certain choices – for example:

- Where exactly should I drill the holes in the wooden pipe to make the notes sound pleasing to the ear?
- Where should the frets be placed in a stringed instrument and at what tension should the strings be set?

He also wanted to keep a record of his musical compositions in order to share them with others and so a range of new notational skills needed to be invented. This chapter has just scratched the surface of this vast and fascinating subject. It has provided a few examples of where mathematical ideas have helped the musician to express his musical yearnings and refine them into a form for performing and sharing with others.

Something for you to try

1 *If a string under tension is plucked, which three key factors determine the pitch of the note produced?*
2 *In which musical scale is the tune 'Auld Lang Syne' written?*

Solutions
1 *The gauge, tension and length of the string.*
2 *A pentatonic scale.*

Chapter 10
Maintaining perspective

Reality is a question of perspective; the further you get from the past, the more concrete and plausible it seems – but as you approach the present, it inevitably seems incredible.

Salman Rushdie

When the artist creates a non-abstract painting or drawing, his aim is usually to represent a three-dimensional image (perhaps a still life, portrait or landscape) on a two-dimensional canvas. In order to achieve this successfully, he has a range of subtle tools at his disposal, many of which have their roots in mathematics.

Foreshortening

Foreshortening is the idea that distant objects appear to our eye to be smaller than objects close up. This principle is evident when you look along the length of a straight road or railway track – the track appears to narrow as it retreats ever further into the distance. The point in the distance where the lines appear to meet is known as the vanishing point.

This idea of foreshortening is the basis of many optical illusions. For example, the one in Figure 10.2 was created by the Italian psychologist Mario Ponzo in 1913. If you measure their heights with a ruler, all four boys in the figure are the same size. But because they

● **Figure 10.1** When you look down a railway track, the tracks appear to narrow.

are placed in a context that suggests 'near' and 'far away', our brain interprets their relative sizes differently – the boy on the right looks huge in relation to the other three.

Earliest records of a serious attempt to depict perspective realistically date back to theatrical productions in ancient Greece in the 5th century

● **Figure 10.2** The foreshortening effect.

BCE. There, people began to develop skills in *skenographia*, which is to do with creating stage sets that plausibly provide the perception of depth. Paintings from the ruins of Pompeii (the Roman town that was buried in the eruption of Mount Vesuvius in CE 79) show evidence that the artists of 1st-century Pompeii also possessed an impressive grasp of perspective.

However, it seems that medieval artists in Europe had to relearn these skills for themselves. European artists before the 14th or 15th century were unable (or perhaps unwilling) to demonstrate full mastery of perspective in their paintings. In many cases it was the spiritual or thematic importance of an object that determined its size on the canvas, rather than its distance from the viewer. Then, as the Renaissance period unfolded, a number of large-scale engineering and military projects enabled many artists of the 15th century to start developing technical skills, which informed their drawing. Other developments also made a valuable contribution – for example, improvements in the design of the telescope and microscope, which went hand in hand with the study of optics (the mathematics of light).

Around 1413, Filippo Brunelleschi painted the outlines of various Florentine buildings onto a mirror, thereby demonstrating the geometrical method of perspective. He also clarified another key principle when depicting perspective – when all the lines of the buildings are extended, they meet in a point that lies on the horizon.

This sketch in Figure 10.3 shows a very long hall with a window in the right wall. By constructing perspective lines, draw another window further down the hallway that appears to be at the same height as the first window.

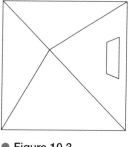

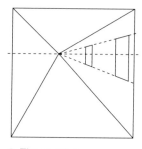

● Figure 10.3   ● Figure 10.4

Solution

Figure 10.4 shows the same picture with the (dotted) perspective lines drawn in and a second window added. Note that the vanishing point is at the end of the hall, where all the lines converge.

Composition and the 'rule of thirds'

An essential part of creating an interesting painting or photograph is deciding where the main subject should be located. This is key to what is known as the *composition* of the figure. A useful general principle of composition is to avoid placing the main subject in the middle of the frame. The so-called 'rule of thirds' is a simple technique for avoiding this and thus making the figure more interesting and dynamic. The idea is to trisect the screen vertically and horizontally, so dividing it into a 3×3 grid of identical boxes. Based on this structure, you are more likely to achieve an interesting composition by observing the following guidelines:

- For a still life or portrait, place your main subject where the lines intersect rather than in the central box.
- For a landscape, place the horizon on either the upper or lower horizontal line.

● **Figure 10.5** Original photo with subjects centred.

● **Figure 10.6** Cropped photo – subjects placed where the lines of thirds intersect.

With most modern digital cameras, a 3×3 grid can be superimposed onto the viewing screen as an aid to composition. Of course, where a digital image has been stored on a computer, the principle of the rule of thirds can be a useful guide when cropping the photo.

A problem with 3-D shapes

The artistic issues raised so far in this chapter have been concerned with the artist's desire to represent three-dimensional objects on a two-dimensional canvas. It's a feature of the way most people learn about mathematics in general, and geometry in particular, that they have to do so by basing their judgements on images in a textbook. This may work well with the geometry of two-dimensional shapes (squares, triangles, circles and so on), but subtle problems are created when studying three-dimensional shapes (cubes, cones, pyramids, and so on). Inevitably, textbook mathematics about three-dimensional shapes represents them on the page as drawings in two dimensions. Unfortunately, such depictions can lay down incorrect intuitions about the properties of the shapes. An example is shown below, based on the properties of a (conical) glass of wine.

Glass of wine

Before exploring the central question about intuitions concerning 2-D and 3-D shapes, let's first establish a relevant fact about the capacity of a conical glass. What is the volume of a conical shape?

Let's work out the capacity of the glass in Figure 10.7 – that is, the volume of air, or wine, that it can contain. It has a top radius, r, of 5 cm and a height, h, of 8 cm. The formula for calculating the volume, V, of a cone is:

$V = \frac{1}{3} \pi r^2 h$.

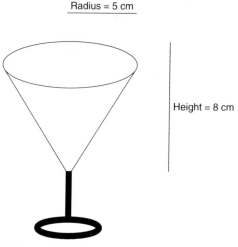

Radius = 5 cm

Height = 8 cm

● **Figure 10.7** These measurements and pi are used to find the capacity of the glass.

Substituting the numbers into this formula gives:

$V = \frac{1}{3} \times \pi \times 5^2 \times 8 \text{ cm}^3$

$= 209.4 \text{ cm}^3$ (rounded to 1 decimal point)

Now suppose you are throwing a party at which the guests are using these conical wine glasses. One of your guests asks for 'just half a glass, please'. To what depth should the glass be filled so that it is half full (i.e. so that there is the same amount of air as wine in the glass)? Which of the four glasses in Figure 10.8 shows the correct answer to this? As a fraction of the height of the conical part of each glass, the wine has been poured: (a) half-way up, (b) two thirds of the way up, (c) three quarters of the way up, and (d) four fifths of the way up. Which would you choose as 'half full'?

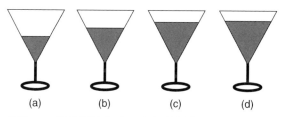

(a)   (b)   (c)   (d)

● **Figure 10.8** Which glass is half full?

You may be surprised to learn that, to fill a conical glass to half of its capacity, you need to fill it to roughly four fifths of its height – i.e. option (d) in Figure 10.8. Most people when asked this question will say either options (b) or (c). If you find this result hard to swallow (sorry about that!), check it yourself using the formula for the volume of a cone given above. If you are interested in checking that this result really is true, have a look at the mathematical solution in the boxed section here.

A mathematical solution to the wine glass problem

As shown, the total capacity of the wine glass in Figures 10.7 and 10.8 is roughly 210 cm^3.

To half fill the glass you will need to pour in 210 cm^3 ÷ 2 = 105 cm^3.

Now consider this conical body of *wine*.

Let its radius = R.

It follows that its height = $^{8R}/_5$. (The explanation for this is as follows. Note that the ratio of height to radius of the original wine glass was 8:5. This ratio will hold for any smaller conical block of wine that the glass contains because all such conical blocks will have the same shape and therefore possess the same proportions.)

We can now write down the following equation, based on the volume of this block of wine that has a capacity of 105 cm^3.

Volume = $^1/_3 × π × R^2 × ^8/_5 R = 105$.

Solving for R gives $R = 4$ cm.

Height of wine cone = $^8/_5 R = 6.4$ cm.

This height expressed as a fraction of the empty glass = $^{6.4}/_8 = 0.8$.

In other words, the wine must fill the glass to 80% (i.e. $^4/_5$) of its height.

So why do people have a poor intuition about this problem? A likely explanation is that they are misled by the diagram, which is a two-dimensional representation of a three-dimensional problem. This means that their intuitive solution is based on comparing areas rather than comparing volumes.

The artist and the illusion of the missing dimension

A key observation of this chapter has been that our intuitions can be fooled when we see three-dimensional objects represented in two dimensions. Because of the way that visual information is received and processed through the eyes, our brains have been trained to make certain adjustments and assumptions when looking at a three-dimensional object and sometimes we can get it badly wrong. This is a problem that our artist has long struggled with and clearly some artistic traditions have coped with it better than others. It has inspired the development of a better understanding of ideas such as foreshortening and perspective as well providing fertile ground for the artist to create optical illusions to confuse and amuse us.

Something for you to try

1 *What word is used to describe a visual effect where an object or distance appears smaller than it actually is because it is angled toward the viewer?*

2 *Suppose you have a wooden cube and you decide to make another one that is twice as big in all dimensions. How does the volume of the larger cube compare with the smaller?*

3 *Two identically shaped plastic bottles of kitchen cleaner hold 500 ml and 250 ml of cleaning fluid, respectively. If you were to compare their heights, how many times taller will the larger bottle be than the smaller one?*

Solutions

1 *Foreshortening.*

2 *The factor by which the volume is increased is $2 \times 2 \times 2$, or 8 times. So the larger brick has a volume eight times that of the smaller brick.*

3 *Let this ratio be X. So, the larger bottle is X times as tall, X times as wide and X times as deep as the smaller one. This means that its capacity is $X \times X \times X = X^3$ times that of the smaller bottle.*

Since the ratio of their capacities = 500/250 = 2, then $X^3 = 2$. Taking the cube root of both sides, $X = \sqrt[3]{2} = 1.26$, approximately. So the larger bottle should be 26% taller (and 26% wider and 26% deeper) than the smaller bottle.

Note that you can check this next time you are in the supermarket – just remember to take your ruler along!

Be an artist

Back in 1959, British scientist and novelist C. P. Snow talked with regret about the breakdown of communication between the 'two cultures' of modern society: science and the humanities. He argued that this great divide was a major obstacle to solving the world's problems. But the idea that we must choose between one or the other presents a false dichotomy. Below are a couple of activities for you to try, which may remind you that in seeking patterns, the artist and the mathematician have more in common than what divides them.

(a) Find a camera and take a series of photographs based on the 'rule of thirds'. If you already have some of your photographs on computer, try cropping them so that the key features conform to this 'rule of thirds'.

(b) Look at some familiar paintings or photographs in a fresh way. For example, try to identify the position of the eye of the artist/photographer. Then check to confirm which parts of the figure show that the artist is looking up and looking down. Also try to pinpoint the position of the source of light by searching for the shadows.

(c) Check out the drawings of Maurits Escher and marvel at his cleverness.

The gambler
Being competitive

The gambler has a fascination with ideas of luck, fate, chance and coincidence. Not only do these ideas point to unknown events that lie ahead, where he simply doesn't know what the next roll of the dice will bring, but also they touch on his interest in competitive game-playing. This section explores situations where the gambler's will to win at all costs meets ideas of probability and chance.

Something the gambler knows better than anyone is that life is uncertain. But how can situations of uncertainty be described and compared? For most everyday situations, chance events can be described and quantified in words – it is *likely* to rain tomorrow, it will be *nearly impossible* to get tickets for this show, there's a *good chance* that I'll pass my driving test this time, and so on. But when the gambler became interested in solving more complex questions about uncertainty, he needed to abandon the rather ambiguous vocabulary of chance and invent a probability number scale.

At times, the gambler finds it hard to distinguish between outcomes that are the result of his own skill and those that can be explained by random chance. What is certain is that he will explain his failures in terms of bad luck and be sure to take full personal credit for his successes! His intuitions about chance events can sometimes let him down, causing him to attribute greater significance to unusual 'coincidences' than might be warranted by a closer examination of the nature of chance.

Occasionally the gambler becomes greedy and resorts to underhand means to win – he starts breaking the rules, being economical with the truth, swinging the lead, dealing off the bottom of the deck, going on the fiddle, otherwise known as cheating. But he'd better watch out because a new breed of forensic mathematicians will be on his trail and he might end up in the dock, up a gum tree, banged to rights, brought to book – or, in a word, busted!

It's not just in casinos and card games that our gambler thrives. He's also drawn to competitions and puzzles and is prepared to overcome his fear of failure to have a go at trying to solve them. In doing so, he is sharpening his mental skills for tackling some of the more serious problems that will crop up in his everyday world.

Chapter 11 • **Betting and gambling**, looks at the gambler's urge to engage in games of chance and how this created the foundations for our better understanding of probability.

Chapter 12 • **Winning: luck or coincidence?**, tries to debunk some popular misconceptions about chance, suggesting, for example, that coincidences happen much more often than we expect.

Chapter 13 • **Cheating**, provides a number of case studies where careful examination of patterns in data has helped to reveal nefarious dealings by cheats.

Chapter 14 • **Competing**, looks at game theory and describes one notorious game where the solution has baffled the minds of many who should have known better.

Chapter 15 • **Puzzling: exercising the curious mind**, provides a selection of some of my favourite puzzles, along with detailed solutions that should help provide insights into how these sorts of puzzles can be tackled.

Chapter 11
Betting and gambling

There is a very easy way to return from a casino with a small fortune: go there with a large one.

Jack Yelton

The words *betting* and *gambling* have a very similar meaning – they refer to the wagering of money on a future event with an uncertain outcome, motivated by the aim of winning a larger amount of money. The gambler's fondness for playing games of chance has a long history. Ancient artefacts for generating random outcomes, such as dice, have been found in China, dating back to around 2300 BCE. A pair of ivory dice made around 1500 BCE were found in Egypt. A clay tablet discovered in one of the pyramids at Giza in Egypt contains writings that describe gambling activity. There is also evidence of various forms of gambling in ancient India, Greece and Rome.

So it would seem that the gambler has existed in most cultures and across many millennia. In the Bible, the Gospel of St John (John 19:23–24) describes how, when Jesus was dying on the cross, the four attending Roman soldiers divided up his garments. However, his tunic was 'without seam, woven from the top in one piece' and so they decided to cast lots for it. There is no record of how they did this but it is likely that they used pebbles or a talus (part of an animal's ankle bone) and rolled them in the manner of rolling dice.

On occasions where rational decision-making has not been adopted or has proved impossible to pursue, problems have often been resolved by the casting of lots (i.e. using the principle of 'let the fates decide'). For example, around the year 1000 CE, there was a dispute between Norway and Sweden about the ownership of the rather obscure island of Hising. As the diplomats failed to resolve the dispute with logic or by deciding entitlement based on precedent, the monarchs of the two countries (both named Olaf, coincidentally) got together to settle the matter with the roll of a pair of dice. The story goes that the Norwegian Olaf won, Norway received the territory, and the two kings departed the best of friends.

In mid-17th-century Europe, interest in games of chance generated a number of questions about gambling probabilities which required rather difficult calculations and this provoked gamblers to seek a better understanding of the mathematics of random events. In 1654, the philosopher and court adviser to Louis XIV, Antoine Gombaud (the self-styled Chevalier de Méré), was interested in the problem of the proper division of the stakes if a game of chance was interrupted. He offered the following problem to the French mathematician, Blaise Pascal:

> Suppose two players, A and B, are playing a three-point game, each having wagered 32 *pistoles*, and are interrupted after A has two points and B has one. How much should each receive?

Gamblers were also interested in comparing the likelihoods of various outcomes when, say, two dice are rolled; for example, is it more likely to achieve a combined score of '10 or 11', or to get a combined score of 7? (The answer is that the latter is slightly more likely than the former – the probabilities are, respectively, $5/_{36}$ and $6/_{36}$.) These sorts of questions required a more systematic approach to thinking about probability than in previous studies and so they led Pascal to build on ideas that were already known about the binomial theorem. (See Chapter 17 for further details of the binomial theorem.)

Blaise Pascal (1623–62)

Pascal was an outstanding French mathematician who excelled in several areas of mathematics. He is best remembered for his contributions to projective geometry and (in association with Pierre de Fermat) to probability theory.

Pascal's mother died when he was only three years old, which resulted in his father educating him and his siblings at home. All the children excelled in their studies but Blaise was a real child prodigy. At the age of 18 he invented a mechanical calculator capable of addition and subtraction, called Pascal's calculator or the Pascaline. Although never a commercial success, this was an important forerunner to modern computer technology. (In his honour, *Pascal* was the name given to a structured computing language that was popular in the 1970s and 1980s.) Two of Pascal's original calculators can be seen at the Musée des Arts et Métiers in Paris and the Zwinger Museum in Dresden, Germany.

Following a brush with death in 1654, Pascal largely abandoned his scientific work, preferring to devote the last eight years of his life to philosophy and theology. From the age of 18 he had endured poor health and, up to his death at the age of 39, he suffered from a painful, nervous ailment as well as debilitating headaches. A post-mortem never fully explained the causes of his ill health but there were suggestions of tuberculosis, stomach cancer and a lesion of the brain.

Dice and coins

The most commonly used artefacts for playing games of chance are dice and coins. So what is it about these objects that makes them so fit for the purpose? Bearing in mind that their function in games of chance is to generate a sequence of random, equally likely outcomes, it is the symmetry of their shapes that makes them ideal choices for this role. The six faces of a perfect cube are all equally likely to remain uppermost after it has been rolled, as are the two faces of a coin when tossed. Other possible outcomes such as the die coming to rest on one of its corners or the coin landing on its edge are so unlikely that they can be ruled out of the equation. What this means is that the chance of getting a particular score (say, a 4) with a single roll of a fair die is one chance in six or, expressed as a fraction, $^1/_6$. Similarly, the chance of getting, say, heads with a single toss of a fair coin is one chance in two, or $^1/_2$.

Of all the topics in mathematics that rest on a person's intuition, the one that does so most uneasily is probability. It seems that most of us, experienced mathematicians included, keep getting it wrong when making intuitive judgements about the likelihoods of chance events.

Here is a short extract from a conversation I had with my daughter, Carrie, when she was seven years old.

Alan: If you throw a dice, which number do you think is hardest to throw?

Carrie: The number you want to throw.

Alan: Why do you say that?

Carrie: Well it seems every time I throw a dice and I want to get a 6 I never get one; I usually get a 1 or a 5.

At the time, my interpretation of Carrie's comments was that she did not understand that each of the six outcomes is equally likely. In particular, she referred to the 6 as being hard to get, which is a common belief. She also seemed to be implying that, in comparison to others, *she* was particularly unlucky in the outcomes that she achieved. However, afterwards, on a more careful re-reading of the entire extract, I began to feel it was I who was failing to grasp the point.

First, Carrie suggested that getting a particular outcome (such as 6) was hard. She was aware that in many board games, this is the desired outcome in order to start the game, which lends it a certain mystique. And, in a sense, she was correct in saying that a 6 is hard to throw; there is only one way of getting a 6 and five ways of getting a not-6, so getting a 6 is five times as hard as getting something else (a not-6). Then there is a second point about a player's likelihood of winning a game of chance. If you are playing against one other player and the game is entirely fair, then you both have a 50:50 chance of winning. But with three or more players, you are less likely to win and more likely to lose the game. For example, with four players, you have a 1 in 4 (0.25) chance of winning and there's a 3 in 4 chance (0.75) of one of the other players winning instead.

I realized that I had rushed to a judgement about Carrie's understanding of probability and that her grasp of these complex ideas was probably more subtle than I had given her credit for. So, as I suggested earlier, intuitions in this area are often faulty, especially when the intuitions are about how successfully mathematics educators grasp the wisdom of their children – sorry Carrie!

The gambler's fallacy

At the time of writing, according to the UK lottery website (www.lottery.co.uk), the lottery number that has come up most often is 38 (with 216 occurrences), while the least commonly occurring number is 20 (with only 152 occurrences). I asked two friends how this information might affect their choice of lottery number next time they played. Peter said, 'Well, I'll choose 38, of course. It has a good track record.' Jannie's reply was very different. 'I'll take 20. It's overdue!' In fact, provided the lottery draw is conducted fairly (which I believe it is), both views are nonsense. Peter and Jannie have both fallen victim to the *gambler's fallacy*.

This fallacy is favoured by gamblers who choose to bet on black at roulette when red has come up, say, five times in a row. In fact, for any given random process (tossing a coin, spinning a roulette wheel, drawing a lottery ball, etc.), the occurrences of all the outcomes are equally likely, regardless of which outcomes have come up previously. The reason is that the outcomes of random processes are *independent* of each other.

People sometimes appeal to the 'law of averages' to justify their faith in the gambler's fallacy. Their reasoning may be that, since the frequencies of all the outcomes will come out to be roughly equal in the long term, there must be something 'in the ether' that causes an 'evening out' effect. But consider what sort of mechanism might be influencing these events to ensure that all the outcomes crop up with the same frequencies. Is there some god of chance pulling the strings behind the scenes saying, 'Well now, that red has come up rather a lot recently; I'd better make the next one black to even it up!' No, this isn't how it works. All we know is that the outcomes are equally likely, but the coin, die or roulette wheel are inanimate and have no memory of what went before. Although in the long term, the patterns may settle down so that the relative frequencies of each outcome are very similar, in the short term you can have no idea what the next toss will bring.

The gambler is self-delusional

The urge to gamble brings together the human instinct for play and the desire to divine our future. The gambler seems to be attracted by a powerful cocktail of greed combined with a fascination about finding out what fate has in store for him. The practice of gambling is so widespread and it generates behaviour that is so addictive, that one can only assume it must be evil! It is a general truism that most gamblers lose more money than they gain (have you ever seen a poor casino owner?). Yet the enthusiastic gambler seems to have one special and enduring quality. This is his aptitude for exercising selective memory; he remembers clearly all his wins but manages to blank out his losses, so that his overall feeling is of having done rather well. And as you will see in the next chapter, what is most reassuring of all is that his losses can be put down to bad luck whereas his wins are down to his skill!

Something to try – your intuitions about chance

Below are ten statements about dice and coins. Use common sense to decide if each one is true or false, and then check your intuitions against the solutions that follow. This might seem simple, but don't be too disappointed if you don't get them all correct!

1   *On a single roll of a fair die, 6 is the hardest score to get.*
2   *On a single roll of a fair die, 6 is harder to get than 'not-6'.*
3   *On a single roll of two fair dice, a combined score of 7 is the most likely outcome.*
4   *Blowing on a die makes the desired outcome more likely.*
5   *Getting a 6 on the first roll of a die makes getting a 6 less likely on the next roll.*
6   *Getting a 6 on the first roll makes getting a 6 more likely on the next roll.*
7   *When you toss six fair coins, exactly three heads and three tails is the most likely outcome.*
8   *When you toss six fair coins, the sequence HHHHHH is a less likely result than HTHTHT.*
9   *When six lottery numbers are drawn, it is less likely that the six numbers will be in sequence than that they will be spread across a wider range.*
10   *When choosing six lottery numbers, you have more chance of winning if your numbers are spread across a wider range than if they are in sequence.*

Solutions
1   *False: with a fair die, all six outcomes are equally likely. The belief that the 6 is 'hard to get' may be linked to the fact that, in many board games, a 6 is the one you want to get, which makes it seem that it will be 'hard'.*
2   *True: there are five ways of getting 'not-6' and only one way of getting 6 so, on a given roll, getting 'not-6' is five times as likely as getting 6.*

3 True: there are six ways of rolling a combined score of 7 (6 + 1, 5 + 2, 4 + 3, 3 + 4, 2 + 5 and 1 + 6) – indeed, there are more ways of rolling a combined score of 7 than any other score.

4 False: there is no evidence that blowing on a die changes the probabilities . . . unless you use this strategy to swap the original die with a loaded one that you have kept up your sleeve! It is possible that this deception is where the myth of 'blowing on the die' comes from.

5 and 6   False: since each roll is independent of all other rolls, whatever outcomes came before shouldn't make any difference to the outcome of the next roll. The belief to the contrary is the basis of the 'Gambler's fallacy'.

7 True: count the number of ways. There are more ways of getting the combination 'three heads and three tails' than any other combination (consider HHHTTT, HTHTHT, HTTHTT, etc., which all give three heads and three tails).

8 False: each of your six tosses is independent of each other toss, so any one sequence is as likely as any other. Despite the result shown in the previous solution, these two outcomes, HHHHHH and HTHTHT, are in fact, equally likely.

9 True: as for statements 3 and 7, it is sensible to ask, 'How many ways. . . ?' There are many, many ways of getting a sequence of numbers that is spread across a wider range, whereas there is only a small number of ways of getting six numbers in sequence (44 ways, in fact).

10 False: the answer to this question parallels the answer to statement 8. Any one selection of six lottery numbers is as likely to win as any other. However, most people who play the lottery don't grasp this idea – and so it actually makes sense to choose six numbers in sequence as your selection because then, if you win the jackpot, there should be fewer other winners to share your winnings with. One caveat is that, apparently, some 300 people each week choose the numbers 1, 2, 3, 4, 5 and 6, so avoid this particular sequence.

Chapter 12
Winning: luck or coincidence?

Of course I believe in luck – how else can I explain the success of people I dislike?

Jean-Michel Cousteau

It's just down to luck

Here are some people's views on whether they believe in luck:

I believe in luck and I also believe in fate. To me, everything happens for a reason and sometimes we're powerless to prevent or change it.

I don't believe in lucky charms like a rabbit's foot or a horseshoe but I do think that sometimes lucky things happen to you – like getting a good hand in cards or winning the lottery.

I don't believe in luck as a force. Most of the important things that have happened in my life are the result of my own good or bad choices. Other things are caused by forces that I can't control but I don't believe it is the same force (luck) every time.

You've got to take it when you find it. Some people see lots of luck and just walk right past it.

The gambler has some subconscious understanding of ideas like luck, chance and fate. Unfortunately, these concepts are not well defined and it is often hard to make sense of what the gambler means when he talks about them. There are two likely ways in which he might be interpreting the word 'luck'. One is 'randomness' – the idea that outcomes are subject to the natural variation that is a feature of random events beyond our control. The second interpretation refers to an undefined 'fate' wherein people's destinies are somehow preordained. With a belief in fate, some people would be deemed luckier than others because 'good luck' is some mystical property that they innately possess more of than 'unlucky' people. A major problem raised by such a fatalistic life view is: if you believe your destiny to be already written in the stars, then why should you make the effort to drive safely, eat sensibly, save money, look after your teeth and generally lead a good life?

Some people say that 'you make your own luck'. I take this to mean that it is more sensible to try to achieve your goals by hard work and seizing opportunities than by sitting around waiting for a lucky break. As Louis Pasteur stated in a lecture at the University of Lille (7 December 1854):

> *Dans les champs de l'observation le hasard ne favorise que les esprits préparés.* (In the fields of observation, chance favours only the prepared mind.)

Coincidence and chance

When people point out a coincidence, the implication is often that such an outcome is so unlikely that it cannot have occurred by chance – there must be some deeper forces at work that have brought the events together. However, the form these deeper forces might take is unclear. For example, some people suggest that accidents (or some other disasters) always come in threes. But what is the causal mechanism that brings about this third disaster in order to fulfil the prediction? The truth is that, if you wait long enough, everything comes in threes!

Yes, there might be some deeper significance in a coincidence, but how would we know if there were? Most of us aren't well equipped to make that judgement because human beings tend to underestimate the frequency of coincidences. This isn't a new idea. Just two thousand years ago the Greek writer Plutarch (CE 46–120) wrote:

It is no great wonder if, in the long process of time, while Fortune takes her course hither and thither, numerous coincidences should spontaneously occur.

Put another way, it would seem that coincidences happen much more often than we expect. Indeed, the most amazing coincidence imaginable would be the complete absence of any coincidence. They are to be expected and require no special explanation.

And yet coincidences fascinate us. Two strangers sitting next to each other on a plane may quickly find some common acquaintance or other fact that links their lives. But this may not be as surprising as it may first appear. Conversations between strangers tend to start out by seeking common ground and sooner or later a shared acquaintance or link of geography or personal history is likely to crop up. Prophetic dreams are also over-rated. Consider that there are 60 million people in the UK, dreaming, on average, 2 hours each night, and each dream lasts between 5 and 20 minutes. By the end of a week, that's getting on for one billion hours of material available to be matched up with some future event in our waking world. Also factor in that our dreams are sometimes triggered by concerns we are already carrying around in our conscious minds and the 'prophetic dream' coincidence suddenly doesn't seem too amazing.

Birthday coincidences

Here's a problem where our intuitions about coincidences may let us down.

The birthday paradox

Imagine that there are 30 people in a room – you and 29 other randomly chosen strangers. What are the chances that at least two people in the room share a birthday? Choose one of these answers:(a) highly unlikely, (b) rather unlikely, (c) about 50:50, (d) greater than 50:50.

The birthday paradox unzipped

Let's do the calculation. To keep things simple, disregard the complication of leap years and assume that the 365 possible birthdays are equally likely and uniformly spread across the year. We'll use the standard numerical measure of probability, which is a number in the range 0 to 1, where 0 corresponds to 'impossible', 1 corresponds to 'certain' and 0.5 is an even chance. You also need to know about combining probabilities: if A is the probability of one event and B is the probability of a second (but unrelated) event, then the probability of *both* events occurring is found by multiplying the two separate probabilities, giving $A \times B$.

With the 30 people in our problem, a good strategy is to start by calculating the chances that *no* two of them share a birthday. Then we'll build up the calculation gradually by inviting each person into the room, one at a time.

The first person enters. It is certain that they don't share a birthday with anyone else in the room (at this stage there is no one else in the room!) so the probability of not sharing a birthday = 1.

The second person enters the room. Note that at this stage only one other birthday has been taken. The probability that the second person doesn't share a birthday with the other person in the room = $1 \times {}^{364}/_{365}$.

The third person enters the room. Now two birthdays have been taken. The probability that they don't share a birthday with either of the other two people in the room is ${}^{363}/_{365}$. The probability that there are no shared birthdays in the room = $1 \times {}^{364}/_{365} \times {}^{363}/_{365}$.

The fourth person enters the room. Now three birthdays have been taken. The probability that they don't share a birthday with any of the other three people in the room is ${}^{362}/_{365}$. The probability that there are no shared birthdays in the room = $1 \times {}^{364}/_{365} \times {}^{363}/_{365} \times {}^{362}/_{365}$.

Continuing in this manner, by the time that the 30th person has entered the room, the probability of no one sharing a birthday = $1 \times {}^{364}/_{365} \times {}^{363}/_{365} \times {}^{362}/_{365} \ldots {}^{336}/_{365}$, which simplifies to 0.29.

By subtraction, it follows that the probability of at least two people sharing a birthday = $1 - 0.29 = 0.71$. So the correct answer to the problem is option (d).

For most people, this is a surprising result. In fact, the break-even number of people for which there is roughly a 50% chance of getting at least one shared birthday is 23 (with a probability of 0.507). What is often underestimated is that there are many possible pairings of the 30 people in the room (many more than 29), so there are lots of opportunities for a birthday to be shared.

Fortune telling

For many centuries, people have amused themselves by having their fortunes told. But why is it still so popular? People who have willingly undergone this experience often admit to pleasure at being the full focus of someone else's attention. Many report that the fortune-teller has made remarkable predictions and insights, based on facts about the person that could not possibly have been known.

So, how is it done? Let's start with a reading that I have specially prepared for you – yes, you, dear reader! You see, I feel we may have known each other in a past life and we have a very special connection . . .

First of all, I think your family is very important to you. But I'm seeing chest pains with a father figure in your family – perhaps your father or grandfather, . . . or it could be an uncle? There's also an older female figure in your life; I think you and she have had some disagreements in the past . . . but she wants you to know that she loved you. Now I see another woman – not a blood relative . . . someone who was around when you were growing up. Was she perhaps a friend of your mother? There's a blackness in her chest . . . was it lung cancer, heart disease, breast cancer. . . ?

Looking at you, I see a very sensitive person. I sense that you sometimes feel rather insecure, especially with people you don't know very well. In your house, I'm seeing a box of old, unsorted photographs. I think that when you were a child, you had an accident involving water.

Are there any surprising insights here? This set of predictions is an example of what is known as a cold reading and it is just one of a variety of techniques used by fortune tellers, psychics and mediums to impress the paying members of the public with their insight and extra-sensory skills.

Clearly, many of these remarks could apply to most people; they are deliberately expressed in such general terms that there is likely to be a grain of truth in some of them for us all. (As an aside, a medium was recently asked to conduct a séance with a studio audience for a live Irish – yes, Irish – TV channel. She closed her eyes and asked, 'Does anyone here know a Mary?'!)

Of course, if we were sitting together, I could pick up much more information about you from your age, sex, body language, manner of dress, hairstyle, educational and regional background and so on. All these factors form a useful database that enables high-probability guesses to be made. Finally, however hard they might try to remain impassive, most subjects subtly betray which predictions are going in the right direction and which are not, so the fortune-teller is quickly able to filter out the dross and follow the body language.

As a teenager I had my fortune read. The most significant feature of the experience for me was how upbeat it all was; it seemed that I was destined for health, happiness and career success. This was all very welcome and I certainly didn't mind crossing the fortune-teller's palm with silver, bathed in the warm glow of such good news!

> A man hears what he wants to hear and disregards the rest.
>
> Paul Simon ('The Boxer')

But do fortune-tellers actually make correct predictions? Certainly they do get it right some of the time. The problem is that we tend to remember the ten correct predictions and conveniently forget the 90 that they got wrong. This phenomenon of selectively remembering the successful predictions and ignoring the rest is sometimes referred to as the Jeane Dixon effect.

Jeane Dixon (1904–97)

Jeanne Dixon was a well-known American astrologer and psychic who achieved fame for her prediction of President J. F. Kennedy's assassination. Her precise prediction was slightly less specific – she said that the 1960 presidential election would be 'won by a Democrat who would then go on to be assassinated, or die in office though not necessarily in his first term.' She is less well remembered, however, for predicting incorrectly that:

The gambler deals with uncertainty

Making life choices is often hard, largely because it normally occurs under conditions of uncertainty. But remember that if you knew an outcome with certainty, there wouldn't be a difficult choice. Sometimes you make a thoughtful and sensible choice that turns out to be wrong. This does not mean that you made a bad decision – just an incorrect one!

So, if all life is a gamble, how should the gambler act in his or her own best interest when making choices? Here are three suggestions.

- In gambling, stop being self-delusional about your success rate and try to keep an honest record of your wins and losses.
- Make a clear distinction between skill and chance and stop taking credit for successes that were outside your control.
- Don't get too excited when you stumble across an 'amazing coincidence' – the chance of it occurring may be greater than intuition might first suggest.

But the last word must go to René Descartes (1596–1650), who wrote in his *Discourse on Method*:

It is a truth very certain that when it is not in our power to determine what is true we ought to follow what is most probable.

1   What do you think is a triskaidekaphobe?
2   You are invited by a friend to play the following game. She tosses two fair coins and explains that there are three possible outcomes – the coins will either come down as two heads, or two tails or one of each. She will bet on 'one of each' and you can take either of the other two outcomes, two heads or two tails. Will you play the game?
3   A fair, symmetrical six-faced die has its faces numbered: 1, 1, 2, 3, 4, 5.
    (a) Before the die is rolled, which number would you bet on and why?
    (b) Let's suppose that the die is rolled and the outcome is 5. What do you now think about the choice you made in part (a)?

Solutions

1   A triskaidekaphobe is someone who is superstitious about the number 13.
2   This is not a fair game! There are actually four equally likely outcomes, not three. These are: HH, TT, HT, TH. Taken together, two of these outcomes (HT and TH) correspond to getting 'one of each' and so this outcome is twice as likely as either HH or TT.
3   (a) The rational choice would be to bet on the '1', since it has two chances to show up and there is only one chance for each other score,
    (b) So it didn't come up – tough! Bear in mind that there are two ways of getting '1', but four ways of getting 'not 1'. Although this means that your chances of losing this bet are double your chances of winning, be pleased that at least you made the right choice – it just didn't work out this time!

Chapter 13
Cheating

I was thrown out of college for cheating in the metaphysics exam – I looked into the soul of the student sitting next to me.

Avy Singer

Although the ancient Greek playwright Sophocles believed that he would prefer to fail with honour than win by cheating, there are many others batting for the other side, ready to win by any means. But just as forensic science has, over the past couple of decades, turned the tables on villains who can now no longer murder and rape with impunity, so forensic mathematics is on the track of 'number cheats'.

Fiddling the figures
Benford's Law

In 1939, Frank Benford, an engineer at the US company General Electric, was playing around with population data for various cities. He noticed a rather interesting fact about these numbers – a surprisingly large proportion of them began with the digit 1, while very few of them began with 9. It must have been a slow day at GEC as Benford decided to press on with his investigations and see whether there was a consistent pattern in all the leading digits of the dataset. He found a very clear pattern – the most commonly occurring first digit was indeed 1, and as he worked through the other first digits (2, 3, 4, etc.) the frequencies of occurrence gradually dropped away.

He wondered whether it was just city population figures that contained this pattern and so he started looking elsewhere. He examined data from newspapers, stock markets and sports publications. He looked at the lengths of rivers and the heights of mountains; they all followed approximately the same pattern, which is summarized in the table below.

Leading digit	1	2	3	4	5	6	7	8	9
Frequency	30%	18%	12%	10%	8%	7%	6%	5%	4%

Benford was able to work out a mathematical formula for the connection between the leading digit, N, and its probability of occurrence, $p(N)$, which is known as Benford's Law:

$$p(N) = \log(N+1) - \log(N).$$

To take a particular example, to find the probability of the leading digit of a number being 1, we substitute the value $N = 1$ into the formula above. This gives:

Probability, $p(1) = \log(1 + 1) - \log(1) = \log(2) - \log(1) = 0.3010 \ldots$ or 30%, rounded to two significant figures.

Of course, not every dataset conforms to Benford's Law. For example, if you collected the heights, in metres, of a large sample of human females, you would find that the vast majority of measures had a leading digit of 1 (i.e. a much greater proportion than the 30% predicted by Benford). Similarly, a dataset of telephone numbers would not conform to the law, for the reason that these numbers are highly constrained by various exclusions and conventions (for example, in the UK, if you include the area codes, all landline numbers have a leading digit of zero). So, Benford's Law doesn't work for numbers controlled to a specific value, or for random numbers. Benford's Law also doesn't work well for small sample sizes.

Although Benford has been given the popular credit for this discovery, the same observation had actually been made over 50 years earlier, by the Canadian Simon Newcomb.

Simon Newcomb (1835–1909)

Simon Newcomb was originally from Nova Scotia. In 1881 he spotted that the first few pages of logarithm books were more well-thumbed than later ones and from this small beginning he deduced the basic principle that is now attributed to Benford. Newcomb published his finding in a short article in the *American Journal of Mathematics*.

Interestingly, Newcomb had very little schooling apart from what he learned from his father, an itinerant schoolteacher. As a young adult, he studied mathematics and physics privately, supporting himself by teaching part-time. Later he got a job in charge of calculations at the Nautical Almanac Office in Cambridge, Massachusetts, which is where he had the opportunity to observe the wear and tear on the logarithm tables used by his team of fellow calculators. Although recognized for his work on astronomy, Newcomb was rewarded for his discovery of Benford's Law by being ignored.

Finding the fraud

In the 1990s, Dr Mark Nigrini from the University of Kansas caused something of a stir by applying a system based on Benford's Law to some fraud cases in Brooklyn. He worked on the principle that if the leading digits of numbers in a dataset such as a tax return were markedly different from those predicted by Benford's Law, this would warrant 'further investigation', with the recommendation of a detailed audit.

Leading digit	Benford's Law (%)	True tax data (%)	Fraudulent data (%)
1	30.1	30.5	0
2	17.6	17.8	1.9
3	12.5	12.6	0
4	9.7	9.6	9.7
5	7.9	7.8	61.2
6	6.7	6.6	23.3
7	5.8	5.6	1
8	5.1	5	2.9
9	4.6	4.5	0

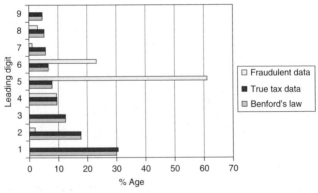

● **Figure 13.1** Application of Benford's Law to tax data. Source: T. P. Hill, 'The First-Digit Phenomenon', *American Scientist*, July-August 1998.

For example, the final two columns of the table here show the percentage occurrences of the leading digits in a set of true tax data (taken from roughly 170 000 inland revenue submissions) and in a set of fraudulent data (taken from a study of cash disbursement and payroll in business). As you can see from the table, and even more dramatically from the chart (Figure 13.1), the true tax data occurrences match the Benford pattern closely, whereas the fraudulent data ones do not. In particular, numbers whose leading digits are 5 and 6 are hugely over-represented in the fraudulent data; and numbers starting with 1, 3, 7 and 9 are lacking.

The patterns that show up in these sorts of investigations are often attributable to situations where certain thresholds are imposed. For example, in a company where there is a £30 upper limit on expenses claims for lunch, it is surprising how many lunch bills come to £29.50. Similarly, in many organizations, payments greater than, say, £100 attract greater attention from accountants than sums just under £100; as a result there are a large number of spurious submissions in the £70–£99 range.

Seven million children go missing!
A feature of Nigrini's forensic method was that he applied it in situations where the cheats had not expected to be caught; their crimes were many but, in the minds of the perpetrators, each one was such a small departure from the truth that surely no one would notice. A statistical crime on a much larger scale took place on the evening of 15 April 1987 when seven million US children disappeared! Was this, as Levitt and Dubner put it in their excellent book, *Freakonomics*, 'the worst kidnapping crime in history'?

This is what actually happened. For the new tax year 1987–88, the Inland Revenue Service had brought in a new rule requiring each dependent child listed on tax forms to be referenced by a Social Security number for that child. Overnight, seven million children who had been listed for the tax year 1986–87 – roughly one in ten of all dependent children in the USA – just vanished. Of course the discrepancy was not necessarily due to fraudulent listing of non-existent children in the previous tax year, to favour the tax liability of the taxpayer, but it seems likely that a fair proportion of the children had been 'fake'.

Cheating teachers

In recent times, as part of measures to improve perform-ance and increase accountability, the 'setting of targets' has mushroomed in many spheres – in health, education, police work and local government, to name just four. Unfortunately there are two undesirable side effects of target setting.

First, targets can never be a perfect match with the underlying goal. However, it is inevitable that people will tend to adjust their performance to meet the targets, which can distort where people put their energies. For example, between 1991 and 1998, a series of standard assessment tests (SATs) was introduced in England to measure the attainment levels of 7, 11 and 14 year-olds. As a result, teachers found themselves under pressure to teach narrowly to the tests, rather than to promote wider and more valuable educational aims.

Second, where people's careers will be publicly judged by the results of tests (for example, educational league tables of SATs results published in local newspapers), there will always be the danger that some will attempt to subvert the system to improve the performance scores by cheating. In 1996, the Chicago Public School authority instigated a new policy whereby schools with low reading scores would be placed on probation, with the threat of being closed down if they failed to show improvement. The seeds were sown for some serious subversion. The story is described in detail by Levitt and Dubner (authors of *Freakonomics*, 2005), who were involved in analysing the data that revealed what was going on behind the scenes.

There was a suspicion that, between the children's completing of the (multiple choice) test papers and the papers being handed over to the educational authority for processing, some doctoring of the answers had taken place. But what sorts of doctoring? Here are some of the patterns that the investigators decided to look for.

- Were there unbroken blocks of correct answers to harder questions at the end of the paper, being scored by weaker students who got low scores earlier in the test with the easier questions?
- Did students from certain classrooms achieve better results than might be expected on the basis of comparisons with their previous performances?
- Were there long strings of correct answers contained within a string of blanks (where the student had not attempted the answer)?

The researchers were able to devise computer analysis tools that tested for these and similar patterns. They concluded that there was evidence of cheating by about 5% of the teachers (that is roughly 200 classrooms). A few weeks after the original test, some retests were carried out for a mix of classrooms – some whose teachers were suspected of cheating and others (chosen as controls) where there was no such suspicion. This time the tests were administered by authority officials – the teachers were not permitted to touch the test papers. The results bore out the suspicions of the researchers; the students in the suspect classrooms did markedly worse than before, whereas in the classrooms chosen as controls the results were pretty much unchanged. In consequence, a number of the cheating teachers lost their jobs and the publicity about the case ensured that the incidence of cheating dropped markedly the following year.

The gambler sometimes deals from a marked deck

Where there is gambling there are, inevitably, winners and losers. Human nature being what it is, if it is possible to become a winner by cheating, someone will try to do so. And where there are cheats, there are suckers waiting to be taken for a ride. (It is said about the world of card games that if, after the first twenty minutes at the table, you don't know who the sucker is, it's you.)

But the good news for Honest Joes like you and me is that cheats are increasingly on the back foot due to recent developments in forensic mathematical techniques. Without the perpetrators being aware of it, their acts of cheating often leave a breadcrumb trail of data that can later be analysed to uncover activities that are suspicious because they contravene certain predictable patterns. Caveat fraudator!

1 Using Benford's Law and a scientific calculator that contains the logarithm command, calculate to 4 significant figures the probability that the leading digit of a number chosen randomly from a dataset is 9.

2 Below are the answers of two students who took the same multiple-choice test consisting of 20 questions. You suspect there may have been some cheating. What evidence can you find for this?

Student X   B, C, C, A, D, E, E, D, E, A, B, E, E, C, A, B, A, E, D, A
Student Y   A, C, B, E, D, C, B, D, A, D, B, E, E, C, A, B, A, E, D, C

Solutions

1 $p(N) = \log (N+1) - \log (N)$.
When $N = 9$, $p(9) = \log (9+1) - \log(9) = \log (10) - \log (9) = 0.0457574906...$, or 0.04576, rounded to four significant figures.

2 The interesting pattern to notice is that the students gave dissimilar answers to many of the questions, apart from a run of nine later (harder) ones, as highlighted below.

Student X   B, C, C, A, D, E, E, D, E, A, **B, E, E, C, A, B, A, E, D**, A
Student Y   A, C, B, E, D, C, B, D, A, D, **B, E, E, C, A, B, A, E, D**, C

It was spotting patterns like this that led to the Chicago detection.

Chapter 14
Competing

*By the time the fool has learned
the game, the players have dispersed.*

African proverb

A key element of game-playing is competition. It is often said that competitiveness (the desire to defeat an opponent in a game) is non-uniformly spread amongst the population – some of us are gripped by the desire to win while others, it would seem, really couldn't care less. However, an individual may have a very laid-back attitude in a gentle game of tennis – but just watch them playing Scrabble or Monopoly and it's a case of 'taking no prisoners'! Also, let's admit: it's easy to demonstrate non-competitiveness in games at which you are patently hopeless anyway, so we shouldn't make too many moral judgements here! Is game-playing a 'good thing'? Well, depending on your point of view, competitive sport is either a safe channel for natural aggression or an incitement to violence and an encouragement for people to impose their will on someone else. Take your choice!

Game theory

In terms of high-conflict competitiveness, one might say that the ultimate game is war, and a great deal of military and academic research has gone into examining the sort of competitive choices people make, based on interpreting the choices taken by others around them. This area of study is now a respectable branch of applied mathematics and goes under the name of 'game theory'. Ideas from game theory have informed our understanding of many fields, including economics, evolutionary biology, computer science and philosophy.

Typically, a game studied in game theory consists of a set of players. Each is provided with a number of possible moves (or strategies) and there will be a clearly defined goal or pay-off. A central question is to do with how one player's behaviour is influenced by attempting to second-guess the behaviour of others around them. A classic game that first appeared in game theory literature around 1950 is known as the prisoner's dilemma.

The prisoner's dilemma

Consider the following scenario. Two suspects of a crime are arrested but the police have insufficient evidence to convict them. The prisoners are separated from each other and invited, in private, to testify against each other. The following three possible outcomes are made known to both prisoners:

- If one testifies against the other and the other remains silent, the testifier goes free and the other receives a 10-year jail sentence.
- If both testify against each other, each receives a five-year sentence.
- If both remain silent, each receives a 1-year prison sentence.

How should the prisoners act?

The four resulting scenarios are summarized in the table below. The two numbers in each cell represent the number of years in jail incurred by A and B respectively. Note that these numbers have been given negative values as they represent a cost rather than a benefit to the two individuals.

	B remains silent	B testifies
A remains silent	−1, −1	−10, 0
A testifies	0, −10	−5, −5

In terms of minimizing their combined cost, the best result for the prisoners is achieved if they both remain silent. This option leads to a combined cost of −1 + −1 = −2 (all three other options lead to a combined cost of −10. The interesting conclusion from the table is that if each player pursues his own self-interest and testifies, this leads both players to be worse off than had they both not done so.

So, why might the ideas behind game theory be useful in the modern world? A major justification is that these models can provide insight into the outcomes and strategies available to individuals and nations in conditions of conflict. If two nations recognize that it is in neither of their interests to go to war, then they may be less likely to initiate hostilities or try to outdo each other in a cripplingly expensive arms race. This concept of mutual deterrence was the guiding principle behind US-Soviet relations during much of the Cold War.

Prisoners and hats

As you saw with the prisoner's dilemma, it's hard to make life-changing choices in circumstances where you don't know what the other key player is going to do. Continuing on the prisoner theme, here is a popular puzzle that also picks up on how your choice is informed by guessing what others are most likely to choose.

The jail is full and when four new prisoners arrive, the jailer realizes he has nowhere to put them. He decides to give them a puzzle – if they succeed they can go free, but if they fail they will be executed (no pressure, then).

Three of the prisoners are placed sitting in a line facing one wall, as shown in Figure 14.1. The fourth prisoner is placed out of sight in an adjacent cell. Each prisoner is given a hat, two of which are red and two blue. The three prisoners on the left can see the hat(s) in front of them but not behind them, and they cannot see their own hat. No communication between the prisoners is allowed.

If any prisoner can work out and say aloud to the jailer what colour of hat he has on his head, then all four prisoners will go free. The puzzle is to work out how the prisoners can escape.

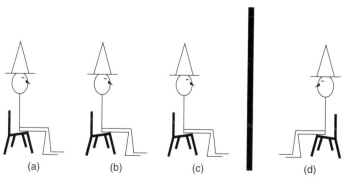

(a)   (b)   (c)   (d)

● **Figure 14.1** The puzzle of the prisoners' hats.

The prisoners' solution

There are two possibilities here, based on whether the colour of hats worn by prisoners B and C are the same or are different. Either way, and assuming that the prisoners behave rationally, they should be able to solve the problem. These two scenarios are set out below.

(a) If the hats worn by prisoners B and C are the same colour

Under these circumstances, prisoner A must take the initiative and speak up. He should realise that the colour of his hat (and that of the solitary prisoner) are the opposite to that of the two hats worn by B and C.

(b) If the hats worn by prisoners B and C are of different colours

This is the more interesting scenario. Under these circumstances, prisoner B must step up to the plate and be the logical one. After a reasonable period of time (say, 2 minutes) has elapsed and prisoner A has not come up with the solution, prisoner B must deduce that the reason for A's silence is that the colours of the hats on prisoners B and C are different. Prisoner B can see in front of him the colour of C's hat, so he can now deduce that his hat must be the opposite colour to that of C.

Note that part (b) of this puzzle is based on an awareness of what someone else would be expected to do (or not do) if acting rationally. Sophisticated games like contract bridge and chess are very much based on this sort of thinking.

The Monty Hall problem

The Monty Hall problem, as it is now known, derives from a 1970s American TV game show hosted by Monty Hall. The show was called Let's Make a Deal and the game was played as follows. A contestant – let's call her Contessa – is shown three doors and is told that behind one door is a car, but behind each of the other two doors is a goat. The host knows what is behind the three doors, but the contestant doesn't. Contessa makes a choice of one of the doors, at which point Monty Hall opens one of the other doors, which he knows will reveal one of the goats. So at this point, Contessa doesn't know whether her initial chosen door is a winner. She is then given a choice: she can either stick with her choice of door, or switch her choice to the other unopened door. Whichever door she now designates (either sticking with her original choice or switching to the other unopened door), it is then opened and Contessa wins whatever is behind it – namely either a goat or a car.

This problem was originally posed in the 'Ask Marilyn' question-and-answer column of the US magazine *Parade*, on 9 September 1990. What is the best strategy for Contessa, to maximize her chance of winning the car? Should she stick with her first choice of door, or switch to the other unopened door, or does it not matter either way? By the way, a reasonable assumption is that, if Contessa initially picks the winning door (with the car behind it), Monty Hall will open one of the remaining two doors randomly (i.e. with equal probabilities).

Play Monty Hall

Now that you know how the game is played, and before reading on, have a go at answering the Monty Hall problem yourself. Also, see if you can come up with a justification for your decision.

The solution to Monty Hall

When it first appeared in *Parade*, the Monty Hall problem generated a lot of controversy. Some people argued passionately that it's best to stick with the first choice and others that it's best to switch, but the majority claimed that it makes no difference to the probability of winning the car whether the contestant sticks or switches. According to cognitive psychologist Massimo Piattelli-Palmarini:

> . . . no other statistical puzzle comes so close to fooling all the people all the time . . . even Nobel physicists systematically give the wrong answer.
>
> Stefan Conrady and Dr. Lionel Jouffe
> *Paradoxes and Fallacies: Resolving some well-known puzzles with Bayesian networks*
> (www.conradyscience.com/index.php/paradoxes)

Most people's intuition leads them to the view that each of the two unopened doors has an equal probability of success and therefore it does not matter whether Contessa sticks or switches. However, this view is wrong. In fact, the rather counter-intuitive solution is that it is better for Contessa to switch her choice to the other door. In fact, switching doubles her chances of winning. Two explanations are set out below.

The common sense explanation

(a) Suppose that your initial choice is the prize door. This has a probability of $1/3$ (i.e. a 1 in 3 chance). If you switch to the other available door, this earns you a goat.

(b) Suppose that your initial choice is a non-prize door. This has a probability of $2/3$ (i.e. a 2 in 3 chance). If you switch to the other available door, you win the prize.

So, since you are more likely to miss with your initial choice of door, and switching from a miss always gives a hit, switching is a good strategy. In fact, you have twice as good a chance of winning the car by switching as you have by sticking.

The tree diagram explanation

If you find it helpful to see solutions visually, the tree diagram in Figure 14.2 may clarify your grasp of the explanation. Here we have assumed that the car is behind door A, but corresponding tree diagrams can be drawn for the other two scenarios where the car is behind door B and door C and the outcome will be the same.

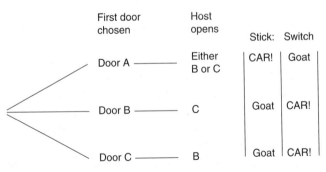

Assuming that the car lies behind Door A

● **Figure 14.2** Tree diagram explanation of the solution to the Monty Hall problem.

The tree diagram shows that a contestant who uses the 'stick' strategy wins a car when their initial choice of door is A and wins a goat when their original choice of door is B or C. The reverse is true for a contestant who 'switches'. This means that there is a 1 in 3 chance of winning by 'sticking' and a 2 in 3 chance of winning by 'switching'.

One reason why most people find this solution hard to accept is that they consider the two unopened doors to be equally valuable. This is not the case. A key element is that the host, Monty Hall, possesses information that the contestant does not. This enables him to open one of those two doors to reveal that it does not hide the prize. Contessa can take advantage of this additional information. Her choice of door A has a 1 in 3 chance of being the winner – that has not changed – but by eliminating door C, the probability that door B hides the prize is $^2/_3$.

My colleague Roger Duke and I have created a computer simulation of this problem at

www.mathsapplets.co.uk

Using our applet, you can set the number of doors to any value from 3 to 9 and explore different strategies. As you will see, the greater the number of doors, the more advantage there is to the strategy of switching.

The gambler second-guesses his opponents

The traditional British attitude to competitive sport has always been to 'play up and play the game' but if you should lose, just remember that 'the game's the thing'. In the USA, sport is often played with a more cutting edge – it's more a case of 'show me a good loser and I'll show you a loser'. Taking risks is an inevitable consequence of living in an uncertain world. But competition brings an added dimension – in a competitive environment, the gambler must attempt to second-guess what decisions his opponents might make, since their choices will affect his own strategic options. This chapter has looked at several examples of problems where the solutions require the solver to try to get inside another person's head.

1   *Each of three people at a party is wearing a different and distinctive hat. They all enter a darkened room, throw their hats into the air and then choose a hat at random. What is the chance that exactly two of them get their own hat?*

2   (a) *In the Monty Hall problem, with three doors, you are twice as likely to win by switching than by sticking. Consider the six-door version where, after your initial door has been selected, four losing doors are opened by the host to reveal a goat behind each one. What is the advantage of switching over sticking in this situation?*

    (b) *Now generalize the problem to n doors.*

Solutions

1   *The probability is zero. If two people retrieve their own hats, the third person must also do so, so getting 'exactly two' successes is impossible.*

2   (a) *In this version you are five times as likely to win by switching than by sticking.*

    (b) *With n doors, you are $n-1$ times as likely to win by switching than by sticking.*

Chapter 15
Puzzling: exercising the curious mind

It is one of man's curious idiosyncrasies to create difficulties for the pleasure of resolving them.

Joseph de Maistre

A major driving force for learning is the learner's curiosity. Curiosity can be observed in all animals but nowhere is it more evident than in the behaviour of young children, eager to discover how the world works. The success (indeed, the very survival) of our species depends on our ability to solve problems successfully and efficiently. Our problem-solving mental muscles need regular exercise, and a good way to get them working is to tackle puzzles of all sorts. On the principle that 'nothing succeeds like success', this chapter provides a variety of entertaining puzzles to help you exercise those mental muscles and keep the problem-solving part of your brain in tip-top condition.

The world's oldest puzzle

This is thought to be the 'loculus' of Archimedes, also known as Archimedes' Box; it was invented by Archimedes around 200 BCE. Similar to the Chinese tangram (which is a square cut into 7 pieces), the loculus consists of a square cut into 14 pieces, as shown in Figure 15.1. The idea is to see how many different ways the pieces can be arranged while still forming a square.

The problem was finally and fully solved in 2003 by mathematician and

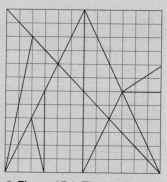

● **Figure 15.1** The loculus: a square cut into 14 pieces.

The puzzles that follow are four of my favourites. Have a go at them and then read the solutions, which I hope will give some helpful general insights into how these types of puzzles might be approached.

Truth and liar

You are in a room with two doors. One door leads to freedom and the other leads to certain death by hungry crocodiles. Standing beside the doors are two individuals – one is a knight, who always tells the truth, and the other is a knave, who always lies. Unfortunately, you do not know which is the knight and which the knave. In order to work out which door to choose, you may ask one of these individuals just one question. What question should you ask?

'Truth and liar' solution

Ask: 'If I were to ask the other individual which door leads to freedom, which one would he point to?' Whether you ask this question of the knight or the knave, the answer you get will be a lie, and so you should choose the door that is not pointed to.

Explanation

If you ask the knight the above question, he will truthfully state the knave's lie, and so the answer you receive will be a lie. If you ask the knave the question, he will lie about the knight's truthful answer, and so the answer you receive will still be a lie.

This strategy can be summarized mathematically as follows.

- Allocate the value 0 to a truthful statement, and the value 1 to a lie. Then:
  - a truthful statement about a lie corresponds to $0 + 1$, which equals 1; and

- a lie about a truthful statement corresponds to 1 + 0, which also equals 1.
- So, whichever order occurs, the answer will always be a lie (i.e. with value = 1).

Slow-burning ropes

You have two ropes (A and B), each of which will burn for exactly one hour. However, they do not burn at a constant speed, so the rate of burning is not proportional to the time elapsed. How can you use them to measure 45 minutes?

'Slow-burning ropes' solution

Set rope A alight at one end while at the same time lighting rope B at both ends. Rope B will take exactly 30 minutes to burn out completely. Immediately light the other end of rope A – it will burn out completely in a further 15 minutes. Now a total of 45 minutes have elapsed.

Explanation

The complicating feature of these ropes, that 'the rate of burning is not proportional to the time elapsed,' is what makes this an interesting puzzle. Here are three further considerations.

(a) If the ropes did burn evenly, the solution would be trivial – simply measure one of the ropes, mark a point three quarters of the way along and set the opposite end alight. When the light reaches the mark, 45 minutes will have elapsed.

(b) The 'uneven rate of burning' feature of these ropes implies that you can only make predictions about time elapsed if a rope is burned through entirely. Realizing this is central to the solution set out above.

(c) In order to check that the solution really does work when the rate of burning is uneven, let us take an extreme case: namely, that the left half of each rope burns through in 10 minutes and the right half burns through in 50 minutes (making 60 minutes in all). We shall also assume that both ropes start with a length of 100 cm, so the rate of burning of the left half is 5 cm per minute and the rate of burning of the right half is 1 cm per minute.

Time (mins)	Rope A	L	R	Rope B	L	R
0	0 → 100			0 → 100		
10	50 → 100			50 → 90		
20	60 → 100			60 → 80		
30	70 → 100			burns out at 70 cm*		
40	80 → 90					
45	burns out at 85 cm					

*Now light the right end of Rope A.

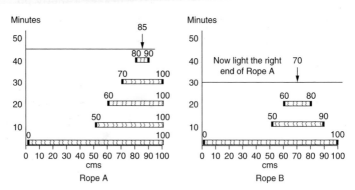

Figure 15.2 How two slow-burning ropes can be used to measure time.

Figure 15.2 shows which sides of the ropes are alight and where they have got to over time.

Nine gold bars

You have nine identical-looking gold bars. Eight weigh exactly 1 kilo each, but the ninth weighs more than 1 kilo. Using a weighing scale with two pans, and carrying out only two weighings, how can you determine which is the heavy gold bar?

(There are several variants of this puzzle – for example, one starts with twelve bars while in another you don't know whether the odd bar is heavier or lighter than the others, but this time you are allowed three weighings.)

'Nine gold bars' solution

Number the bars 1, 2, 3, . . . 9 and arrange them into three groups, 1–3, 4–6 and 7–9.

Place bars 1–3 on one pan and 4–6 on the other. If they balance, go to A below; if they don't balance, go to B below.

A If bars 1–3 and 4–6 balance, the heavy bar must be in the 7–9 group. Choose any two of these bars (say, 7 and 8) and put one in each pan. If they balance, the heavy bar is number 9; if they don't balance, you can see which of the two bars (7 or 8) is heavier.

B If bars 1–3 and 4–6 don't balance, you can see which of the two groups contains the heavy bar (say, 4–6). Choose any two of these bars (say, 4 and 5) and put one in each pan. If they balance, the heavy bar is number 6; if they don't balance, you can see which of the two bars (4 or 5) is heavier.

Explanation

The type of thinking required to solve this puzzle is based on the idea of *branching* (i.e. it contains statements in the form, 'if this, then do that, otherwise do the other'). You can bring clarity to branching problems by setting out the options in the form of a tree diagram, as in Figure 15.3.

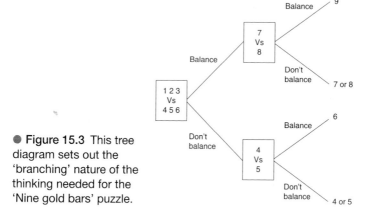

● **Figure 15.3** This tree diagram sets out the 'branching' nature of the thinking needed for the 'Nine gold bars' puzzle.

Crossing the river

There are many forms of problems involving river crossings (for example, the now rather politically incorrect 'missionaries and cannibals' one). The version below is one of the best known and was apparently a particular favourite of Lewis Carroll, author of *Alice's Adventures in Wonderland*.

A farmer went to market and purchased a fox, a goose and a bag of corn. His journey home involved crossing a river so he hired a small boat. However, the boat could only carry himself and one of his purchases – the fox, the goose or the bag of corn. If left alone, the fox would eat the goose, and the goose would eat the corn.

How could the farmer carry himself and his three purchases to the far bank of the river, and keep all of them intact?

'Crossing the river' solution

Step 1: Take the goose over
Step 2: Return
Step 3: Take the fox or corn over
Step 4: Bring the goose back
Step 5: Take the corn or fox over
Step 6: Return
Step 7: Take the goose over

Explanation

A common trick of mathematicians when tackling problems set within some sort of scenario is to strip away the context and so reduce the detail to the bare minimum. This approach, sometimes called 'mathematical modelling', can make it easier to see an underlying structure and, with a bit of luck, may allow you to spot that the problem is essentially one of a known type. A further advantage of modelling problems in this way is that it may provide you with a method that allows you to tackle much harder versions of the same problem.

Looking at the 'Crossing the river' puzzle, the three items could be replaced by numbers: 3 = fox, 2 = goose and 1 = bag of corn.

Six combinations can be identified, which are:

- each item left on its own (three of these); and
- the items arranged in pairs (also three of these).

Expressed in numbers, these six situations correspond to: {1}, {2}, {3}, {1,2}, {2,3}, {1,3}.

Of these six situations, only two - {1,2} and {2,3} - are dangerous, so these are the ones to avoid. In other words, two adjacent numbers must not be left together unsupervised. Notice that both of these dangerous combinations involve number 2 (the goose) combined with one other item – which explains why, in the solution above, the goose gets to do so much travelling (it has a tendency either to eat or be eaten!).

The two tables in Figure 15.4 provide a summary of the seven steps in the two possible solutions (depending on whether the corn or the fox is taken over first in Step 3). Note that the shading on a cell shows the location of the boat (left or right) at that step.

Step	Left	Right
0	123	
1	13	2
2	13	2
3	3	12
4	32	1
5	2	13
6	2	13
7		123

Step	Left	Right
0	123	
1	13	2
2	13	2
3	1	23
4	12	3
5	2	13
6	2	13
7		123

● **Figure 15.4** (a) Solution 1: the corn (item 1) is taken over in Step 3. (b) Solution 2: the fox (item 3) is taken over in Step 3.

Something more for you to try

If you are keen to explore more logical puzzles, you will find a wide selection on the web – http://www.cut-the-knot.org/ would be a good starting place.

The gambler enjoys tackling puzzles

Some people say they dislike tackling puzzles and problems. Often this response derives from a lack of confidence in their problem-solving skills – they don't think they're very good at it. The gambler, on the other hand, doesn't fear the unknown. He is happy to embark on a problem or puzzle where the outcome is uncertain, and is prepared to take the risk that he might not succeed. This type of willingness to take risks and the perseverance to keep trying when you get stuck are valuable life skills. I believe that they lay down useful strategies, helping to train the mind and keep it active and resilient for tackling the more pressing real-life problems we may face in the future.

Be a (better) gambler

Most people would agree that 'luck' refers to occurrences that are beyond their control. What there is less agreement about is whether such events are purely random or actually controlled by some external force. This book has suggested that many people have a dodgy grasp of ideas like luck, chance and coincidence. If you are one of those people, you may be at a serious disadvantage when it comes to gambling, because your instincts may not lead you to make sensible decisions. To help you think a little more about these questions, here are two statements about chance that are wrong. Check that you understand the underlying fallacies. If you are unable to explain why the statements are wrong, you might find it helpful to skim through the five 'Gambler' chapters again, for enlightenment.

(a) On average, when a fair coin is tossed, heads and tails come up roughly the same number of times. If you have just tossed five heads in a row, your next toss is more likely to be tails.

(b) When two fair coins are tossed, there are three equally likely outcomes – two heads, two tails and one of each.

Finally, here is a life-or-death brain-teaser. You are given 50 black marbles, 50 red marbles and two empty bowls. You are asked to divide the 100 marbles into the two bowls in any way you like, provided you use all the marbles. You will then be blindfolded and the bowls will be mixed around. Still blindfolded, you must choose one bowl and remove one marble from it. If this marble is black, you will live, but if the marble is red, you will die. How should you divide the marbles up so that you have the greatest probability of choosing a black marble?

Solution
Into one bowl, place a single black marble. The other bowl will contain the remaining 99 marbles (50 red and 49 black). If you happen to select the first bowl, you are certain to get a black marble. If you select the second bowl, your chances of getting a black marble are roughly 0.5 (actually 49/99). So, arranging the marbles in this way increases your chances of survival from 0.5 to roughly 0.747 (i.e. $0.5 \times 1 + 0.5 \times 49/99$).

The scientist
Understanding how my world works

Things didn't start out too well for the scientist. In his attempts to find out how the world worked, he found himself looking in the wrong places. He wasted a lot of time examining goat entrails and studying the alignment of the stars and planets to find explanations for everyday earthly happenings. His conclusions were too often drawn on the basis of a vague instinctive feeling or a strange sensation 'in his bones'.

Religious leaders too often got in on the act, threatening him with dire punishment if he dared to disseminate new theories that they felt contradicted 'God's truth', revealed exclusively to them. But slowly the scientist began to block out the siren voices and realize that the only sensible way to establish the truth or falsehood of an idea was on the basis of the *evidence*. He began to ask questions like 'I wonder what would happen if. . .?' and 'Under what conditions does that happen?' These questions led him to start searching for understanding by conducting well-designed experiments; he started to use careful measurements, and to include control groups, and became open to the possibility that there might be alternative explanations for the phenomena he observed.

The Scientist chapters of this book explore some of the big ideas on which the principles of scientific thinking are founded.

Chapter 16
Measuring: very large and very small

If you cannot measure it,
you cannot improve it.

Lord Kelvin

A history of measurement

In his quest to find out how the world worked, the scientist quickly discovered two important principles. One was not to take other people's word for it. So, if you have doubts about the prevailing explanation for anything – from the shape of the Earth and its location within the universe to the basic laws of nature, then get out there and find out for yourself! Secondly, the scientist realized that a key to understanding lay in the careful measurement of the thing you are interested in. To slightly adapt Lord Kelvin's words quoted above, if you cannot measure it, you cannot properly understand it.

From the earliest times in the development of human society, the scientist exchanged information about the objects and events in our shared world with others around him. At its most basic, this meant agreeing on the names of these objects. This gave rise to one of the simplest forms of measurement – known as measuring on a *nominal* (i.e. naming) scale. However, names alone do not capture the subtle and changing nature of the world and what it contains. It was inevitable that our scientist would want to compare objects by their size and this required measures that included the notions of 'greater than', 'less than' and 'equal to'. The scale that results from these sorts of comparative measures is known as an *ordinal* (i.e. ordering) scale. Many dimensions can be compared in this way – length (longer than), time (later than), weight (heavier than), temperature (hotter than), and so on.

Inevitably again, the scientist needed to invent some sort of *numerical* scale and, for each dimension under consideration, a fundamental unit of measure needed to be agreed. Not surprisingly, the earliest units for measuring length were borrowed from human body parts – the everyday rulers that humans carry around with them at all times. For example:

- An inch was the thickness of a man's thumb, or the length of the forefinger, from the tip to the first joint.
- A foot was . . . well, that one's obvious.
- A yard was the length of a man's stride, or the distance from the tip of a man's nose to the end of his outstretched arm (I can remember, as a child, going to markets where cloth merchants sold material in yards using this measure).
- Another unit of length commonly used around the world was the cubit (the length of a man's forearm, or the distance from the tip of the elbow to the end of his middle finger).

How big was Noah's ark?
According to Genesis 6:13-16:

> The length of the ark [shall be] three hundred cubits, the breadth of it fifty cubits, and the height of it thirty cubits . . .

Working on the basis that a cubit is about 18 inches, this means that the ark would have been 450 feet long, 75 feet wide and 45 feet high. As a basis of comparison, the dimensions of a standard soccer pitch are 105m by 68m, or roughly 350 feet by 250 feet. As you can see from the sketch in Figure 16.1, this ark of Noah's was a serious boat!

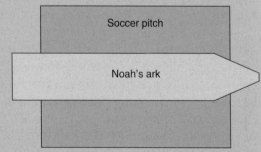

● **Figure 16.1** The size of Noah's ark compared to a soccer pitch.

Regardless of how tall or short people are, because humans all share a similar shape, their individual body proportions are roughly the same. So, for most people, the length of their foot is roughly twelve times the thickness of their thumb. Also the length of their stride is roughly three times the length of their foot. These body ratios would have given rise to the connections between the units – for example:

- 12 inches = 1 foot;
- 3 feet = 1 yard;
- 1 cubit = 1½ feet, and so on.

As the scientist's world became more complex, the need grew for greater precision and consistency in measurement. Eventually the benefits of convenience of everyday units based on the body were outweighed by their main disadvantage – that no two inches, feet, cubits, etc., could be relied upon to be exactly the same. Attempts were made by many civilizations to standardize them. For example, there is considerable architectural evidence from various cross-referenced sources that the Egyptian royal cubit was between 20.61 and 20.63 inches in length (just over 52 cm), a unit that remained virtually unchanged for 3000 years. It was subdivided into 7 palms, each of which contained 4 digits, giving a 28-part measure in total. The standard Roman cubit (the *cubitus*) was equal to 17.4 inches (roughly 44 cm), and was subdivided into 6 palms.

Horses and ponies

Traces of the ancient measures are evident today in the equine world, where horses and ponies are still measured in 'hands'. For example, here is an advertisement from www.horsemart.co.uk:

8 yrs 15.2 hh Bright Bay Irish Sport Horse – Hertfordshire

This eight-year-old horse is 15 hands high (hh) and 2 inches, measured from the ground to the highest point of the withers (where the neck meets the back). A hand is taken as the width of the palm, sometimes including the thumb when closed against the palm, and is equal to 4 inches (101.6 millimetres). So the height of Bright Bay is 15 hands (60 inches [152.4 cm]) plus 2 inches (5.1 cm), making a total of 62 inches (157.5 cm).

The metric system

The metric system of measurement, based on the metre as the standard unit of length, was adopted in France in 1793. The metre was chosen to be one tenth-millionth part of the distance from the North Pole to the Equator when measured on a straight line running along the surface of the Earth through Paris. All other units of length were in multiples of ten – for example, there are ten metres in a dekametre, a hundred metres in a hectometre, and a thousand metres in a kilometre. Going the other way, there are ten decimetres in a metre, a hundred centimetres in a metre, and a thousand millimetres in a metre. One metre is just a little longer than a yard – approximately 39.37 inches.

Two excellent features of the metric system make it much more attractive than the imperial system of measurement that I was taught in school. First, unlike the imperial measures, where the conversion units could be 3, or 12, or 14, or 16 or 20 or . . . well, anything, metric units are converted just by multiplying or dividing by powers of 10. In a decimal world, this simply involves moving the decimal point – for example, a length of 1357 m is the same as 1.357 kilometres, and so on.

Second, whatever the dimension being measured, a standard unit is allocated and, thereafter, all other units are defined according to a standard set of prefixes. These are:

deca- = 10, hecto- = 100, kilo- = 1000, etc., and
deci- = $^1/_{10}$, centi- = $^1/_{100}$, milli- = $^1/_{1000}$, etc.

For example, the gram is the standard unit of weight, so 1 kilogram equals 1000 grams and a milligram is one thousandth of a gram.

SI units

A major update of measuring units took place in 1960 with the establishment of a modern international system of measuring known as SI units (from the French, *Le Système International d'Unités*). It was established by the 11th General Conference on Weights and Measures and is now an agreed standard throughout most of the world. The General Conference meets on a regular basis with the twin aims of ensuring a wide dissemination of the SI system and modifying it as necessary to reflect the latest advances in science and technology. For scientists, the great advantage of the SI system is that whether they are working in Belfast, Beijing or Buenos Aires, they can be confident that when they refer to 1 kilometre or 1 gram or 1 degree Celsius, everyone else will understand exactly what they mean.

Very large and very small numbers

Although there are many circumstances where precise information is required to resolve a problem, most of the time an approximate figure is good enough for our purposes. So, being able to make a rough estimate, or perform an approximate 'back of an envelope' calculation, is a useful skill to help us get a feel for the order of magnitude involved. When estimating weights, many people think of a bag of sugar as an example of 1 kilo or, going back to old-fashioned imperial units, they think of a 6-foot policeman as a handy template for estimating heights. However, when the quantities under consideration involve huge or very tiny numbers, it is not so easy to find suitable 'common-sense' templates for making ballpark estimates.

In his entertaining and informative book *A Short History of Nearly Everything* (Black Swan, 2004), Bill Bryson provides a variety of imaginative templates to help us think about very large and very small numbers. Here are four of his examples:

- Astronomers today believe that there are perhaps 140 billion galaxies in the visible universe . . . If galaxies were frozen peas, it would be enough to fill a large auditorium – . . . say . . . the Royal Albert Hall (page 169).
- A typical atom has a diameter of 0.00000008 cm . . . Half a million of them lined up shoulder to shoulder could hide behind a human hair (page 176).
- An atom is to a millimetre as the thickness of a sheet of paper is to the height of the Empire State Building (page 177).
- [On how far back is the Cambrian era, the first geological period of the Paleozoic Era, lasting from

about 542 million years ago to 488 million years ago]
If you could fly backwards into the past at a rate of
one year per second, it would take you about half an
hour to reach the time of Christ, and a little over three
weeks to get back to the beginnings of human life.
But it would take you twenty years to reach the dawn
of the Cambrian period (page 395).

Some guesstimates for you to try

*Fortunately, making estimates is a skill that can quickly improve with
practice, particularly when there is a calculator to hand. Here are some
for you to work on.*

1   *A driver at the port of Dover, just returned from France, was
    found to have one million cigarettes in the back of his van. When
    questioned, he claimed that these were for his personal use. By
    making a common-sense assumption about average tobacco
    consumption, estimate roughly how many years his haul could
    be expected to maintain his smoking habit. Options: 1 year, 10
    years, 30 years, 80 years, 140 years.*

2   *How many years will it take for one billion seconds to tick
    by? (Note that modern usage of the word billion means one
    thousand million.) Options: 1 year, 10 years, 30 years, 80 years,
    140 years.*

Solutions

1   *Assume an average smoker's consumption of 20 cigarettes per
    day, which means an annual consumption of $20 \times 365 = 7300$
    cigarettes. Divide this number into one million: the cigarette haul
    would be expected to last him roughly 137 years, so the nearest
    option is 140 years.*

2   *Number of years that are equivalent to one billion seconds =
    $1\,000\,000\,000 \div 60 \div 60 \div 24 \div 365 = 31.7$ years approximately,
    so the nearest option is 30 years.*

    *Back in Chapter 5 you read about some numbers like the googol
    and the googolplex, which are so large as to be 'beyond our
    imagination'. The scientist is often confronted with numbers
    so huge or so tiny that they are hard to make sense of using
    conventional number notation. Here are some examples.*

Very large

- *The number of bits, in standard SI usage, on a 1 terabyte
  (1 Tbyte) computer hard disk is 10 000 000 000 000.*
- *The number of cells in the human body is more than
  100 000 000 000 000.*
- *The observable universe is 93 000 000 000 light years across,
  which is equivalent to 880 000 000 000 000 000 000 000 000*

metres, and contains about 50 000 000 000 000 000 000 stars. (Note that one light year is the distance travelled by light in one year and has a value of roughly 9 460 000 000 000 metres.)

Very small
- *The wavelength of green light is 0.000 000 55 metres.*
- *The time taken by light to travel one metre is roughly 0.000 000 003 seconds.*
- *The radius of a hydrogen atom is 0.000 000 000 025 metres.*

Scientific notation

As you may have observed from the examples above, very large and very small numbers are not suited for being written in conventional notation. When they are written in that way, it is difficult to get a sense of their size and so comparisons are difficult to make. A better approach is to express them in a different format, known as *scientific notation* (also known as standard form).

To write a conventional number in scientific notation, express it as a number between 1 and 10, multiplied by a power of 10. For example, for numbers larger than 1:

380 is written as 3.8×10^2
5170000 is written as 5.17×10^6

and so on. For small numbers (numbers less than 1) the power of 10 takes a negative value. If you are unsure about this idea, note that one tenth ($^1/_{10}$) is equal to 10^{-1}, one hundredth ($^1/_{100}$) is equal to 10^{-2}, and so on. So, for example:

0.38 is written as 3.8×10^{-1},
0.000473 is written as 4.73×10^{-4}.

The main benefit of displaying very large or very small numbers in scientific notation is that it makes them easier to read, and you can tell the order of magnitude at a glance (rather than having to count zeros). If you can lay your hands on a scientific calculator, you will find it an entertaining medium for exploring scientific notation. A special feature of these calculators, and a reason why they are called 'scientific', is that they automatically jump to scientific notation when displaying very large or very small numbers.

The scientist sizes up the world

The scientist has long been fascinated by natural phenomena and over several millennia has created and refined a set of useful tools to help him describe and explain them. In his quest for answers to some really big questions, he has also developed a system of acquiring knowledge based on observation, experimentation and measurement; this format for conducting investigations is often referred to as the *scientific method*. It rests on the important principle that the observer and the phenomena being observed should be kept separate, which means that if another scientist in another part of the world looks at the same thing using the same method, the same outcome should result.

This chapter has focused on one strand of the scientific method – measurement. Because the scientist often has to deal with very large and very small numbers, he has devised an alternative way of writing numbers, known as scientific notation.

Something for you to try

1 An electron's mass, in conventional notation, is roughly:
   0.000 000 000 000 000 000 000 000 000 000 910 938 22 kg.
   What is this in scientific notation?

2 The Earth's mass in scientific notation, is approximately 5.9736×10^{24} kg. What is this in conventional notation?

3 The population of the UK is roughly 60 billion. How many people would you expect to die in the UK each day?

4 The world's smallest guitar, the nano guitar, is at Cornell University; it is made from silicon and is 10 micrometers long. Each of the six strings is about 50 nanometres (or about 100 atoms) wide. An ordinary guitar is roughly 1 m long. How many times bigger is it than the nano guitar?

Solutions

1 Roughly $9.1093822 \times 10^{-31}$ kg.

2 About 5 973 600 000 000 000 000 000 000 kg.

3 Let's assume an average lifespan of 70 years, so each year roughly $^1/_{70}$th of the UK's population dies. That means that each day the fraction is $^1/_{70 \times 365}$. The UK's population is roughly 60 million, so the daily number of deaths is 60 000 000 $\times$ $^1/_{70 \times 365}$ or roughly 350.

4 An ordinary guitar is roughly 100 000 times bigger than the nano guitar.

Chapter 17
Understanding families: the binomial distribution

> *My friend has a baby. I'm recording all the noises he makes so later I can ask him what he meant.*
>
> Stephen Wright

Compared to what?

Imagine the following scenario. The scientist has just carried out an experiment and collected relevant data and now is sitting staring at a mass of figures wondering what to make of them. This is a common enough scenario for scientists at all levels of sophistication; they want to make decisions informed by evidence, but sometimes the evidence is messy and difficult to interpret.

Having faced this situation many times, the scientist discovered a way of dealing with the problem. He worked out the following important principle for designing experiments: where possible, include a *control* element against which to compare the data collected in the experiment. Sometimes the control takes the form of a second sample, a group of people randomly selected to reflect accurately the characteristics of the wider population. An alternative to setting up a control group as a basis of comparison is to ask 'What result would I expect to get by chance alone?' In this chapter we look at this second path; and the particular model of chance to be considered here is called *the binomial distribution*.

Is it a boy or a girl?

There are many myths surrounding what determines the sex of a baby. For example, some people suggest that the sperm for male children come from one testicle, and sperm for female children from the other one. This is a mistaken theory – in fact, men who have had one testicle removed surgically produce, on average, equal proportions of male and female babies. The only truth in this theory is the link with the father – a baby's gender *is* determined by their father, but for a completely different reason. If the father provides an X chromosome, the baby will be female, and if he supplies a Y chromosome, the baby will be male. Because the mother can provide only an X chromosome, she cannot have the same influence over the sex of her child.

The chance of an unborn child being a girl is slightly lower than of it being a boy – approximately 0.48 compared with 0.52. However, the survival rates of boys are lower, right through early childhood and into the teenage years, due to the following factors:

- Boys have a higher death rate if born premature.
- Rates of Sudden Infant Death (SID) syndrome are 50% higher in boys than girls.
- As teenagers, boys die at twice the rate of girls.

As a result of these factors, by their mid-thirties, women slightly outnumber men. Overall, then, the differences in the sex balance are small and for simplicity the probabilities of the baby being a girl, P(G), and a boy, P(B), are usually taken as equal: i.e. P(G) = P(B) = 0.5.

The extent of the difference in the boy/girl ratio is not fixed. The disparity decreases for older mothers and for women with larger numbers of children. There are also ethnic differences – Chinese and Filipino women have a relatively high ratio of boys to girls, while for American Indian mothers it is lower.

Now here's another myth. Let's say you already have five children, all of whom are girls, and you discover that number six is on the way. Many people believe that the sixth one is more likely to be a boy. This is incorrect for similar reasons to those explained about the 'gambler's fallacy', in Chapter 11. Although there are patterns that characterize the girl/boy combinations in families with five children, these will not influence the outcome when it comes to predicting the sex of the *next* child that you have.

The pattern of sex composition of children in a family is similar to the pattern of outcomes (heads and tails) when a fair coin is tossed. In statistics, this pattern is called *binomial* – literally, 'two names' – because there are only two possible outcomes. In these two examples (sex at birth and outcome when tossing a coin), the probabilities of both outcomes are equal.

A common and incorrect assumption is that the outcomes of a binomial situation must *always* be equally likely. This condition of equal-likelihood is not a requirement, however, and there are many other binomial situations where the two possible outcomes are not equally likely. Here is a simple example: consider the rolling of a die; we normally think of this as having six equally likely outcomes, each with a probability of $1/_6$. Now let's simplify this scenario so that the six outcomes are reduced to just two outcomes that are not equally likely – for example, getting a six and getting a not-six, which have probabilities $1/_6$ and $5/_6$, respectively.

The binomial pattern

The binomial pattern provides a good model of the sex composition of the children in a family. Let's investigate the sorts of family compositions that this produces, starting with a small family of just two children. These outcomes can be simulated by tossing a pair of coins. Each coin can produce either 'heads' or 'tails' and these outcomes correspond to, say, 'girl' and 'boy', respectively. In order to generate the sex compositions for a large number of two-child families, you would need to toss a pair of coins many times.

Imagine that you toss two fair coins 100 times and count the frequencies of the following three outcomes: 'both heads', 'both tails', 'one of each'. Roughly how many would you expect to get for each outcome?

A common belief is that these three outcomes must all be equally likely but this is incorrect. The explanation is that there is only one way of getting two heads, HH, one way of getting two tails, TT, but two ways of getting one of each, HT and TH. So getting one of each is actually twice as likely as getting one of the other two outcomes. I ran this as a simulation on a spreadsheet and got the results of six runs shown in Figure 17.1. As you can see, the pattern roughly matches the underlying probabilities of 0.25, 0.5 and 0.25 but the outcomes are not exactly equal to these proportions – due to natural variation, the results will vary a bit each time the simulation is run.

Run	Both tails	One of each	Both heads
1	16	52	32
2	21	60	19
3	21	52	27
4	26	48	26
5	24	56	20
6	28	49	23

● **Figure 17.1** Outcomes of tossing a pair of coins.

And so it is with the sex composition of families – the underlying proportions remain but, particularly for small sample sizes, there will be a fair degree of variation. In fact, this is one reason why most of us have an imperfect intuition about these things. We can observe family compositions around us but our sample of experience is relatively small and so any underlying patterns are masked by the sort of variation that is inevitable with small samples. As a result, many people are prepared to believe that it is possible to predict the sex of the unborn child by observing the contours of the bump on the mother's tummy or by dangling a needle above the bump to see how it swings. Some of these predictions do turn out, by chance, to be correct, but in our dealings with predicting the sex of babies we just haven't drawn from a large enough sample of experience to test whether the predictions score better than just random guesses. If we were to conduct a more scientific test that involved a larger sample size and was based on unambiguous measurement, we would all be able to spot that these theories are bunkum!

Astra can see into your wallet
Before the days of ultrasound scans, which can predict a baby's sex scientifically and accurately from about 20 weeks in the womb, mothers were at the mercy of scam merchants for this sort of information. A

typical scam would work like this. An advertisement would be placed in a newspaper, such as:

Astra can see into your womb.
Predict the sex of your unborn baby
Only £20; money-back guarantee.

Along with the all-important £20 note, the mother would be asked to send in some personal artefact (perhaps a lock of her hair, a fingernail cutting, or a sample of her handwriting – it really didn't matter what she sent to Astra since it was going to be consigned to the dustbin anyway). Back would come an envelope – either pink or blue – with the prediction inside. Now, let's say that 100 mothers were foolish enough to part with their money in this way. In roughly 50 % of the cases, Astra would get it right, so there's £1000 already safely stashed in Astra's pocket. And what of the remaining 50 or so mothers who were sent an incorrect prediction? Well, they've just had a baby and their life is pretty chaotic, so it's a safe bet that they are unlikely to be saying, 'Now, where did I put Astra's address so I can claim my £20 back. . . ?'.

The other child

Here is a little puzzle that is trickier than might at first appear. Suppose that Mrs Smith has two children and at least one of them is a girl. What is the probability that the other child is a boy?

Solution

If your answer was 0.5 (i.e. 50:50), you are in good company, as this is the most common answer . . . but I'm afraid it's wrong. Figure 17.2 shows the four possible girl/boy combinations for two children, GG, GB, BG and BB. We are informed that there is at least one girl so we can disregard the BB combination and focus just on the three shaded combinations, GG, GB and BG. These three combinations are equally likely so there is a 1 in 3 chance of each occurring. In two of these combinations (GB and BG) there is one girl and one boy, so the 'other child' is a boy; in one of the combinations (GG) the 'other child' is a girl. We can now answer the question – the probability that the other child is a boy = $^2/_3$.

	Second child	
First child	GIRL	BOY
GIRL	GG	GB
BOY	BG	BB

● **Figure 17.2** Possible girl/boy combinations for two children.

The binomial distribution

The expected pattern of boy/girl births or head/tail outcomes on the toss of a coin is referred to as the binomial pattern or the binomial distribution. As with many ideas in mathematics, our understanding of this concept derives from the coming together of two related ideas, one in pure mathematics and the other in probability. Much of our understanding of this important idea derives from the work of the giant of British science, Sir Isaac Newton.

Sir Isaac Newton (1643–1727)

It is generally agreed that Isaac Newton was the outstanding scientific mind in British history. His work in physics, mathematics, astronomy and philosophy made a huge contribution to our understanding of science, most of which is still relevant today. His great work, usually referred to as *The Principia* (published 1687) is the cornerstone of our understanding of gravity, the laws that determine the motion of objects and much more.

Newton built the first reflecting telescope and explained how a prism separates white light into the many colours that form the visible spectrum. In mathematics, he broke new ground in the understanding of many important topics, including differential and integral calculus, and – as explained in this chapter – he developed the generalized binomial theorem.

Isaac was born in a small village in Lincolnshire, the son of a wealthy farmer who died three months before Isaac's birth. As a boy, Isaac was skilled at creating mechanical toys. He once made a hot air balloon, which he released along with the family cat as 'navigator'. Neither the balloon nor its navigator were ever seen again. Although he was briefly engaged at the age of 19, he never married, preferring to devote all his energies to his studies.

It seems that we may have the Great Plague to thank for Newton's contribution to the binomial theorem. While the plague was in full swing in 1665, he retreated to his family's country manor in Woolsthorpe, Lincolnshire. Over the next two years, he made good use of the peace and quiet of this retreat to work on his theories, including a proof and extension of the binomial theorem.

A very brief explanation of the binomial theorem

This theorem is based on finding a way of expanding the algebraic expression $(p + q)^n$. Building it up one step at a time, we can set out the simple examples where $n = 1, 2$, and 3.

When $n = 1$, $(p + q)^1 = p + q$.
When $n = 2$, $(p + q)^2 = p^2 + 2pq + q^2$.
When $n = 3$, $(p + q)^3 = p^3 + 3p^2q + 3pq^2 + q^3$.

What Newton achieved was to come up with a general rule that enabled the expansion of any expression of the form $(p + q)^n$ for any value of n.

Now we travel across the English Channel to Paris. In the same year (1665), a posthumous Treatise on the Arithmetical Triangle (*Traité du Triangle Arithmétique*) was published, based on the work of the French mathematical genius Blaise Pascal (1623–62), whom you read about in Chapter 11. The great insight of the Treatise was to adapt Newton's rather unexciting algebraic expansion to calculate probabilities from the binomial distribution. This connection can be illustrated by considering the possible boy/girl combinations of a family of three children. This family has four possible boy/girl *combinations*: GGG, GGB, GBB and BBB. However, these combinations are not all equally likely. While the GGG and BBB combinations can crop up in only one way, the other two can each crop up in three ways, or *permutations*. That is, the combination of 'two girls and a boy' could be GGB, GBG or BGG. Similarly, the combination of 'one girl and two boys' could be GBB, BGB or BBG.

Now let's relate this to Newton's binomial expansion. Let the probability of getting a girl be represented by the letter g and the probability of getting a boy be represented by the letter b (in this particular example, both g and b have a numerical value of roughly 0.5). Pascal could see that a family of three children could be represented by the expression $(g + b)^3$ and the four terms in its expansion enabled him to calculate directly the probabilities of each separate boy/girl combination. Thus:

$$(g + b)^3 = g^3 + 3g^2b + \mathbf{3gb^2} + b^3.$$

To focus on just one of the terms in the expansion (marked in bold) the gb^2 term corresponds to the combination 'one girl and two boys'. It has a coefficient of 3 because there are three ways that this term can appear (GBB, GBG and BGG). By substituting the values for b and g (which are both approximately equal to 0.5), we can work out that, for a family of three children, the probability of getting one girl and two boys = $3 \times (^1/_2) \times (^1/_2)^2 = {}^3/_8$.

The scientist weighs up probabilities

Often a scientist is in the position of conducting an investigation into whether or not a particular intervention or treatment actually 'works'. Typically, his decision is made on the basis of comparing the outcome with what he would expect to have happened if he had done nothing. This sort of comparison is embodied in the following little rib-tickler:

> With proper medication, influenza usually lasts about a week, but left to its own devices it can drag on for a full seven days.

If, as is sometimes the case, there is no difference between the results of the 'treatment' and the 'no-treatment' samples, then he will conclude that the treatment/intervention would not be worth pursuing. Unfortunately, the fact of natural variation complicates things a lot when making decisions like these; sometimes a randomly chosen sample can contain very high or very low scores *just by chance alone* and this tends to mask possible differences due to the treatment. At the very heart of this tricky decision lies the question, 'How likely is it that I would get a result as extreme as this by chance alone?' This is a question about probability and it was as a result of such an approach to the making of scientific decisions that probability models like the binomial distribution were invented.

These ideas about making comparisons in situations where there is already a degree of random (natural) variation are continued in Chapter 18.

1 *If two fair coins are tossed, what is the probability that they both come up tails?*

2 *If three fair coins are tossed, what is the probability that they all come up the same?*

3 *The binomial expansion corresponding to the boy/girl combinations for a family of five children is:*
$(g + b)^5 = g^5 + 5g^4b + 10g^3b^2 + 10g^2b^3 + 5gb^4 + b^5$

 (a) *Which term of the expansion corresponds to the combination, 'one girl and four boys'?*

 (b) *How many times more likely is it to get the combination 'three girls and two boys' than for all five children to be of the same sex?*

Solutions

1 Let the probability of getting heads be h and the probability of getting tails be t.
Tossing two coins can be represented by:
$(h + t)^2 = h^2 + 2ht + t^2$.
The final t^2 term of the expansion corresponds to the outcome 'both tails'. Since $h = t = \frac{1}{2}$, probability 'both tails' $= (\frac{1}{2})^2 = \frac{1}{4}$.

2 Tossing three coins can be represented by:
$(h + t)^3 = h^3 + 3h^2t + 3ht^2 + t^3$.
The first and last terms of the expansion together correspond to the outcomes 'all heads' or 'all tails'. This gives:
$h^3 + t^3 = (\frac{1}{2})^3 + (\frac{1}{2})^3 = \frac{1}{8} + \frac{1}{8} = \frac{1}{4}$.

3 (a) The term corresponding to the combination, 'one girl and four boys' is $5gb^4$.

 (b) The probability of 'three girls and two boys' is:
$10g^3b^2 = 10 \times (\frac{1}{2})^5$.
The probability of all five being of the same sex is:
$g^5 + b^5 = 2 \times (\frac{1}{2})^5$
So, the first outcome is five times as likely as the second.

Chapter 18
Grasping variation: the normal curve

To compare is not to prove.

French proverb

This chapter develops some of the ideas raised in the previous chapter, where the scientist attempts to make comparisons in order to test whether or not one particular set of data is bigger than another. Where Chapter 17 explored the binomial model as a useful basis of comparison, this chapter turns to explore the normal distribution. You may find some of the ideas in this chapter more challenging than those in previous chapters. However, I hope you can stick at it, as there are important concepts here that will lead you to the very heart of what statistical decision-making is all about.

Is it bigger?

A key feature of thinking scientifically is to ask questions in the form, 'Is this bigger/faster/hotter/denser/ than that?' We cannot make comparisons like this without taking measurements (you may remember the quotation from Lord Kelvin at the start of Chapter 16: 'If you cannot measure it, you cannot improve it').

Some questions of comparison are easy to answer. For example: Can a cheetah run faster than a snail? Clearly, you can give a confident 'Yes' to this. Of course, you might want to be slightly pedantic and say, 'But not all cheetahs run at the same speed', and similarly, 'But some snails are quicker than others.' These statements are true, but you can be confident that the slowest, laziest, most laid-back cheetah who ever sported a pair of shades can still outrun the fastest snail in the world, because the difference between the running speeds of these two species is so huge that it trumps any possible variations within them.

Now let's look at a question where the differences are not so clear-cut: Are men taller than women? The answers to this and similar questions tend to be in the form, 'sometimes', or, 'more often than not'. Although, on average, men are taller, the point is that not all men are taller than all women. Unlike with the cheetah and the snail, the large degree of variation in men's and women's heights means that there is considerable overlap between the two.

Two important statistical ideas that enable us to get a handle on these sorts of comparisons are *location* and *variation*. The location of a dataset refers to where its numerical values are located – it can be thought of as where the average value lies. Variation, on the other hand, describes how widely spread the values in the dataset are. In general, differences between two datasets are clear-cut when the differences in location are large but the extent of variation in each is small. Conversely, it is much harder to conclude that there is a difference between two sets of measures when their locations are quite close together and there is a wide degree of variation in each.

The normal curve

An interesting and almost universal property of data collected from nature is that the values tend to be concentrated in the middle of the range, with much sparser concentrations at the extremes on either side. You might like to pause briefly to check that this statement accords with your own experience. For example, let's stay with human height – a relatively large proportion of the heights of the adult population fall into a middle band of, say, 1.60m to 1.90m. Taking equal bandwidths on either side, there are far fewer adult human heights in the band below it (1.30m to 1.60m) or the band above it (1.90m to 2.20m).

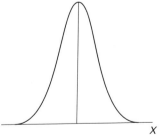

● **Figure 18.1** The normal curve often gives a good description of data that cluster around the mean.

A similar property applies to other datasets from nature – the weights of robin eggs, the length of sycamore leaves, body temperatures of iguanas or the gestation periods of African elephants, for example. The pattern that describes the distribution of each of these datasets can be approximated to the bell-shaped curve shown in Figure 18.2, which is known as the *normal curve*. For these datasets, you need to imagine that a large sample of measures has been taken. In each case, the numerical values are placed along the horizontal axis (marked here with *X*) and the height of the curve at any point is a measure of the relative frequency of the corresponding *X* value.

The ideas of location and variation are central to the normal curve: the location of the data values determines how far to the right the curve lies on the horizontal axis – i.e. large-valued datasets produce distributional curves that are further to the right. The degree of variation in the dataset is represented by how widely spread the curve is. Where there is little variation in the values, the normal curve is narrow with a squashed appearance; but if the values vary a lot, the curve is widely spread (as shown in Figure 18.2). More specifically, the position of the curve is determined by the *mean* of the dataset while its shape is determined by a measure of spread, of which the best known is the *standard deviation*.

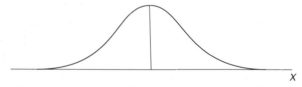

X

● **Figure 18.2** A normal curve with a wide spread, indicating a lot of variation in the data values

Abraham de Moivre (1667–1754)
The first discovery of the normal curve is attributed to French-born mathematician Abraham de Moivre. He is known for his work on his eponymous theorem, which links trigonometry and complex numbers. But, like a number of eminent mathematicians of the 18th century, de Moivre also had a passion for games of chance. A typical gambler's question of the time was, 'If a fair coin is tossed 100 times, what is the probability of getting 60 or more heads?' The mathematical idea that underpins this question is the binomial distribution (which was described in the last chapter). De Moivre's problem here was that, for a number of tosses as large as 100, the calculations were very lengthy. It was his work on questions like these that led de Moivre to discover the following important fact: as the number of tosses is increased, the shape of the binomial distribution approaches a smooth curve – the

normal curve. By exploiting this observation, de Moivre's calculations were greatly simplified by the use of the *normal approximation*.

As a footnote, in the final weeks of his life, de Moivre noticed that he was sleeping 15 minutes longer each day. By extrapolation, he predicted that 27 November 1754 would be the day on which he would achieve 24 hours sleep each day and that this would therefore be the day of his death. His prediction was exactly correct!

The intelligence quotient

A classic example of a measure that has been constructed around the properties of the normal distribution is the intelligence quotient (IQ) test. When administered to the general population, IQ scores are designed to produce data that display the normal pattern characteristic of the bell-shaped curve, with a mean of 100 and (usually) a standard deviation of 15. For example, imagine randomly selecting one person at a time from the general population and measuring their IQ score. Typical values will be 113, 94, 134, 89, 79, 103 and so on – i.e. values that are spread around the overall mean of 100 but initially with no clear pattern (apart from the obvious fact that the scores are scattered on either side of 100). However, as the sample size is increased, an underlying pattern will start to take shape to match the normal curve. You will see the central values close to the mean of 100 become taller; the extreme scores (those greater than 130 and less than 70, say) will crop up only rarely. Figure 18.3 (a) and (b) show typical patterns for sample sizes of 10 and 50.

By the time you have recorded the IQ scores of, say, 10 000 people, the match with the normal curve becomes clearly apparent. In general, the larger the sample, the better the match to the normal curve.

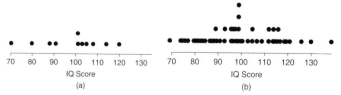

● **Figure 18.3** Typical IQ score patterns for sample sizes 10 and 50. (a) Sample size = 10; no clear pattern. (b) Sample size = 50; the beginnings of a central peak.

Areas under the curve

The importance of de Moivre's breakthrough in identifying the normal curve was that the properties of the curve could be used to estimate the likelihoods of getting particular values from the populations from which datasets were selected. This opened up many possibilities in terms of statistical interpretation for scientific decision-making. Specifically, it allowed decisions to be made about observed data on the basis of linking it to the probability of getting such results from the parent population *by chance alone.*

For example, let's return to de Moivre's problem of the number of heads to expect when a fair coin is tossed 100 times. Imagine carrying out this experiment a very large number of times, on each occasion recording the number of heads – perhaps getting scores like 58, 41, 55, 52, 43, and so on. If we were to plot these scores as a bar chart then, as with the example of the IQ scores above, the normal distribution pattern would slowly emerge. By the way, you don't actually have to do this experiment in order to create this particular curve – it is really an imaginary curve, the existence and properties of which are created mathematically, rather than empirically.

Using this imaginary normal curve as a good approximation to the bar chart of 'heads from 100 tosses of a coin', the mean number of heads is 50 and the standard deviation is 5. A property of the normal distribution is that approximately 95% of the values lie within 2 standard deviations on either side of the mean, so 95% of the values could be expected to lie between 40 and 60 heads. Since the curve is symmetrical, it follows that the remaining 5% of the values are equally divided, with a 2½% tail on either side. So, the chance of getting more that 60 heads is roughly 2½%, as are the chances of getting fewer than 40 heads.

As you can see, this normal curve provides a useful short cut for working out how likely certain outcomes are. This is the big idea that underlies statistical testing. There are statistical tables that make this translation between particular values and the corresponding probability of getting such values from a parent population by chance alone. If the observed value corresponds to a very unlikely or untypical result, we will be encouraged to reject the hypothesis that it has come from the population in question. But the point here is that knowing about the properties of the normal curve allows us to make decisions quantitatively, based on measures of probability.

A feature of the discussion above is that we were operating with populations that could be assumed to be normally distributed. Of course, it is often the case that a data value is not drawn from such a population. How then can these ideas be relevant when conducting tests on the patterns displayed by values that do not belong to this normally distributed pattern? The secret is to work with the sample mean, because sample means do have a strong tendency to follow a normal pattern. This is explained by a very clever law known as the *Central Limit Theorem*, described as follows by the statistician Sir Francis Galton in his book, *Natural Inheritance* (1889):

> The law would have been personified by the Greeks and deified, if they had known of it. It reigns with serenity and in complete self-effacement, amidst the wildest confusion. The huger the mob, and the greater the apparent anarchy, the more perfect is its sway.

The Central Limit Theorem

Imagine choosing random samples of, say, ten people at a time and finding the mean intelligence scores of these ten people. These mean scores will tend to cluster much more closely to the population mean of 100 (typical values might be 98.1, 103.2, 101.7, 99.2, and so on). The Central Limit Theorem makes two claims in relation to situations such as this, where repeated samples are taken from a population:

(a) The sample means will tend to cluster more closely around the population mean than would the individual values. (Indeed, the larger the size of sample from which the mean is calculated, the more marked this clustering will be.)

(b) Regardless of the underlying pattern of the original data from which the samples were taken, the set of sample means formed by repeated sampling will tend to conform to a particular pattern known as a normal model.

The scientist loves approximating to the normal

The story goes that the English monarch, George III, decided to take up the violin and engaged as his tutor one of the finest violinists of his day, the German virtuoso Johann Salomon. After a few lessons, the king asked Salomon how he thought he was coming on. 'Well, your majesty', the virtuoso replied, 'all violin players can be divided into three classes. The first class cannot play at all; the second class contains all those who play very badly; and the third class consists of those who play well. Your Majesty has already managed to advance to the second class.'

Like Salomon, the statistically aware scientist devotes considerable energy to devising categories for his data and then making comparisons between them. This chapter has been about the method of statistical decision-making that scientists regularly employ, which is based on an important statistical model known as the normal distribution.

And by the way, if you felt that the link between the Salomon story and the central themes of this chapter was rather tenuous, you would be correct! In my defence, you deserve an amusing anecdote at the end of this tricky chapter and anyway it made *me* laugh! I should say that, of the many branches of mathematics in existence, statistics is the one that I find the most interesting and entertaining. But you need to bear in mind that there are three types of statistician – those who can count and those who can't!

Something for you to try

1   *Which words are needed to fill the two blanks in the following sentence?*
    The _____ of a dataset refers to where its numerical values lie, while _____ describes how widely spread the values are.
2   *Based on knowing that the mean and standard deviation of IQ scores are 100 and 15, respectively, roughly what proportion of the population would you expect to achieve IQ scores of between 70 and 130?*

Solutions
1   *location, variation.*
2   *Roughly 95% of the population of a normal distribution lie within 2 standard deviations on either side of the mean. Since the standard deviation of IQ scores = 15, the interval 70–130 should contain roughly 95% of the IQ scores of the general population.*

Chapter 19
Calculating with machines

There will still be things that machines cannot do. They will not produce great art or great literature or great philosophy; they will not be able to discover the secret springs of happiness in the human heart; they will know nothing of love and friendship.

Bertrand Russell

A very brief history of calculating machines

Since ancient times the scientist has made his discoveries by careful measurement and the interpretation of his results by calculation. As his calculations became more complex, so the need grew to find ways of performing them more quickly and accurately. In Chapter 3 you read how John Napier's work on astronomical calculations led him to use logarithms to speed up calculations. Chapter 11 referred to the calculator invented by Blaise Pascal, known as the Pascaline. But many other important steps have been taken on the way to developing the modern computer, of which just a small selection are covered here.

Jacquard's punched cards

In 1801, Joseph-Marie Jacquard, a weaver from Lyons in France, developed the idea of punched cards – a development that was to become central to the operation of the early electronic computers in the 20th century. Jacquard's 'cards' were actually small sheets of hardboard with strategically positioned holes drilled through them to match a particular weaving pattern. These boards were inserted into his loom in the correct sequence, enabling the automation of his settings for the weaving process.

Babbage's difference engine

Londoner Charles Babbage (1791–1871) is often described as the 'father of computers'. During Babbage's time, computers were commonly found in towns and cities all over the UK, but they were of the human kind, employed by companies and in science laboratories to perform arithmetical calculations. However, being human is to err, and Babbage wanted to create a machine that eliminated human error in calculation. In 1822, he began work on designing a 'difference engine' – a monstrous beast that would contain some 25 000 parts, weigh 13 600 kg and stand 2.5 metres high. It was called a difference machine because it used a principle known as the method of 'finite differences', an approach that avoided the need for the two most error-prone operations of multiplication and division. Yet many technical problems prevented Babbage from completing this first machine. Government funding was withdrawn and he set to work designing a faster, sleeker model 2. A mere 153 years later, in 2002, Difference Engine No. 2 was built exactly to Babbage's original drawings. It consists of 8 000 parts, weighs a mere 4 500 kg (about 5 tons) and can be seen at the Computer History Museum in London – a sight no Victorian ever had the opportunity to enjoy! This device can perform calculations to 31 figures, which, in terms of precision if not portability, knocks modern pocket calculators into a proverbial cocked hat.

Ada Lovelace (1815–52)

Ada lovelace (née Byron) was the only (legitimate) child of the poet Lord Byron. Having hoped for 'a glorious boy', he failed to demonstrate any paternal feelings towards his daughter and when he died nine years after her birth, they had rarely if ever met. Ada was taught privately in mathematics and science and became an outstanding mathematician. She was fascinated by Babbage's calculating machine and was able to see possibilities for its use that Babbage could never have imagined. For example, she speculated that the engine might compose elaborate and scientific pieces of music. Her ideas about the use of the machine formed the foundation for the programming of computers and she is often referred to as the first computer programmer. She was the subject of a 1997 movie, *Conceiving Ada*, and featured significantly in *The Difference Engine*, a book by William Gibson and Bruce Sterling. On 27 November 1852, Ada Lovelace died, aged 36, from uterine cancer, not helped by extensive bloodletting by her doctors.

Enigma and Colossus

An Enigma machine is a device used for the encryption and decryption of secret messages. These machines were used commercially during the 1920s but were developed for military purposes by the Germans and used extensively in the Second World War. The Enigma is famous mainly because Polish, American, but principally British code-breakers were able to crack its secrets and so decrypt a huge number of German messages. They were supported in their efforts by the development of the Colossus computer – the first of these was operational in February 1944 and by the end of the war, there were ten in place. The Colossus used a large number of valves, which took the form of vacuum tubes, and the data were fed in via paper-tape.

It should be pointed out that American and Polish accounts of the relative contributions of their respective countries to cracking the Enigma code will be rather different! However, no one questions the remarkable contribution made by the British mathematician Alan Turing and his team based in Bletchley in Buckinghamshire. It has been estimated that their ground-breaking work on the Enigma, codenamed ULTRA, shortened the war in Europe by two years.

Transistorized computers

Invented in 1947, transistors replaced the vacuum tube valves in computers over the following decade. Transistorized computers could pack tens of thousands of binary logic circuits into a small space, and so a computer's size and cost were greatly reduced. Since then, and up to the present time, circuit boards have become ever smaller, cheaper and more reliable (according to Moore's Law, the number of transistors that can be placed inexpensively on an integrated circuit has approximately doubled every two years). The Microsoft CEO, Bill Gates, has famously stated that, 'If General Motors had kept up with technology like the computer industry has, we would all be driving $25 cars that got 1000 MPG.'

Programming a computer

Today many people make their living writing computer programs for a variety of purposes. At a high level of complexity, programs need to be created in order for the operating system of the computer itself to work. Computers run a variety of sophisticated applications such as word-processing and spreadsheet packages and these too have been created on the basis of computer programs. But the majority of commercial computer programs are designed for functions such as payroll and personnel management, health advice and, of course, computer games.

If you have never tried your hand at creating a simple program, be reassured that it can be a highly satisfying exercise that most people could do at some level. All you need to get started is a little technical knowledge of the particular programming language you are working in and a clear head to enable you to organize the instructions logically. Here is a simple example based on using the programming language known as BASIC (an acronym for Beginner's All-purpose Symbolic Instruction Code). The example uses a reduced form of BASIC which can be found in a graphing calculator such as the Texas Instruments TI-84 Plus.

This example program is entitled 'Temperature Convert'. It invites the user to enter a temperature in degrees Celsius and it will then give back that same temperature converted to degrees Fahrenheit. (Pretty exciting stuff, huh?) The program consists of a title (TEMP_CONVERT) and two lines of instruction, called program lines. Note that both of the program lines start with a colon:

```
PROGRAM: TEMP_CONVERT
: Input "CELSIUS?", C
: Disp "FAHRENHEIT", 1.8*C+32
```

Line 1 of the program is an *Input* command that uses the letter C as the variable for the input. It also contains the word 'CELSIUS?' inside quotation marks. When this line is executed, two things happen. First, 'CELSIUS?' is displayed on the screen. Second, the input command will invite the user to enter some numerical value, which will be the temperature in degrees Celsius that he/she wants to convert (this invitation will usually show up in the form of an on-screen flashing cursor). When this number (say, 20) has been keyed in, the machine will keep a mental note that 20 is now the current value of C and then the program moves on to line 2.

Line 2 of the program is a *Disp* (display) command which displays two things. First it displays the word 'FAHRENHEIT' inside quotation marks. Second, it displays the numerical value of 1.8*C+32, where the value of C is the one already entered in line 1 (in this example, C = 20). So, in this case it will display the number 68 (i.e. 1.8×20 + 32).

Two programs for you to identify

Look at the two (untitled) programs below and try to work out what they do.

Program A
: Input "LENGTH?", L
: Input "WIDTH?", W
: Disp "PERIM", 2(L+W)

Program B
: Input "MILES?", M
: Input "HOURS?", H
: Disp "SPEED", M/H

Solutions
Program A calculates the perimeter of a rectangle using the formula: *Perimeter = 2(Length + Width)*.
Program B calculates the average speed in miles per hour using the formula: *Speed = Distance ÷ Time*

Binary numbers

In the binary system we count on our fists instead of on our fingers.

Author unknown

You just have to examine a computer keyboard to see that numbers, letters, punctuation marks, etc., can all be entered, and so it might seem that a computer is able to understand all this varied sort of information. However, your computer can only do this because of a translation process going on deep inside its brain; and, at this most fundamental level, the computer can only process information in the form of a sequence of on/off pulses. Each pulse is referred to as one *bit*, so a bit is the most basic atom of computer information. These bits are generated in batches of eight, each batch being one *byte*. Normally a byte is coded as a sequence of 0s and 1, where 0 represents pulse *off* and 1 represents pulse *on*.

Let's take a particular example:

The letter 'capital E' is coded by the byte 01000101.

So, the eight pulses used by the computer to represent this character are:

off, on, off, off, off, on, off, on.

And another example:

When you press the space bar, it sends the byte 00100000.

Here the pulses are:

off, off, on, off, off, off, off, off.

Numbers that are composed of just zeros and ones are called binary numbers. In the same way as everyday numbers operate to a base of 10, binary numbers are based on the number 2. Base ten numbers require ten separate digits: 0, 1, 2, 3, 4, 5, 6, 7, 8 and 9, but binary numbers need just the two digits, 0 and 1.

In order to understand the meaning of the digits in a binary number, it is helpful to consider how base 10 numbers are arranged. Here is the number 'thirty five thousand, six hundred and twenty nine':

35 629.

From left to right, the place value of each digit in this number is:

10 000, 1000, 100, 10 and 1.

As you can see, these are ordered in decreasing powers of 10 – i.e. 10^4, 10^3, 10^2, 10^1 and 10^0. The same idea holds for binary numbers, but with a 2 instead of 10 for each digit. So, again reading from left to right, the place values of an eight-digit binary number are:

2^7, 2^6, 2^5, 2^4, 2^3, 2^2, 2^1 and 2^0.

Let's apply these place values to the binary number corresponding to a capital 'E' on the computer, 01000101. It becomes:

$$0\times2^7 + 1\times2^6 + 0\times2^5 + 0\times2^4 + 0\times2^3 + 1\times2^2$$
$$+ 0\times2^1 + 1\times2^0$$

which simplifies to $64 + 4 + 1 = 69$.

In fact, all computer characters can be translated into a base-10 number by this method – clearly they are much easier to remember in the conventional base-10 form.

Taking another example, the binary code for the 'space' character is 00100000, which translates to base 10 as follows:

$$0\times2^7 + 0\times2^6 + 1\times2^5 + 0\times2^4 + 0\times2^3 + 0\times2^2 + 0\times2^1$$
$$+ 0\times2^0 = \text{the base-10 number 32.}$$

The complete classification of the binary codes for computer characters is known as the ASCII (pronounced 'ass-key') code, which is an acronym for American Standard Code for Information Interchange.

To end this chapter and as your reward for reading this far, here is a binary joke.

I bought a book called 1001 things to do in binary but when I got it home I could only find nine things in it.

The scientist does it on a computer

In August 2010, three computer enthusiasts (IT professionals Chris and Helen Colvin from Iowa, USA, and systems analyst Daniel Gebhardt from Mainz in Germany) donated the down time on their home computers to support the exploration of the galaxy. They discovered a rare and exciting astronomical object – a disrupted binary pulsar – which was probably created as a result of the collapse of a massive star.

One of the big changes that has taken place in my lifetime has been the rise and rise of cheap but powerful calculating machines. This, combined with the rapid growth in the range of applications offered by a domestic computer, has resulted in a transformation in how the scientist, both amateur and professional, sets about investigating the world. Today our researcher can confidently key his data into a machine, knowing that he will get back an accurate collection of summaries, graphs, charts, correlations and statistical tests in a couple of nano-seconds. Of course, sheer computing power alone does not ensure that a sensible question has been posed or that the collected data were valid in the first place (in computing parlance, GIGO stands for 'garbage in, garbage out'). However, in a world where the majority of the world's population either own or have access to a powerful computer, the possibilities for more discoveries in the future are exciting and expanding. The future for the scientist has never looked so good!

Something for you to try

1 *What do you think this program will do?*
```
:Input T
:If T >12
:T−12→T
:Disp T
```
2 *The ASCII code for the open bracket sign, (, is 0101000. What is this in base 10?*
3 *The ASCII base-10 code for the letter capital T is 84. What is this in binary?*

Solutions
1 *This will convert time, T, from 24-hour to 12-hour notation.*
2 *In base 10, the number is 40.*
3 *1010100*

Chapter 20

Approaching limits: the story of calculus

The mathematics of limits underlies all of calculus. Limits allow us, in a sense, to zoom in on the graph of a curve – further and further and further ad infinitum – until it becomes straight. Once it's straight, regular-old algebra and geometry can be used. This is the magic of calculus.

Mark Ryan, *Calculus for Dummies*

Discrete and continuous

An important distinction that the scientist is required to make on a regular basis is between quantities that change *discretely* and those that show *continuous* change. Here is a simple example to illustrate the difference. Shoe sizes (e.g. sizes 4, 4½, 5, . . .) are an example of a discrete measure, whereas foot length measures (e.g. 28.4 cm, 31.9 cm, . . .) are continuous. With a discrete measure like shoe size, there is only a finite number of possible measures between, say, size 4 and size 7, whereas, with foot length there is an infinite number of possible lengths between, say, 25 cm and 28 cm.

The discrete/continuous distinction is a useful one beyond the confines of mathematics or science textbooks – for example, it can be helpful when trying to decide on the correct word in an everyday situation. In one of my local supermarkets, the express check-out displays a sign stating that it can be used by customers with '5 items or less' in their basket. Another supermarket in my town has a similar arrangement to hasten the throughput of lighter shoppers, but its sign reads '5 items or fewer'. Which word is correct here, 'fewer' or 'less'? We (should) use 'fewer' in situations where there are items that can be enumerated or counted. So, 'fewer' applies where the measurement is discrete. 'Less', on the other hand, is reserved for continuous measures – we say that one glass contains <u>less</u> water than another, but there are <u>fewer</u> marbles in this glass than that one. The correct supermarket sign, therefore, is the one that reads '5 items or fewer'.

Try using the discrete/continuous distinction to help clarify the difference between the meanings of 'how much?' and 'how many?'.

Solution
'How much?' is a question that relates to continuous measures (how much wine is in the bottle?), whereas 'how many?' is asked about a discrete measure (how many glasses will we need for the party?).

Zeno's paradoxes

The discrete/continuous distinction is an idea that has been well understood and much debated for over two thousand years. Zeno of Elea (an Italian-Greek colony, now known as Velia in southern Italy) lived around 450 BCE and belonged to the Eleatic School of philosophy. He suggested that however much you might subdivide a unit of measurement, it can never be used to represent a continuous measurement such as length or time. He made his point by means of a series of clever paradoxes, of which the best known is Achilles and the tortoise.

Achilles and the tortoise

In a race between the tortoise and Achilles (the fleet-footed Greek warrior), the plodding tortoise is given a head start. Achilles tries to catch the tortoise up, but each time he reaches a point where the tortoise has already been, the tortoise will have moved on. So, however swiftly Achilles runs, he can never overtake the tortoise.

The Greek philosopher Aristotle (384–322 BCE) summed up Zeno's paradox as follows:

> In a race, the quickest runner can never overtake the slowest, since the pursuer must first reach the point

whence the pursued started, so that the slower must always hold a lead.

One approach in the refutation of this paradox is to argue that Zeno has broken the problem into a series of catch-ups, in such a way that no one of them can enable Achilles to reach the tortoise. He does this by arranging it so that the catch-ups get shorter and shorter. This is mathematically equivalent to you walking towards a precipice in a series of ever-shorter steps, each one half the length of the previous one. The reason you never fall over the precipice is that, for a finite number of steps, the sum of the series $\frac{1}{2} + \frac{1}{4} + \frac{1}{8} + \frac{1}{16} + \ldots$ is always less than one.

But let's look at the question from a different point of view. Instead of taking ever shorter steps, take steps of equal duration (say, one minute each) and you will see that there is indeed a point where the tortoise is overtaken by Achilles. This is easiest to see with a numerical example. Let's assume that the tortoise is given a 5-metre lead and travels at a steady 1 metre per minute. Achilles, confident of his forthcoming victory, strolls along at twice the tortoise's speed – 2 metres per minute. Their progress is summarized in the table below. This shows that, when the problem is cast in intervals of equal duration, Achilles does indeed catch up with the tortoise (after 5 minutes) and overtake it.

Time (mins)	0	1	2	3	4	5	6	7
Tortoise's position (m)	5	6	7	8	9	10	11	12
Achilles' position (m)	0	2	4	6	8	10	12	14

Newton and Leibnitz

A key idea underpinning this paradox of Zeno's is the notion of a limit. In mathematics, a *limit* is a value that a function or sequence 'approaches', getting closer and closer but never quite reaching it. Limits are essential to the understanding of calculus and, since calculus is one of the most important mathematical developments of the past three or four hundred years, this is where the story now takes us.

The first thing to say about the birth of calculus in the late 17th century is that it did nothing for the entente cordiale between England and France. In the red corner was (Sir) Isaac Newton (1642–1727) from Lincolnshire – a moody and anti-social individual who preferred not to publish his ideas as he had a particular aversion to having them criticized. In the blue corner was a German from Leibzig but based in France (*allez les bleus!*), the prolific Gottfried Wilhelm Leibniz (1646–1716). Unlike Newton, Leibnitz is remembered for his positive attitude to life. For example, he took the view that our universe was 'the best possible one God could have made' (well done God!).

These two contemporaries were working on essentially the same problem at the same time. Newton almost certainly came up with a solution before Leibniz, but Leibniz published first and, egged on by their patriotic followers, each side accused the other of plagiarism. The disagreement grew to a row and ended up in an intellectual war which lasted for decades and isolated English mathematicians from the exciting developments opened up by their European colleagues in the years that followed. Both Newton and Leibnitz developed their own notations for calculus but it is the notation of Leibniz that has stood the test of time.

So, Isaac and Gottfried, what was this calculus thing anyway?

What is calculus?

A central question that was bothering European mathematicians around the end of the 17th century was to do with *rates of change* – for example, rates of growth, velocity (which is the rate of change of distance) and acceleration (which is the rate of change of velocity). Here is a simple example to illustrate how their thinking may have proceeded.

If I am travelling at, say 40 mph, I can understand this in terms of the distance I would travel (40 miles) if I kept going at this speed for one hour. But what if I want to know what is happening *at a particular instant*? One way of getting a handle on this is to reduce the time interval from one hour to something much less. For example, by repeatedly halving the interval:

- I would travel 20 miles if I kept going at this speed for ½ an hour;

- I would travel 10 miles if I kept going at this speed for ¼ of an hour;
- I would travel 5 miles if I kept going at this speed for $^1/_8$ an hour; and so on.

But for Newton and Leibnitz, 'an instant' was not a finite interval; they wanted to solve the harder problem of defining speed over an interval that is zero in length. Clearly, over an interval of zero time, zero distance will be travelled, so we are left with speed as $^0/_0$, which doesn't make mathematical sense. Newton referred to these vanishingly small intervals as fluxions, based on the idea of a quantity flowing towards zero but never actually getting there. The Irish mathematician George Berkeley referred to these fluxions rather sniffily as 'the ghosts of departed quantities'.

The area of mathematics concerned with working out the rate of change in zero time is referred to as *differential* calculus and the mathematical procedure required to find the rate of change of an algebraic function is known as *differentiation* or *finding a derivative*. The procedure of differentiation can be reversed and this gives rise to what is known as *integration* or *finding an integral*, a branch of mathematics called integral calculus. These two faces of calculus are enshrined in the 'Patter song' from *The Pirates of Penzance*, written by W. S. Gilbert and A. Sullivan towards the end of the 19th century:

I'm very good at integral and differential calculus;
I know the scientific names of beings animalculous:
In short, in matters vegetable, animal, and mineral,
I am the very model of a modern Major-General.

The technique of differentiation

As a technique for calculating rates of change, differentiation proved to be the key to the mathematicians' problem of finding the gradient of a curve at a given point on the curve (which reduces to the problem of finding the gradient of the tangent to the curve at that point). For functions of the form, $y = x^n$, the derivative (written as $^{dy}/_{dx}$ and spoken as 'dee y by dee x') is:

$$^{dy}/_{dx} = n \times x^{n-1}.$$

For example, consider the curve of the function: $y = x^3 - x^2$.

Using the rule for differentiating described above, we get this expression for the derivative:

$$^{dy}/_{dx} = 3x^2-2x.$$

In order to work out the gradient of the curve for a particular value – say, $x = 4$, simply substitute this value into the expression for the derivative. In this example, the gradient at $x = 4$ is $3\times(4)^2 - 2\times4 = 48 - 8 = 40$.

Applications of calculus

No branch of mathematics has opened more doors to understanding across so many fields of application and study than calculus. Calculus has a major role to play in astronomy, economics, biology, mechanics, physics and much more. It has also enabled the development of other important fields of mathematics such as analysis (the mathematics of continuous change). Here are just some of the achievements that would not have been possible without calculus:

- calculating the trajectories of space rockets;
- determining the paths of aircraft to avoid them crashing into each other;
- modelling how the sizes of animal populations change over time; and
- predicting the spread of disease.

The scientist knows his limit

The idea of a limit has importance across a wide range of human experience. For example:

- Is life expectancy approaching a limit?
- Are sporting achievements (high jump, long jump, throwing, putting, running speed and so on) approaching a limit?
- Is there a frontier or limit to the understanding of science itself?

These are questions with no easy answers, but the idea of a limit is an important and useful one that can help us shape our understanding of the world. It was to handle problems involving limits that calculus was invented and this branch of mathematics remains central to the work of scientists and engineers today.

1   Which of the following are discrete and which are continuous
    measures?
    (a) the number of days in a week on which one takes exercise;
    (b) the gestation period of a bird;
    (c) dress sizes (06, 08, 10, 12, etc.);
    (d) waist measurements, in cm.
2   Consider the graph of the function $y = x^2$.
    (a) What is the derivative, dy/dx?
    (b) What is the gradient of the tangent to this curve at the points
        where $x = 3$ and $x = -2$?

Solutions
1   Discrete measures: (a) and (c). Continuous measures (b) and (d).
2   (a) $dy/dx = 2x$
    (b) When $x = 3$, $dy/dx = 2 \times 3 = 6$.
        When $x = -2$, $dy/dx = 2 \times -2 = -4$.

Be a scientist

No doubt, one could list many remarkable discoveries, made over
the centuries, for which the scientist takes most of the credit: DNA,
anaesthetics, the theory of evolution, electricity, fingerprinting, the
computer, the Internet, the one-wheeled motorcycle (yes, really!) . . . the
list goes on and on. But if I had to choose one thing that represents
the scientist's greatest contribution to humanity, it would probably
not be any particular discovery but rather the way that the scientist
goes about discovering things. This is usually referred to as the
'scientific method'. It can be broken down into roughly seven steps,
which are illustrated below using a very simple example.

1 Make an observation	My torch (flashlight) isn't working.
2 Ask a question	What is wrong with it?
3 Form a hypothesis	The batteries are dead.
4 Find a method of testing	If the batteries are replaced, it should work.
5 Conduct experiments	Replace the old batteries with new batteries.
6 Gather and analyse results	Check whether it works.
7 Reach a conclusion	If it works, the problem is solved.

Of course, at the final stage, if the torch still did *not* work, you would
need to go through the seven-step procedure again, using another
hypothesis.

To be a scientist is to tackle problems in this systematic way. Try it
the next time you have a practical problem to solve. You should find
that, particularly at steps 5, 6 and 7, a number of mathematical and
statistical big ideas will crop up naturally.

The environmentalist
The Earth in balance

One thing that is certain and fixed about the natural world is that it is always changing. Since earliest times, the life of the environmentalist has been closely tied to the growth and development of the plants and animals around him. Crucially, of course, these have been his source of food, but they also formed his landscape and provided his sense of what the Earth looked like. No doubt his initial quests were largely practical: Where do these berries grow? Where might that lion be hiding? and so on.

As his curiosity grew, his questions became more general:

- Where am I likely to find more of these sorts of berries?
- What would happen if I planted this seed in the ground?

And these would have been further refined to questions such as:

- What type of habitat tends to support these sorts of berries and why?
- What conditions best support the growth and development of this plant?
- What are the most effective ways of farming livestock?
- What will I do when these resources run out?

Particularly in his search for answers to the more general questions, the environmentalist has turned to mathematics. The next five chapters introduce a selection of mathematical ideas that give a better understanding of growth and change in nature. You are invited to see the world now from the point of view of someone with an interest in patterns in nature and a concern for the future of the planet.

Chapter 21
The Fibonacci sequence

Mathematics is the science of
patterns, and nature exploits just
about every pattern that there is.

Ian Stewart

Let's say hello to our fifth character. Like the explorer, the artist, the gambler and the scientist, he too makes extensive use of mathematical ideas in pursuit of his particular interests – which, in his case, are his love of the natural world and his deep concern about the health of planet Earth and its inhabitants. Like the other characters in the book, he is curious about the patterns and regularities that he observes around him, but his attention is particularly focused on nature. He is the environmentalist.

In Chapter 8 you read about the golden rectangle, which is proportioned so that the length of the longer side is roughly 1.618 times that of the shorter side. This proportion is usually known by the name 'golden ratio'. You read there that many ancient artists and architects believed that its properties were so perfect that it must have come from God (hence its alternative name, the divine proportion). The number corresponding to the golden ratio, 1.618 . . ., has inspired curious minds from many fields – mathematics, art, music and architecture, to name just four. The ratio was known about by the ancient Greeks Pythagoras and Euclid, who were both aware that it cropped up in the pentagram (five-pointed star). Euclid referred to it as the 'extreme and mean ratio' and devised a means of constructing it from a line segment using just compasses and a straight edge. It is normally referred to with the Greek letter phi (φ). Its numerical value is $(1 + \sqrt{5})/2$, which approximates to 1.618033989. However, like the numerical value of π, the decimal expansion of φ goes on forever.

You will be revisiting φ in this chapter and in Chapter 22, but rather than viewing it this time with an artist's eye you will see where it connects with nature and the environment. Let's start in the garden with a look at some of the patterns contained in the arrangement of leaves and petals.

Flower patterns

Why is a four-leafed clover considered lucky? The likely answer is that getting four leaves is rather unusual (most clovers have only three). In fact, if you count the petals on any flower (or the number of leaves on a plant), you will rarely find 4, 6 or 7 while numbers like 3, 5 and 8 are more likely. For example, the lily and the iris have 3 petals, the buttercup, wild rose and larkspur have 5, and delphiniums have 8. Pineapples display their scales in spirals of 8 and 13. Sunflower seeds contain patterns of bigger numbers of spirals – like 21 and 34.

● **Figure 21.1** A primrose has five petals.

These same numbers occur in the arrangements of the leaves or thorns around the plants' stems. For example, try choosing a starting leaf and count it as zero. Then, as you work along and around the stem, count the number of leaves you meet until you encounter a leaf pointing in the same direction as the starting one. More often than not you will find that its number is one of those listed in the sequence 2, 3, 5, 8, 13, . . . These numbers are part of a mathematical sequence that provides fascinating insights into patterns in nature, art and architecture and also occurs in classical theories of beauty and proportion.

Have a look at the number sequence: 1, 1, 2, 3, 5, 8, 13, 21, 34, 55 . . .
What do you think the next two numbers in the sequence might be?
(Hint: try looking at the numbers in consecutive groups of three.)

Solution
Each new number in the sequence is found by adding the two previous
numbers. So the next number must be 89 (i.e. 34 + 55), and then 144
(55 + 89) and so on.

The pattern of numbers was given prominence when
it was written about by the Italian mathematician Leonardo
Fibonacci, around 1200 CE, and today the sequence is referred
to as the Fibonacci sequence. In Dan Brown's novel *The
Da Vinci Code*, the Fibonacci numbers crop up as a code to
unlock a holy vessel. Fibonacci first mentioned the sequence
in a puzzle he posed about breeding rabbits:

> A man had one pair of rabbits together in a certain
> enclosed place, and one wishes to know how many are
> created from the pair in one year when it is the nature of
> them in a single month to bear another pair, and in the
> second month those born to bear also.

From *Liber Abaci* (*Book of Abacus* or
Book of Calculation), 1202

A careful reading of this translation of Fibonacci's rabbits
problem reveals the following two underlying conditions:

- When mature enough to breed, each pair of rabbits
  gives birth to one other pair every month.
- The rabbits are mature enough to breed after one month.

Based on these assumptions, it is possible to work out
the number of pairs of rabbits month by month, as follows.

- At the start of month 1, there is one pair of immature
  rabbits.
- Over the first month the original pair matures, so at
  the start of month 2 there is still a single pair.
- The first gestation of this pair occurs over month 2,
  so at the start of month 3 there are two pairs – the
  original pair and a pair of babies.
- By the start of month 4 a second pair of babies is born from
  the original pair and there are now three pairs of rabbits.

- By the start of month 5 the two pairs of mature rabbits have each produced a new pair of babies, and the pair of babies has matured, making 5 pairs in all.
- One month later there are 8 pairs, 5 mature and 3 immature.

So, month by month, the number of rabbit pairs so far are: 1, 1, 2, 3, 5 and 8. At the start of month 7 there are 13 pairs, in month 8 there are 21 pairs, and so on.

Although Fibonacci's rabbit problem seems a little artificial, its underlying solution provides an excellent explanation of the patterns shown by many growing things. If you think of how a twig forms branches, for example, there is, typically, a year of maturation followed by a year in which it forms a new branch (to form two twigs). Each subsequent new twig will then take one year to mature and then branch to form a new twig, as shown in Figure 21.2.

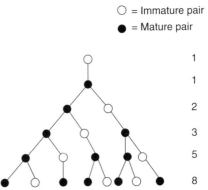

○ = Immature pair
● = Mature pair

1
1
2
3
5
8

● **Figure 21.2** Fibonacci's breeding rabbits.

Leonardo Fibonacci (c.1170– c.1250)

Leonardo Pisano Bogollo was a mathematician of many names, including Leonardo of Pisa and Leonardo Fibonacci, but today he is normally referred to simply as Fibonacci. He was born in Pisa, Italy, the son of a wealthy merchant, Guglielmo Fibonacci, who ran a trading post. Travelling around the Mediterranean on trips with his father enabled Leonardo to broaden his horizons and learn about alternative mathematical ideas such as the Hindu-Arabic numeral system (which made arithmetic much more efficient than working with Roman numerals). His main contribution to mathematics was the writing and publication of a book on arithmetic, *Liber Abaci*, which drew together ideas on many topics including number systems, fractions, prime numbers and irrational numbers. The book also included geometric proofs and a study of simultaneous linear equations. He devoted an entire chapter to his 'rabbits' problem, which gave rise to the sequence of numbers that today bears his name.

The golden rectangle revisited

Another application of the Fibonacci sequence crops up in the topic of proportion. As you saw in Chapter 8, the shape of a rectangle is defined by its 'aspect ratio' – i.e. the length divided by the width. You may remember that the *shape* of the rectangle is independent of its size – you can scale it up or down and it will maintain its shape.

You are now asked to look at several rectangles whose dimensions are taken from pairs of consecutive numbers from the Fibonacci sequence. As you move through the numbers, you'll gradually see that the overall shape of each new rectangle starts to settle down to one with very special proportions. Figure 21.3 shows the first six rectangles that can be created in this way (I've also scaled them so that they are all of roughly similar size).

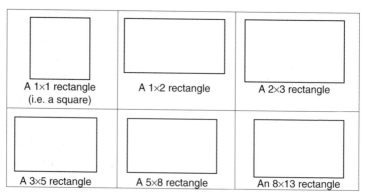

● **Figure 21.3** Rectangles drawn with side lengths that are two consecutive numbers from the Fibonacci sequence.

As you can see, the rectangles gradually start to take on the same basic shape. Continuing this process will produce rectangles that look more and more like each other in shape. Ultimately, if you were to keep going and could perform your measurements accurately enough, the ratio of the length to the width of the rectangles (i.e. their aspect ratio) would get ever closer to 1.61804 . . . As explained in Chapter 8, this number is known by several names, such as the 'golden ratio' and the 'divine ratio', and by the Greek letter Φ (pronounced 'phi'). The calculations for the aspect ratios of the first twelve such rectangles are shown in the table below.

Rectangle	1×1	2×1	3×2	5×3	8×5	13×8
Aspect ratio	1/1 = 1	2/1 = 2	3/2 = 1.5	5/3 = 1.67	8/5 = 1.6	13/8 = 1.625

Rectangle	21×13	34×21	55×34	89×55	144×89	233×144
Aspect ratio	21/13 = 1.61538	34/21 = 1.61905	55/34 = 1.61765	89/55 = 1.61818	144/89 = 1.61798	233/144 = 1.61806

The evidence of these examples indicates that the rectangles do look progressively more and more 'golden' as we work along the sequence. This property of the Fibonacci sequence confirms its special connection to Φ, which is that, as you move along the Fibonacci sequence, the ratio of each value to the one that precedes it gets ever closer to Φ.

The environmentalist retraces the artist's path

In Chapter 8 (and elsewhere) we considered how exploring different rectangular shapes led the artist to discover a particular one that seemed so special that it was thought by many to have mystical or God-given properties. This was the rectangle whose proportions were defined by the so-called 'golden ratio', which has a numerical value of roughly 1.618. Remarkably, the very same number crops up in many diverse situations, including a variety of contexts in the world of the environmentalist.

In this chapter, the story began with Fibonacci's breeding rabbits. This example may be a bit artificial – for instance, it is built on the assumption that each birth consists of exactly two rabbits, one male and one female. The problem was adapted from breeding rabbits to cows by an English creator of puzzles, Henry E. Dudeney (1857–1930). He made it more realistic by focusing on the number of female cows, as follows.

If a cow produces its first she-calf at age two years and after that produces another single she-calf every year, how many she-calves are there after 12 years, assuming none die?

If you want to follow up more of these natural contexts for the golden ratio, there are many excellent examples at: http://www.maths.surrey.ac.uk/hosted-sites/R.Knott/Fibonacci/fibnat.html

1 The 20th number in the Fibonacci sequence is 6765. Given that the value of φ is approximately 1.61804, what do you think are the values of the 19th and 21st numbers in the sequence?

2 The reciprocal of a number is 1 divided by that number. Use your calculator to find the reciprocal of φ. Can you spot a pattern in the result?

Solutions

1 Remember that the ratio of successive numbers in the Fibonacci sequence is equal to φ. Therefore the value of the 19th number in the sequence is approximately equal to:

6765 ÷ 1.61804 which, rounded to the nearest whole number gives 4181.

The value of the 21st number in the sequence is approximately equal to:

6765 × 1.61804, which, rounded to the nearest whole number gives 10 946.

2 The reciprocal of φ, or $φ^{-1}$, has a numerical value of approximately 0.618033989. The interesting pattern is that this value equals φ − 1. If you wish to play around with this relationship, you get:

$1/φ = φ − 1$

Multiplying both sides of the equation by φ and rearranging gives the equation:

$φ^2 − φ − 1 = 0$

If you now refer back to the section headed A mathematical aside on calculating the value of φ (Chapter 8), you will observe that this is the very equation from which we worked out the 'true' value of φ. So this explains why the relationship that $1/φ = φ − 1$ must be correct, as it is only a restatement of the initial formula for calculating the value of φ.

Chapter 22
Spirals

The growth of understanding follows an ascending spiral rather than a straight line.

Joanna Field

Many of the vast array of beautiful natural patterns have simple mathematical properties. This chapter takes a close look at spirals and shows their links with Fibonacci numbers and the golden ratio.

First, we need to be clear what we mean by a spiral. A *spiral* is a two-dimensional curve that starts from a central point and gets progressively further away as it revolves around the point. Now imagine that the spiral is made of light wire that is fixed at the centre and stretched in the third dimension. It is now a *helix*.

There are many different types of spiral, including the Archimedean spiral, the Euler spiral and Fermat's spiral. Perhaps the most interesting one is the logarithmic spiral, not least because it crops up so often in nature and also has many connections to the Fibonacci sequence and the golden ratio.

Any *two starting numbers*

In Chapter 21 you saw that, as you move along the Fibonacci sequence, the ratio of each value to the one that precedes it gets ever closer to Φ. As an aside, let's see what happens if we start the process with any two randomly chosen numbers, not taken from the familiar 1, 1, 2, 3, 5, 8, . . . pattern. Let's start with, say, 3 and 11. Based on the principle that the next number is formed by adding the previous two numbers, the sequence becomes:

3, 11, 14, 25, 39, 64, 103, 167, ...

Now, let's work out the ratios of consecutive numbers:

$11 \div 3 = 3.667$
$14 \div 11 = 1.273$
$25 \div 14 = 1.786$
$39 \div 25 = 1.560$
$64 \div 39 = 1.641$
$103 \div 64 = 1.609$
$167 \div 103 = 1.621$

As you can see, these ratios appear to be settling down, albeit fairly slowly, to the value of Φ of 1.618. . . And if you choose to extend the pattern, you will find that the approximation to Φ gets ever closer as you move along the terms of this sequence. For example, the 21st value of this particular sequence is 86 958, the 20th value is 53 743 and their ratio is 1.61803398. So this points to a surprising result: no matter which two starting numbers you choose to generate a Fibonacci-like sequence, the ratios of pairs of consecutive values always get ever closer to Φ.

Spiralling plants

One wonder of nature that has intrigued naturalists is the spiral pattern of the arrangement of seeds in a sunflower head. Typically there are two interweaving sets of spirals, one set running clockwise and the other anticlockwise. The exact number of spirals varies, but in general there

● **Figure 22.1** Sunflower head.

are either 21 and 34, or 34 and 55, or 55 and 89, or 89 and 144. These numbers may, by now, be familiar to you.

The same pattern crops up with pinecones, which have either 8 spirals from one side and 13 from the other, or 5 spirals from one side and 8 from the other (one of these is marked in Figure 22.2). Another example of where these patterns occur in nature is the number of diagonals in a pineapple, which is typically 8 in one direction and 13 in the other. In both of these examples (and there are many others in nature), the numbers involved are all from the Fibonacci sequence 1, 1, 2, 3, 5, 8, 13, 21, 34, 55, 89, . . .

An obvious question that the environmentalist was fascinated to explore was why so many plants form their leaves around the stem in this sort of pattern. The explanation is almost certainly to do with maximizing the amount of sunlight that falls on each leaf. If plants formed these leaves in a more uniform pattern, with each new leaf directly above the previous one, the upper leaf would shield the lower one, reducing the amount of sunlight

● **Figure 22.2** A pinecone with one of the spirals marked.

it received. Roses have five leaves every two turns, asters have eight leaves for every three turns and almond trees have thirteen leaves for every five turns – all numbers from the Fibonacci sequence.

In fact, the story is even more complex and amazing than this. The rotational angle of leaves around a stem, which maximizes the amount of sunlight falling on each leaf, turns out to be 137.5° and this angle is known as the 'golden angle' because of its close mathematical connections to Φ, the golden ratio. For example, if you draw a circle and construct two radii containing an angle of 137.5°, the ratio of the lengths of the two arcs formed on the circumference are in the golden ratio, as is the ratio of the complete circumference to the length of the larger arc.

Self-similarity

The technical term for the sort of spiral found in many natural forms (such as pinecones and sunflower heads) is the *logarithmic* (or equiangular or growth) *spiral*. It was first described by Descartes and later investigated in detail by Jacob Bernoulli, who named it *Spira Mirabilis*, the 'marvellous spiral'. What particularly impressed Bernoulli about its pattern of growth was that, with each successive loop, the size of the spiral would increase but its shape remained unchanged. This property is known as self-similarity.

Self-similarity can be found not just in spirals but also in other growth patterns. A property of some plants is that the shape of the whole is the same as that of one or more of its parts. For example, if you were to zoom into a branch of a fern, you would find that it has exactly the same shape as the original fern. Continue zooming into a sub-branch and then a sub-sub-branch and so on, and you would see the same underlying shape. This property of self-similarity is the central idea of a general type of geometric shape known as a *fractal* and you can read more about fractals in Chapter 25.

Discovering the logarithmic spiral

We all know, roughly, what a spiral shape looks like. But the environmentalist began to observe that not all spirals were identical. In order to be able to differentiate one natural spiral pattern from another, he needed to learn more about the factors that affect their shape. Once these key defining factors had been identified, it became possible to create a mathematical model for all possible spirals.

Algebraically, the underlying equation looks like this:

$$r = e^{a\theta}$$

where r is the radius (i.e. the distance from the centre to a point on the spiral); θ (pronounced 'theta') is the angle from the x-axis; and a is a constant that determines how tight the spiral is. (Note that, like π and Φ, e is an irrational number. It is known as Euler's number and has a numerical value of approximately 2.718281828459045235360287471352 7…)

As can be seen from the formula of the logarithmic spiral, its basic form is 'e raised to a power', which indicates that the spiral's growth has an exponential component. (Exponential growth is the subject of the next chapter.) For spirals there is an exponential relationship between the growth of the radius, r, and the angle, θ. Since logarithms and exponentials are closely connected (one is the inverse of the other), this explains the use of the word 'logarithmic' in the name of this spiral.

Figure 22.3 shows what a logarithmic spiral looks like. It will, of course, continue forever. As Descartes observed, if you draw a straight line from its centre, this line cuts all parts of the curve at the same angle – and it is this property that provides a clue to explain how a peregrine falcon flies as

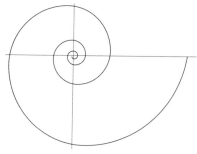

● **Figure 22.3** A logarithmic spiral (source: http://mathworld.wolfram.com/LogarithmicSpiral.html)

it hunts other birds. Rather than swooping in a straight line, the falcon follows a flight path that is a close approximation to a logarithmic spiral. By taking this path, the falcon is able to observe its prey at the same angle throughout the attack, thereby improving its accuracy.

Another interesting fact about this curve is explained by its property of self-similarity. If you were able to hover above it, and rise vertically upwards, extending the spiral outwards as you did so, you would see the same shape, however far you travelled upwards. This effect can be simulated using the zoom facility on a computer.

How to construct a logarithmic spiral
One way of creating a logarithmic spiral is to enter its formula into a computer graphing package or graphical calculator. But here is another way.

As accurately as possible, construct a golden rectangle (i.e. with sides in the approximate ratio 1.618:1). Next mark onto the rectangle a square, as shown (unshaded) in Figure 22.4 (b). A special property of the

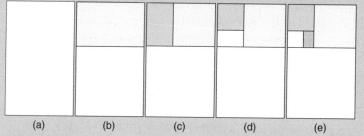

● **Figure 22.4** A series of golden rectangles: a starting point for constructing a logarithmic spiral.

golden rectangle is that the smaller rectangle that remains (shown here at the top) is also a golden rectangle.

Now repeat the process several times, each time marking a square onto the new rectangle to create another smaller golden rectangle. Figures 22.4 (b)–(e) show the first four stages of this process.

Now construct, within each square, a quarter circle, centred at its appropriate corner. You should end up with a curve similar to the one shown on the stained glass design in Figure 22.5, which is a good approximation to the logarithmic spiral.

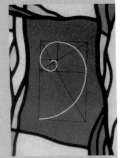

● **Figure 22.5** A logarithmic spiral in stained glass, by Roger Sargent.

The logarithmic spiral also underlies the shapes of many biological structures, including the shells of molluscs. Figure 22.6 shows a sectional slice through a fossil of the shell of a beautiful sea creature called a nautilus. Notice that all the chambers have an identical shape and each one is a scaled-down version of its larger neighbour – by the scale factor of the golden ratio.

● **Figure 22.6** A nautilus shell showing a logarithmic spiral.

The environmentalist models spirals

Around us we observe a vast array of natural patterns, but in order to be able to classify and compare them, the environmentalist needs to know more precisely what he is looking at. This chapter has shown you a formal algebraic model for defining spirals, which has enabled a meaningful investigation into spirals in nature and laid the groundwork for discovering why these particular patterns actually exist at all. You have also seen how the twin ideas of the Fibonacci sequence and the golden ratio are as common in the natural world as they are in art and architecture.

1   Explore the web to investigate how patterns in the world of the honeybee connect to the Fibonacci sequence and φ.

   For example, in a honeybee colony, the female bees (queens and workers) have two parents, a drone and a queen. However, since drones hatch from unfertilized eggs, they have only one parent, two grandparents, three great-grandparents, five great-great-grandparents and so on – yes, it is the Fibonacci sequence.

   Also, if you divide the number of female bees by the number of male bees in any given hive, you will get a number very close to 1.618.

2   Can you find any body proportions that lie close to the value of φ? For example, based on measurements of your own body, find the following ratios:

   (a) the length of your arm (from shoulder to fingertips) and the length from your elbow to your fingertips;

   (b) your height and the length from your belly button to your feet.

Chapter 23
Exponentials

The greatest shortcoming of the human race is our inability to understand the exponential function.

Albert A. Bartlett, physicist

Every spring there is a particular day when I smell the garden and say to myself, 'Now it's finally here – this is what I spent the whole winter looking forward to!' You don't need to be wearing a badge labelled 'professional cultivator of the soil' to appreciate the miracle of plant growth. Given the right sort of conditions (soil, water, warmth from the rays of the Sun), a tiny seed transforms itself magically, with little need for further human intervention. But to maximize yields and ensure disease-free crops, the environmentalist needs to explore a range of research questions about how and under what circumstances living things grow.

Growth

Our environmentalist is aware that plants, animals and their populations grow in different ways at various stages of their development. Some go through periods of steady growth, whereas others start slowly and then grow faster and faster. But to be able to make predictions and so anticipate and cater for future needs, the environmentalist will turn to mathematics to create a variety of models for growth. After a little tweaking and fine-tuning, he will use these models to describe and then, hopefully, explain what is going on when natural phenomena change over time.

The particular model covered in this chapter is *exponential growth*, which is characterized by a fixed-percentage increase each time period. Its key feature is that, as the values get bigger, this percentage represents, in absolute terms, a bigger and bigger amount, and so the amount of the increase is itself increasing all the time. As you will see shortly, this can mean that exponential growth can quickly 'go through the roof', in ways that may take your breath away.

First, however, let's go back to the 19th century and look at the gloomy predictions of the Reverend Thomas Malthus (1766–1834). At a time when the world's population was around one billion – just one seventh of what it is today – Malthus could see that human population growth was increasing in a way that would soon outstrip our capacity to feed ourselves. This idea can be reduced to a graph, as in Figure 23.1. It shows two types of growth (albeit measuring different things). For subsistence, measuring food production, growth is represented by a straight line and therefore can be described as linear – each year the amount of subsistence increases by a fixed amount. Population growth, on the other hand, is shown by an upwardly curving (exponential) pattern – each year the population size increases by an ever-increasing amount.

At some point, the exponential growth shown by the population curve will overtake the linear growth shown by the subsistence line. As Malthus expressed it, 'the power of population is indefinitely greater than the power in the earth to produce subsistence for man'. In fact, Malthus's predictions turned out to be basically correct, as was his view that it would be the poor who would bear the brunt of the shortfall.

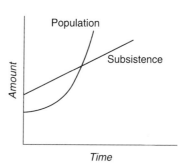

● **Figure 23.1** Population outstripping subsistence.

Doubling

One of the simplest examples of exponential growth is successive doubling. Here are a couple of questions to get you thinking about the effects of doubling.

1   Imagine a pond containing a lily pad that doubles in size every day. After 30 days, the pad completely fills the pond. After how many days was the pond exactly half full?

2   Imagine tearing a large sheet of paper in half and placing one half on top of the other. Then tear the two pieces in half and stack them together, making the pile four pieces high. Continue in this way until you have made 50 tears. Estimate the height of the paper pile and choose one of the following answers that is closest to your estimate: (a) roughly 20 cm, (b) roughly 50 cm, (c) roughly 1 metre, (d) more than 5 metres.

Solution

1   It would be tempting to answer 'after 15 days', but that would be wrong! If the pond is full after the 30th day, it would have been half full one day earlier (remember that it doubles in size every day), so the correct answer is 'after 29 days'. Note that it would have been one quarter full after 28 days and only one eighth full after 27 days.

2   The correct answer here is (d), more than 5 metres. In fact, as you will see from the following 'back of an envelope' calculation, it is a lot more than this!

After 1 tear, the number of sheets of paper = 2.

After 2 tears, the number of sheets of paper = 2^2 = 4.

After 3 tears, the number of sheets of paper = 2^3 = 8 . . .

After 50 tears, the number of sheets of paper is $2^{50} = 1.13 \times 10^{15}$.

Using conventional notation, this is 1 130 000 000 000 000 pieces of paper. Such a column of paper would be roughly 1.13×10^8 km (i.e. 70 million miles) tall – a distance equivalent to a journey of 130 trips to the Moon and back!

Here is a story about the perils of doubling. The king invited the creator of the game of chess to choose a reward for his invention. The man cunningly asked the ruler for some grains of rice according to the following rule: 1 grain for the first square of the chess board, 2 for the second one, 4 for the third and so on, doubling the number of grains each time until all 64 squares were accounted for.

The king had not heard of exponential growth and so foolishly agreed to the arrangement. The total number of grains of rice would come to:

$$1 + 2 + 2^2 + 2^3 + 2^4 + \ldots + 2^{63}$$

This is a lot of rice. In fact, the amount of rice on the last square alone (2^{63} grains) is approximately 40 times what could be grown in a single harvest, if all of Earth's arable land could be devoted to growing rice!

As can be seen from the paper tearing and chessboard examples, repeated doubling can quickly bring about mind-blowing levels of growth. This probably explains why there is a common misconception, seen particularly in the media, that exponential growth and very rapid growth mean the same thing. The confusion here is between the *rate* of growth and the *amount* of growth in each time period. To take a simple example: a regular growth of, say, 0.01 % each time period will bring about only small changes at first, yet the growth model is still exponential. It is true that, eventually, even small exponential growth rates will indeed produce rapid growth but in the short term, the increases can be extremely modest.

> ## Compound interest
>
> A more down-to-earth context for exponential growth is in calculating how money grows in a bank account if allowed to remain undisturbed gathering interest. What makes this scenario one of exponential growth is that the interest rate is a fixed percentage, and the amount of interest is calculated on an ever-increasing amount of investment (i.e. on the capital plus the accumulating interest). So every year, as the amount of interest grows, the growth of money in the account increases by a larger and larger amount. If you would like to explore the mathematical equation that describes the exponential model of growth, the compound interest formula is a good place to start, and these ideas are provided in the appendix to this chapter (A formula for exponential change).

Exponential decay

The exponential model for growth is based on the repeated multiplication of a number that is larger than 1. This number is the scale factor. For example, in the case of 4 % growth, the scale factor would be 1.04, while for a growth rate of 1.17 % the scale factor would be 1.0117.

When the scale factor is a number just *less* than 1, the effect is a form of exponential reduction, known as *exponential decay*. Under conditions of exponential decay, the amount of decrease reduces step by step

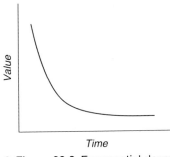

● **Figure 23.2** Exponential decay.

but by successively smaller amounts. You can see that the corresponding graph (Figure 23.2) flattens out to the right.

An everyday example of exponential decay is depreciation – for example, the depreciation of the monetary value of a vehicle over time. The key pattern is that the vehicle undergoes the largest amount of depreciation in the first year, less in the second year and progressively less in each succeeding year.

A more interesting application of exponential decay is a method used for estimating the dates of objects, known as *carbon dating*. This technique is a valuable tool in testing potential forgeries, be they the Turin Shroud or bottles of wine claimed to be of a particular vintage. (Recent attempts to carbon-date wine suggests that up to five per cent of the vintage wine sold is faked!) The mechanism works as follows. When plants grow, they absorb carbon dioxide. As a result of photosynthesis, they acquire an amount of the isotope Carbon 14 (written ^{14}C) that matches the amount of ^{14}C in the atmosphere. When the plant dies, its ^{14}C starts to dissipate in a very predictable way that can be modelled by exponential decay. By taking a sample of the plant, measuring the fraction of the ^{14}C remaining, and comparing this to the amount expected from atmospheric ^{14}C, it is possible to estimate the year in which the plant died. This method can be used to date any organic material – for example, the plant used to create the cloth from which the Turin Shroud was made or the grapes used to make authentic 'vintage' wine.

Something for you to try

1 Which of the following statements about exponential change is true?
   A Exponential growth always means rapid growth.
   B Exponential growth is where the percentage rate of change each time period is fixed.
   C Exponential growth is where the percentage rate of change each time period is continually increasing.

2 (a) For what range of values of the scale factor will the exponential change be one of growth?

2 (b) For what range of values of the scale factor will the exponential change be one of decay?

Solutions

1 Statement (a).

2 (a) Growth occurs where the scale factor is greater than 1.
   (b) Decay occurs where the scale factor is between 0 and 1.

The environmentalist learns a lesson about exponential growth

One lesson learned by the environmentalist in recent centuries has been about the danger of introducing a particular species into a new environment. Two recent examples are the introduction of the rabbit to Australia from Europe in 1859 and the introduction of the grey squirrel into the UK from the USA in the late 19th century. The environmentalist discovered, too late, that where the conditions are favourable to the introduced species, it can undergo a population explosion where numbers double every few years, resulting in the displacement or elimination of indigenous species.

In this chapter, the environmentalist has learned about the astonishing effects of the exponential growth model and how easily it can 'go through the roof', even when the under-lying scale factor is quite modest.

> The mathematics of uncontrolled growth are frightening. A single cell of the bacterium E. coli would, under ideal circumstances, divide every twenty minutes. That is not particularly disturbing until you think about it, but the fact is that bacteria multiply geometrically: one becomes two, two become four, four become eight, and so on. In this way it can be shown that in a single day, one cell of E. coli could produce a super-colony equal in size and weight to the entire planet Earth.

> Michael Crichton, *The Andromeda Strain*
> (Dell, NY, 1969), p. 247

Chapter 24
Chaos

Ne'er cast a clout till May be out.

Traditional British proverb

The proverb above advises you not to discard your winter clothing until the May blossom appears, after which, presumably, you have a reasonable guarantee of warm weather. Ah, the weather! It seems that no nation in the world talks or cares more about the weather than the British. Perhaps this obsession has its roots in our geography, as Britain's island status, latitude and close proximity to the Atlantic Ocean all make its weather so changeable and unpredictable. But does knowing about the future weather actually matter? Surely it's not just so we can finalize barbecue plans for the weekend or decide which factor of suntan lotion to take on holiday? No, it is our agricultural roots that helped to set the weather as the jewel of our conversational crown. Weather forecasting is traditionally about farmers and gardeners making important decisions to protect and nurture their crops and maximize their yields.

Talk about the weather

There is a certain charm in the many country sayings about weather prediction, but do they actually work? Here is one you may have come across. It is based on which tree comes into leaf first in spring – the oak or the ash – as an indicator of the amount of rainfall we should expect.

Oak before ash, in for a splash;
Ash before oak, in for a soak.

The German version of this rhyme is:

Grünt die Eiche vor der Esche,
hält der Sommer große Wäsche.
Grünt die Esche vor der Eiche,
hält der Sommer große Bleiche.

In Norway it is:

Ask før eik blir steik
Og eik før ask blir plask.

The fact that this proverb crops up in several countries might appear to lend support to the truth of its central claim . . . were it not for the fact that the German and Norwegian rhymes have it the other way around from the British one! In fact, statistical investigations demonstrate very little evidence for the suggestion that years in which the ash appears before the oak have higher rainfalls. The only pattern there is real evidence for is that years in which March temperatures are high also tend to be years when oak precedes ash by a considerable margin. However, in recent decades, oak has preceded ash in almost every year and so, due to global warming, it is increasingly unlikely for ash to precede oak in the foreseeable future.

Much as we might like them to possess some sort of universal truth, the sad fact is that the claims of many of our ancient folk sayings don't stand up to close scrutiny. Weather forecasting has come a long way since the days in which the delight of shepherds was to observe a 'red sky at night', and this shift is largely down to the invention of the computer. Meteorological offices around the world invest a lot of time and money creating mathematical models of weather patterns, which are then run through sophisticated computer simulations. While they find it relatively easy to predict what the weather will be like tomorrow, predicting it for one week or one month ahead is extremely difficult. There are so many variable factors that change from day to day that it is difficult to find reliable data for long-term forecasts. In fact, as you will see shortly, even tiny aberrations in the initial data can result in huge discrepancies in the final prediction and this is where chaos theory comes in.

Chaotic behaviour

In the 19th century it was generally believed that the universe was fairly predictable; provided you could measure the inputs, a model of it could be created that ran strictly on scientific principles. Isaac Newton referred to this theory as the 'clockwork universe' – a perfect machine governed by the laws of physics that could model the behaviour of the solar system. On a less cosmic scale, it was clear that a simple mechanism like the free pendulum operated according to simple and predictable laws of motion and energy. This view of science is known as *deterministic* because of its idea that, provided you have precise measures of your input variables, the outputs can be predicted (determined) with perfect accuracy. So, a system is deterministic if its current state completely defines its future, unaffected by external random events.

Now spin forward to the mid-20th century and the early days of using computers to model weather patterns. One day in 1961 the American meteorologist Edward Lorenz was working in his laboratory in the Massachusetts Institute of Technology (MIT). He fed his input value into the computer and went off to make a cup of coffee, leaving the computer running. When he returned he found a very unexpected result and one that appeared to contradict an earlier finding. Despite the fact that he was using the same model as before and had fed in essentially the same input data, the result was completely different. How could this be?

On closer examination of his print-out, he spotted that this time his initial input value, 0.506, had been entered to just three-figure precision, whereas previously he had used six figures: 0.506127. But why should this make any substantial difference? After all, if a sprinter runs a 100m race on two occasions, setting off, say, 0.1 seconds later in the second race than in the first, we might expect the two running times to be very similar, with the second just slightly slower. The point here is that, while some systems are relatively insensitive to variations in the initial conditions, others are highly sensitive. Of course, the idea that small actions can result in large consequences is not particularly new or surprising, as this 14th-century proverb observe:

> For want of a nail the shoe was lost.
> For want of a shoe the horse was lost.
> For want of a horse the rider was lost.
> For want of a rider the battle was lost.
> For want of a battle the kingdom was lost.
> And all for the want of a horseshoe nail.

What surprised Lorenz and his colleagues was the scale of the effect resulting from such a tiny perturbation in the input to his weather program. This became known as the *butterfly effect*. The term derives from a short story about time travel written by Ray Bradbury and published in 1952. 'A Sound of Thunder' tells how, in a prehistoric era, time-travelling hunters accidentally kill a butterfly – a seemingly trivial event whose consequences ultimately affect the language and politics of our present world. As chaos theory gained wider popularity, the term 'butterfly effect' really caught the public imagination after Philip Merilees gave a talk to the American Association for the Advancement of Science in 1972, entitled 'Does the flap of a butterfly's wings in Brazil set off a tornado in Texas?'

Another metaphor that tells a similar story is pouring a glass of water onto the top ridge of the Rocky Mountains. Move the glass a few centimetres to the west and the water makes its way to the Colorado River, ending up in the Pacific Ocean. Move it slightly the other way and it flows to the Mississippi River and on to the Atlantic Ocean. In practice, chaos tends not to be linked to one single 'tripping point' but to a pattern involving a long series of 'iterative' steps, where each new output is fed back into the process to become the next input value. Iteration is a very important idea in mathematics and is explored now.

Iteration

Have you ever wondered how calculators and computers perform calculations involving awkward numbers? For example, how do they work out the square root of 367.1296 or the logarithm of 91834.267? Rest assured that they do not already possess a data file containing the square root, cube root, logarithm, etc., of every possible number that you might feel inclined to feed in. No, they have something much better – each function is represented by a procedure (known as an algorithm), which will work out, from first principles, the square root, logarithm, etc., of any number to an appropriate level of precision. (In the case of scientific calculators, this is usually 15 or 16 figures, which are subsequently rounded and displayed to ten.)

A common approach used by calculator designers to create acceptably precise calculations for a particular function is to reconfigure the function in question into the form of a mathematical formula so that it becomes the sum of a sequence of numbers, each one having a numerical value smaller than the one that preceded it. So, the further you work along the sequence collecting terms and adding them into your summation, the closer the approximation will be to the true value.

Another way of making these sorts of approximations is to use *iteration*. With this approach you need to set up the desired solution – let's call it x – as an iterative equation, which is of the form $x = f(x)$, where $f(x)$ is some function of x. Typically you start by feeding in a starting value for x (call it x_1) into $f(x)$ and what you get out is a new value for x, called x_2. This value is then fed into $f(x)$ once more and the third value, x_3, is produced. If the iterative equation has been set up sensibly, each succeeding value of x should, quite quickly, get ever closer to the true value of x.

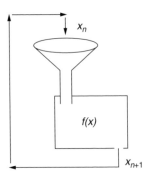

● **Figure 24.1** Iteration: the latest output becomes the next input value.

Here is an example of iteration to solve the equation we used to calculate the value of the golden ratio φ in Chapter 8: $x^2 - x - 1 = 0$.

Step 1

Set up the equation in the form $x = f(x)$. This can be done as follows: Add $x + 1$ to both sides, giving: $x^2 = x + 1$.

Then take the square root of both sides, giving: $x = \sqrt{x+1}$.

This is now in the form $x = f(x)$, where $f(x) = \sqrt{x+1}$.

Step 2

Choose a starting value, say $x = 3$, which means setting $x_1 = 3$. Feed this value into the right-hand side of the iteration equation. This gives:

$$x_2 = \sqrt{x_1 + 1} = \sqrt{3+1} = \sqrt{4} = 2.$$

(Note: we can ignore the alternative square root, -2.)

Repeat the process, now using this output value 2 as the next input value, and so on.

$$x_3 = \sqrt{x_2 + 1} = \sqrt{(2 + 1)} = \sqrt{3} = 1.732050808.$$

$$x_4 = \sqrt{x_3 + 1} = \sqrt{(1.732050808 + 1)} = \sqrt{(2.732050808)}$$
$$= 1.65289165.$$

$$x_5 = \sqrt{x_4 + 1} = \sqrt{(1.652891650 + 1)} = \sqrt{(2.652891650)}$$
$$= 1.628769981.$$

etc.

$$x_9 = \sqrt{x_8 + 1} = \sqrt{(1.618350337 + 1)} = \sqrt{(2.618350337)}$$
$$= 1.618131743.$$

$$x_{10} = \sqrt{x_9 + 1} = \sqrt{(1.\,618131743 + 1)} = \sqrt{(2.618131743)}$$
$$= 1.618064196.$$

As can be seen from the similarity in the values of x_9 and x_{10}, the values have started to settle down. Ten or eleven iterations later and the values have settled down as far as nine figures ($x_{19} = 1.618033990$ and $x_{20} = 1.618033989$) and this will be a sufficiently precise solution to the original equation for most purposes.

Something for you to try

Setting up a spreadsheet to solve equations iteratively is normally quick and painless. Fire up a spreadsheet and follow the instructions below to solve, iteratively, the same equation: $x^2 - x - 1 = 0$.

Into cell A1 enter the starting value, 3.

Into cell A2, enter the iterative formula: =SQRT(A1+1).

(Note that the command 'SQRT' is square root and the value A1 corresponds to the starting value, x_1, which in this case is 3.)

Cell A2 will now display the value 2, which is x_2.

Reselect cell A2 and fill down* as far as cell A20. The cells A1:A20 will now display the results of the first twenty iterations.

Conditions for chaotic behaviour

In this chapter, three conditions for chaotic behaviour have been explored. First, there must be a system that follows strict rules – like Newton's clockwork universe – where each step is well defined and there is no random element. Second, there needs to be a high level of sensitivity to initial conditions, so a tiny adjustment to the starting value could make a huge difference to the final outcome. Third, the well-defined steps themselves need to be of a non-linear form, to enable very rapid and extreme swings. Exponential models, for example, have this property, but the one most commonly associated with chaotic behaviour is the iterative model – a pattern of change in which each new output feeds back into the calculation to become the next input, and so on ad infinitum. These three conditions all pertain to weather forecasting, which is why chaos theory has such relevance in meteorology. Chaos theory has applications across many fields, including physics, medicine, computing and tectonics (the study of the Earth's continental plates).

The most commonly held misconceptions about chaos theory are that it is all about disorder and that we can conclude that ordered systems are impossible to achieve. The implication is that determinism is bunk and attempts to model complex systems are a waste of time. These views are wrong as they confuse the outcomes with the mechanism that produces them. We should not lose sight of the fact that deterministic theories such as the ideas of Newton have been highly successful at enabling us to gain a better understanding of the world around us. While the values generated in a system where chaos theory applies may look disordered, it is actually operating under strict rules and is not subject to random fluctuations. So, the real meaning of the 'chaos' in chaos theory is 'apparent chaos'.

A footnote on the meaning of life

Chaos theory has helped to shed light on a surprisingly wide range of issues that touch on the big existential questions that bother the curious human mind. For example, the discovery that extreme complexity can result from the operation of simple rules has helped to knock on the head the creationist argument that our world is so complex that it could not just have happened by chance and therefore must have been put together by an intelligent designer. Secondly, chaos theory offers a neat extension to Darwin's ideas on natural selection. Chaotic activity has enabled the formation of a multiplicity of natural forms, while natural selection puts each alternative to the test. The outcome is that those forms that adapted best to their environments have thrived, at the expense of the others that failed to make it.

The environmentalist tries to predict the future

One of the main reasons why chaos theory is so popular with the environmentalist is that it provides him with valuable insights into the science of prediction. Like the rest of us, the environmentalist is obsessed with predicting the weather, but he does it for the good reason that he needs to know about optimal conditions for planting and harvesting. Over the longer term, the environmentalist has many deeper questions about how our climate is changing, and whether this will affect what he should choose to plant in the future.

A relatively new branch of mathematics, chaos theory appears at first to challenge the more traditional and deterministic view that the laws of science and mathematics are highly predictable. What the environmentalist has discovered is that, in some fields, the laws of science still operate pretty much 'like clockwork'. However, in others (like weather prediction), the underlying relationships are extremely sensitive to tiny perturbations in the input values and, over the longer term, the end result can turn out to be a long way away from where the mathematical model had predicted.

1   Which words describe the following?
    (a) a system where there is no randomness and the output values
        can, theoretically, always be predicted from the starting values;
    (b) a system where each new output is fed back to form the next
        input;
    (c) a procedure for solving a problem, expressed as a sequence of
        instructions.

2   To find the numerical value of $\sqrt{2}$, you can attempt to solve the
    equation $x^2 = 2$.
    This can be rearranged into the following iterative formula:

$$x = x - \frac{x^2 - 2}{2x}$$

Based on the spreadsheet method, use this iterative equation to
work out the value of $\sqrt{2}$ to ten figures.
How many iterations are required to reach this level of precision?

An aside on creating iterative formulas:

Rearranging simple equations such as $x^2 = 2$ into a form suitable
for efficient iteration can sometimes be quite tricky. But if you feel
the urge to try a little light algebra, try the reverse – have a go at
simplifying the iterative formula above and see if you can end up
with $x^2 = 2$.

Solutions

1   (a) deterministic; (b) iterative; (c) algorithm.
2   Enter the starting value, say 2, into cell B1. In cell B2 enter:

    $=B1-(B1\wedge2-2)/(2*B1)$

(Note that the '$\wedge$' symbol raises to a power.)
Then use 'fill down' to confirm that the solution settles down to a
value of 1.414213562.
This turns out to be a very efficient algorithm, which achieves
10-figure precision after just five iterations.

Chapter 25
Fractals

*I never saw an ugly thing in my life:
for let the form of an object be what it
may – light, shade, and perspective will
always make it beautiful.*

John Constable (British landscape painter,
1776–1837)

Modelling nature

From my schooldays, I remember being impressed by
the poetry of Gerard Manley Hopkins. His works seem to
invite you to read them aloud. For example, his short poem
'God's Grandeur', written in 1877, which can be found at:
http://www.poetryfoundation.org/poem/173660

Hopkins berates us humans who have done our best to
wreck the magnificence of the world, God's grandeur.

The beauty of nature has been extolled by humankind
for as long as history records. Like Hopkins, artists and poets
in the past have tended to give the credit to God and have
not asked detailed questions about the mechanisms that have
created the natural marvels. That changed in the mid-20th
century, when the environmentalist and the mathematician
started to come together in pursuit of a common goal – to
find ways of describing, in simple terms, the mechanisms that
produce such features as the markings on a leopard's skin or
the particular shape of a bird's wing.

One outstanding mathematician and creative thinker who
pushed this idea forward was Benoît Mandelbrot, a French/
American mathematician who was particularly interested
in finding mathematical models for the patterns and shapes
of the real world. As well as coining the word 'fractal', he
opened up a way of seeing the complexity of the natural

world as something that could be modelled by a few simple equations.

Self-similarity

The idea of self-similarity was described in Chapter 22, in the context of spirals in nature. Self-similarity is the property where the shape of the whole is the same as that of one or more of its parts. So, if you were to zoom into a branch, then into a sub-branch, then a sub-sub-branch and so on, you would keep seeing the same underlying shape. The importance of self-similarity is that it appears to be one of nature's most favoured design principles, and it is a central feature of how fractals are structured.

Now consider the shoreline around Great Britain and imagine how you might go about estimating its length.

Depending on how large a 'step size' you use, you will get a different answer every time. For example, let's suppose you were to take giant steps, each of 200 km. This would give an estimate for the length of coastline of approximately 2400 km. Now reduce the step size to, say, 50 km. With this smaller step size, it becomes possible to follow some of the more intricate contours of the coastline, as a result of which the estimate goes up to roughly 3400 km. Suppose you decide to use even greater precision by undertaking the journey on foot and so are able to reduce the unit size to a single metre. Your walk will take you around many twists and turns that weren't visible before, as a result of which your estimate may have increased to something in excess of 4000 km. So, big inlets contain several smaller inlets, each of which contains yet smaller inlets, and so on. It turns out that coastlines are another example of self-similarity and therefore are fractal in their form.

Other examples of self-similarity include the shapes of ferns and broccoli florets; and the branching of our circulatory systems, from major arteries to tiny capillaries. Snowflakes often display self-similar branching patterns or crystals within crystals. On a more cosmic scale, there is the arrangement of galaxies – a single galaxy will usually be found within a small cluster, which itself is part of a larger cluster, which is nested within a super-cluster, and so on. This phenomenon is often likened to the arrangement of Russian dolls, which is a nested set of dolls within dolls, each similar in shape but different in scale only.

Iteration again

Chapter 24 showed that when a particular combination of circumstances is present, the application of even a simple rule repeated over and over can quickly produce chaotic and unpredictable outcomes. The sort of rule that can generate chaotic outcomes is one based on iteration. Iteration is a repetitive procedure where each new output in turn feeds back into the calculation to become the next input, and so on.

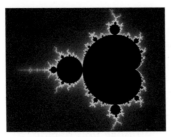

● **Figure 25.1** The fractal known as the Mandelbrot set.

As well as contributing to chaotic behaviour, iterative procedures can also lead to the creation of surprising patterns which, when plotted graphically, can form beautiful geometric shapes known as fractals. (In fact, although human understanding of chaos theory and fractals evolved separately, they are now seen as being closely connected.) The so-called father of fractal geometry, Benoît Mandelbrot was a major figure whose vision and originality of thinking about patterns in nature helped bring this branch of mathematics into being.

The joy of creating a fractal on a computer (using suitable fractal generation software) is that it makes it easy to explore self-similarity. Zoom into a tiny section of the picture by creating a box around it and see elements of the original pattern in the new picture. There is no limit to how deeply you can continue to zoom in, except of course for your patience. If you keep going, it is inevitable that you will eventually uncover parts of the Mandelbrot set that no one has seen before!

● **Figure 25.2** 'Fractal Star'—from the *Beauty of Maths* collection by Sheila Graham.

Image compression

An obvious question to ask about fractals is 'What is the point of them?' Clearly it is possible to create a fractal picture on a computer, but why should anyone want to? One answer is that it enables the creation of fractal art. But there are many more practical applications of fractals, of which the compression of digitized computer images is a useful and highly profitable example.

As you read this, look at your surroundings and examine closely the surface of any object that you see – perhaps a table top or the floor under your feet or, if you are out of doors, the sky. On close examination, you may find it is possible to break up the overall picture into smaller components that can be made to look similar to each other. It may be necessary to rotate or reflect one of the sub-images or scale it up or down in size in order to make it match another one. It is plausible to imagine that, if you keep going, you will eventually be able to carve up the entire picture in this way, reducing it to multiple copies of a single sub-image. If this sub-image can be created by a single fractal equation, then repetitions of the entire floor or tabletop or sky can be coded in terms of this equation – once the first one is in place, each of the others simply requires an instruction about its location, orientation and size.

This is a simplified version of how fractal image compression works. It is a technique that is increasingly being used to compress digital images so that they can be stored and transmitted more cheaply and quickly. By contrast, traditional image compression formats such as the industry-standard JPEG (Joint Photographic Experts Group) use a compression technique based on discarding parts of the image that the human eye cannot easily discern. Based on this principle, the greater the compression, the more information must be discarded. Fractal compression has several advantages over JPEG and similar formats. First, once the fractal codes are in place, the image is scaleable in size, which means that you can zoom in on a fractal image with no loss of resolution. In practice, the constraint on zooming is affected only by the amount of available memory in the user's computer. Second, fractal compression is more efficient in terms of the compression ratio that it allows. For example, JPEG images will start to give a pixellated (i.e. blocky) appearance with compression ratios greater than about 20, but good resolution is possible with fractal compression at ratios of 100 times or greater. Finally, while the fractal compression of a digital image takes a long time, the decompression process is very rapid, so from this point of view it is highly user-friendly.

1   *A feature of broccoli is that the whole plant has the same shape as its florets which, in turn, have the same shape as the sub-florets, and so on. What term is used to describe this property?*

2   *Name the two formats for digital image compression mentioned in this chapter.*

Solutions

1   *self-similarity.*

2   *Fractal compression and JPEG were the two mentioned in this chapter – there are many others!*

The environmentalist uses fractals to model the world

In a chapter this length, it has not been possible to do justice to the huge and rapidly growing area of mathematics known as fractals or fractal geometry. What began as a branch of geometry that enabled the environmentalist to model shapes in nature has mushroomed into a wide variety of applications that its inventor, Benoît Mandelbrot, could never have predicted. Fractal geometry is now used in film and TV to create convincing special effects such as landscapes, lunar scenes, mountain ranges and coastlines. Ever more efficient fractal techniques are used to model natural objects, producing images that can be stored and exchanged in the form of high-resolution files that consume relatively low levels of computer memory.

Be an environmentalist

It is believed that the phrase 'Think globally, act locally' was first coined by the Scottish town planner and social activist Patrick Geddes nearly a century ago. Today the mantra is used to encourage people to consider the health of the whole planet while at the same time doing their bit to protect their own community. Undoubtedly, the Earth and its millions of other inhabitants (the many species of plants and animals who share it with us) need our help and there's no shortage of practical ways to lend a hand. However, environmentalism is not a religion and it is not about coercing others into your way of seeing the world. If you decide to become more active in the rapidly growing environmentalist movement, your two most valuable weapons are a driving passion to do something worthwhile and a well-researched understanding of how the world works. This may mean that you will spend less time hugging trees and more learning about biology, chemistry, ecology and, yes, mathematics.

Here are three of the many questions about the environment that you may be interested in following up. All of them will inevitably extend your mathematical understanding in some way.

- How is pollution harming our planet?
- Should farmers be allowed to kill badgers to protect their cattle from disease?
- Is global warming a serious risk to the planet's long-term survival or is it part of the cycle of natural global change?

The philosopher
Communicating effectively with others

You could never accuse the philosopher of being a very practical person! While the other five members of our family were out there 'doing', he was sitting indoors, quietly reading or just thinking. But where he excels is in the clarity of his thinking. He could be described as someone who truly 'says what he means and means what he says'. And for that we value his contribution to our quality of life.

Clarity of expression is achieved in two stages. First you must think through carefully what points you wish to make and then you must choose your words carefully so that you communicate the ideas clearly to others. These steps require the following elements for which the philosopher gets much credit: *logical thinking*, and *precision* in the use of language.

Unfortunately, the long wordy arguments of the philosopher can sometimes be hard to follow and there are great benefits to be had in learning to express them concisely. This is where the mathematician can be of help; by translating wordy statements into a shorthand notation (he usually calls this algebra but it can also take the form of charts and diagrams), he can make an entire idea plain to see at a glance.

Over many centuries, mathematics has evolved into a form that is both *concise* in its notation and *precise* in its meaning. These are the signature features of mathematical language and provide what many consider to be its two key strengths – manipulability of the ideas being expressed and almost total freedom from ambiguity. Of course, in order to reap these benefits, you do need to have some grasp of the basic conventions of mathematical language and notation. These final chapters look at some of the forms of communication that mathematics does particularly well, including proof and logic.

Chapter 26
Whispering: secrets and codes

I would imagine if you could understand Morse Code, a tap dancer would drive you crazy.

Mitch Hedberg (American comedian, 1968–2005)

In these final five chapters you are invited to enter the world of the philosopher and consider how the questions he asks are supported by mathematical forms of expression and ways of thinking. A feature that the philosopher shares with the mathematician is that ideas need to be communicated in forms that are clear and unambiguous. But in this particular chapter, on secret codes, those are precisely the qualities he is seeking to avoid!

The life that I have

The Life that I Have is a poem which was written during the Second World War by cryptographer Leo Marks. He wrote it as a poem code for the French spy Violette Szabo, who was subsequently captured, tortured and killed by the Nazis. The story of her life and death was told in a 1958 film, *Carve Her Name with Pride*. You can find the poem widely online.

● **Figure 26.1** Violette Szabo, who died in 1944.

The poem-code system works on the basis that only the sender and receiver know the poem. To create a message, the agent, who has learned the poem by heart, chooses a set number of words (say, 5)

at random from it and allocates a number to each letter from the chosen words. These numbers are then used as a key to encode the message. Each poem-code message starts with five letters showing which five words of the poem have been used.

What made this code particularly hard to crack was the fact that Marks's poem was original, unpublished and known to no one else. Previous attempts tended to base codes on well-known published verse by authors such as Shakespeare, Racine, Molière and Keats, and many agents came to grief when the enemy discovered the source

● **Figure 26.2** Leo Marks holding a silk coding sheet.

of their text. In his book *Between Silk and Cyanide* (London: Harper Collins, 1998), Marks describes his wartime experiences as a cryptographer in the Special Operations Executive and includes a moving account of his briefing of Szabo, prior to her first mission.

Marks's earlier coding maps were printed on silk so that they could be concealed easily in clothing. To ensure that no code was used twice, the operatives would use one key, send the message, and then cut off and burn the relevant strip of code alphabet.

Simple codes

From ancient times, restricted information could always be whispered into the ear of a trusted confidante; it was when the secret had to be written down that the problems really began. How could you be sure that it wouldn't fall into the wrong hands? Thus began the invention of codes, out of which has grown a huge multi-billion industry, referred to today as *cryptography*. The process of creating a coded message is called *encryption*, while the process of turning it back into the original message (i.e. de-coding it) is *decryption*.

Have a look at this message and see if you can decrypt it.

20 8 5 13 15 14 5 25 9 19 9 14 20 8 5 3 12 15 3 11.

This has been written in what is probably the simplest sort of code, based on substitution, where each number corresponds to the position of the letter in the alphabet:

1	2	3	4	5	6	7	8	9	10	11	12	13
A	B	C	D	E	F	G	H	I	J	K	L	M
14	15	16	17	18	19	20	21	22	23	24	25	26
N	O	P	Q	R	S	T	U	V	W	X	Y	Z

Using this chart, the message above can be quickly decoded as follows: becomes:

20 8 5 13 15 14 5 25 9 19 9 14 20 8 5 3 12 15 3 11
T H E M O N E Y I S I N T H E C L O C K

As codes go, this is as easy as it gets! You can make it harder by shifting each number along by a certain number of places – say, four places to the right, as follows:

5	6	7	8	9	10	11	12	13	14	15	16	17
A	B	C	D	E	F	G	H	I	J	K	L	M
18	19	20	21	22	23	24	25	26	1	2	3	4
N	O	P	Q	R	S	T	U	V	W	X	Y	Z

Using that code, see if you can crack this message (you can find the solution at the end of this chapter):

23 9 18 8 22 9 13 18 10 19 22 7 9 17 9 18 24 23.

This type of transposition was popular with the ancient Roman military and is often called the Caesar Shift cipher, or simply the Caesar cipher. Of course, decoding it's fine if you happen to know that the shift is, say, four steps to the right. But what if you didn't know this? One strategy might be to try every possible shift and see which ones form recognizable words. This might sound a tall order – there are, after all, 25 possible shifts. But with the aid of a computer you can quickly execute each shift in turn, checking the resulting letter sequences against the computer's resident dictionary.

Yet another possibility presents itself. What would happen if you were to allow the order of the alphabet to be mixed up *in any permutation*? There would be 26 ways of choosing the first letter, 25 ways of choosing the second, 24 ways of choosing the third, and so on. This yields a total of $26 \times 25 \times 24 \times \ldots \times 1$ possible transpositions, which is a number known in mathematics as 'factorial 26,' and written '26!' It is a truly huge number, with a value of roughly: 400 000 000 000 000 000 000 000 000.

If you devoted, say, one second to trying each possible permutation, it would take roughly a billion times the lifetime of the universe to check them all!

Decoding by letter frequencies

A second and surprisingly powerful, strategy for cracking the above type of code is to exploit certain known facts about letter frequencies. For example, the most commonly used letter in the English language is 'e', which crops up, on average, 12.702 % of the time. The second most commonly used letter is 't' (9.056 %), while the least commonly used letter is 'z' (0.074 %). Figure 26.3 shows the relative frequencies for each letter in the English language – the taller the bar, the greater the relative frequency. As you can see, the five vowels (a, e, i, o, u) tend to come up more often than the consonants. Clearly, words like 'the' and 'a' crop up often, so the frequencies of the letters in these words (a, t, h and e) will be bumped up accordingly. Also, the letter s is often used at the end of nouns to make them plural, so this too has a fairly high relative frequency.

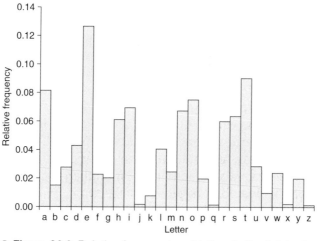

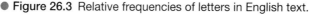

● **Figure 26.3** Relative frequencies of letters in English text.

So how is this information useful to cryptographers? The answer is that by counting how often each of the characters in the coded message occurs and matching this information to the chart of relative frequencies of letters, they can make a reasonable deduction about which letters are being used. For example, there is a good chance that the code-character occurring most frequently corresponds to the letter e. To take the example of the coded message, 'the money is in the clock', here are the frequencies of its 20 letters.

Letter	e	t	h	o	n	i	c	m	y	s	l	k
Frequency	3	2	2	2	2	2	2	1	1	1	1	1

You can see that, in this short message, the letter e does indeed occur more frequently than any other. In practice, with very short messages like this, the patterns may not match well with the chart; in general, the longer the message, the better the match.

The arrival of public key cryptography

Let's now bring the story of cryptography into modern times. While military espionage is still a major field for creating and cracking codes, the secret world of banks and industry has become a money-spinning new environment for cryptography. In this digital age, all information that you might wish to communicate can be reduced to numbers. Encoding your message then involves performing some calculation that will alter these numbers. To decode the message, simply reverse the calculation. However, since the recipient needs access to the reversal key, much time and effort were necessary to ensure that these keys were distributed securely. Right up to the 1970s, carefully vetted dispatch riders would set off with the reversal keys locked in briefcases, to distribute them *in person* to each customer. Then, with the invention of public key cryptography in 1977, all that changed.

The only way to avoid having to convey a key personally to your customer would be to make it publicly available. However, this wouldn't appear to make sense, as the key would then be available to any Tom, Dick or Harry who could use it to read your secret message. One possible solution might be to provide the key for people to *encrypt* any message that they wanted to send you, while the key to *decrypt* these messages would be held only by you. You may be thinking that, surely, making the encryption key public would automatically enable anyone to decrypt your messages, simply by reversing the procedure. To take a simple example, if the publicly available procedure for encryption was 'multiply by 1379', Tom or Dick or Harry would simply divide by 1379 to return to the original message. What was needed, therefore, was a *one-way* procedure – one that would allow anyone to use your code to encrypt a message that they wanted to send to you, but where the procedure could not be reversed and so could not be decrypted. This would be a bit like mixing some red and yellow paint (to get orange) – easy to do but very hard to undo!

For a long time, the problem of coming up with a suitable one-way function was thought to be insoluble, but it was finally cracked in August 1977 by three young American mathematicians, Ronald Rivest, Adi Shamir and Leonard Adleman. Their solution effectively laid off hundreds of briefcase-wielding dispatch riders around the world. Their RSA algorithm (RSA being an acronym made from their surnames) provided a calculation that allowed messages and data to be easily encoded and yet remain impossible to decode by anyone other than the owner of the reversal key. This discovery opened up possibilities that even the three authors could not have imagined. In fact, shortly after details of their system were published, a representative of the National Security Agency knocked on their door. He informed them that the US government classified cryptography as a *munition* and if their publication were to be mailed overseas, they would be prosecuted for illegal arms dealing!

The RSA system was based on the multiplication of two extremely large *prime* numbers. First, here is an illustration of why it works.

Consider two prime numbers, say, 523 and 1039. With the aid of a calculator, multiply them: $523 \times 1039 = 543\,397$.

Now give this answer, 543 397, to your most mathematically skilled friend and ask him or her to reverse the process – i.e. to factorize this number and retrieve the original two prime numbers. But don't hold your breath waiting, as this is not easy.

Now imagine choosing two really large prime numbers, each over 400 digits long. This is considerably harder – in practice it is impossible! It has been estimated that to factorize their product and retrieve the original numbers, using the fastest computers in the world, would take something in the order of a billion years.

The process of multiplying two large prime numbers is known as a *one-way function*: the calculation is easy to perform but (virtually) impossible to reverse. And this is the principle on which public key cryptography is based. Of course, it would only take one mathematician to work out how to factorize the product of two large prime numbers for the entire e-banking system to collapse overnight, but fortunately that doesn't seem likely in the foreseeable future.

An alternative history

Although Rivest, Shamir and Adleman got the credit for their RSA algorithm, there is an alternative history to public key cryptography. An English cryptographer, James Ellis, actually solved the core problem in 1970. He shared his ideas with colleagues Clifford Cocks and Malcolm Williamson and by 1975 they had all the main details sorted out. However, as they were working at the British Government Communications Headquarters (GCHQ) at the time, they were sworn to secrecy and so never got the recognition they deserved.

As has been discussed in this chapter, codes have been used for thousands of years to transmit secret messages, whether for reasons of military or commercial advantage, giving rise to a huge and growing field of cryptography. Codes today affect practically all aspects of our lives – for example, barcodes in pricing and stocktaking, codes for locks and safes, codes for brevity (musical notation and knitting patterns, for example), the ASCII code for codifying characters on a computer, codes for communication (semaphore, Braille, …) and much more.

The philosopher knows how to keep a secret

An encryptor, or creator of codes, tries to understand the logical processes likely to run in the minds of others and seeks ways of subverting these. A decryptor, or cracker of codes, tries to get into the mind of the encryptor and second-guess what tricks he might be using to try to throw others off the scent. But to be successful at what they do, both players in this little drama require a good logical awareness, combined with the ability to think laterally.

Back in Chapter 4, prime numbers were referred to as the 'building blocks' of the number system. You can now start to see that primes have a practical as well as a philosophical value; they are the mathematical cogs that form the machine of modern cryptography.

Something for you to try

1   Can you crack this code?
    The letters of the alphabet were numbered in order, 1 to 26. For letters a to i, the single digits 1 to 9 were used. For the other letters (which all correspond to two-digit numbers) a zero was placed between the two digits. Thus, the code for the third letter, C, is 3 and for the twelfth letter, L, is 102. Use this code to crack the following secret message:
    203110420054312002039200881052001910821102102105105104109101 91 0210210911061061022059104520320010 5104
    What is the point of inserting the zero into the two-digit numbers?
2   The number 1541 is the product of two 2-digit prime numbers. What are they?
3   You are told that a certain code is based on the fact that the number 17855 is the product of two unknown prime numbers. Why might you not be impressed with this code?

Solutions

1   The message relates to a story in Chapter17. The role of the zero is to isolate the codes for each separate letter – otherwise you would not know whether the code 12 meant AB or L.
2   23 × 67 (Hint: the answer ends in a 1, so either the numbers both end in 9 or one ends in 3 and the other 7. From here on it is a question of being systematic and using common-sense 'order of magnitude' estimates.)
3   Any number ending in 5 must have 5 as a factor. So 5 is the first prime. If the number is the product of two prime numbers and one is 5, the other can be obtained by dividing 17855 by 5, which gives 3571. This code is too easy to crack!

Chapter 27

Are you sure? Beginnings of mathematical proof

*No way of thinking or doing, however
ancient, can be trusted without proof.*

Henry David Thoreau

Telling arguments

Usually, in most everyday situations, proving something
to be true with absolute certainty is an impossible task. There
are often definitional ambiguities and uncertainties about
the underlying assumptions, which make it hard to come up
with a convincing, watertight argument about the truth or
falsity of a statement. One of the joys of experiencing a world
created by the philosopher is that he presents an imaginary
set of circumstances in which these problems of ambiguity
and uncertainty largely disappear. The philosopher can state
clearly, at the outset, the nature of the objects he is dealing
with (in the case of mathematical objects, these could be
integers, real numbers, circles, rectangles and so on). He
can make statements about them that are both precise, in
their clarity, and concise, in their form of expression. Finally,
he can apply forms of mathematical argument that anyone
versed in its language and notation can understand. Perhaps
it is not so surprising, then, that some philosophers prefer to
stay within the ivory tower of mathematical certainty rather
than to venture out into the dangerous unpredictability of
cocktail-party conversations!

So what is the nature of mathematical communication
and why should we bother about it? The idea that 'the
medium is the message' was introduced in 1964 by Marshall
McLuhan, in his book *Understanding Media: The Extensions
of Man*. McLuhan was suggesting that the form in which a
message is communicated has a crucial effect on the message

itself; and indeed that the medium of communication is as important a subject of study as the message it is used to convey. There are interesting parallels in how mathematics is viewed, learned and used. It is an unfortunate fact that the experience of most school-learned mathematics is as a medium alone. Mathematics is a language with its own vocabulary and syntax, but for many people, the mastery of this language is the only goal on offer – rarely, if ever, do they get to use this mathematical language to solve problems and express ideas for themselves.

The next three chapters look at mathematical communication but with a clearer sense of purpose. Chapters 27 and 28 explore the idea of proof – a topic of great interest to the philosopher. It is also a central idea in mathematics and one that is strongly supported by appropriate use of mathematical language. In these two chapters you will not only get an opportunity to become better acquainted with mathematical language but you will also see it being used to a purpose in tackling mathematical proofs.

Patterns

From an early age, Carl Friedrich Gauss (1777–1855) was a precocious talent in mathematics. The story goes that while at primary school, he and his classmates were instructed to add together all the whole numbers from 1 to 100 (presumably an exercise designed by their teacher, J. G. Büttner, to keep them quiet for an hour or so). But much to Herr Büttner's disappointment, Carl came up with the answer in a matter of seconds. So how did the young prodigy do it?

1 to 100: Try it yourself!

Before reading on, you might like to spend a few minutes trying to work out how young Gauss managed this feat.

Like all successful mathematicians, Gauss was more interested in finding patterns and applying general principles than in spending time on boring, mechanical calculations. He had immediately spotted that if the numbers are taken in pairs, 1 and 100, 2 and 99, 3 and 98, and so on, each of these pairings adds up to 101. For the numbers 1 to 100, there are clearly 50 such pairings, so the answer must be 50 × 101, which equals 5050.

What set Carl Gauss apart from his classmates was that his attention was on the general rather than the particular. In mathematics, arithmetic is about performing calculations with particular numbers whereas algebra can be used as a means of codifying and investigating the general patterns that lie underneath particular calculations. It is the thrill of discovering a generality that excites mathematicians most. But when they have discovered some general pattern, they need to be able to convince themselves and then convince others that it is *always* true and not just for the particular cases they have looked at. Sometimes this can be done with a straightforward general argument in words, but more often than not it is presented in the form of algebra. Whichever method you choose, remember that proofs must provide you with an argument that covers all possible cases.

Finding proofs

Below is a simple mathematical statement that looks as though it might be always true but which will require proof.

The sum of any two odd numbers is always even.

First let's choose some particular numerical examples to help get a feel for what the statement is about.

- Choose the odd numbers 3 and 7: 3 + 7 = 10, which is even.
- Choose the odd numbers 19 and 9: 19 + 9 = 28, which is even.
- Choose the odd numbers 101 and 327: 101 + 327 = 428, which is even.

So it does seem that this statement might be true, but remember that three examples do not constitute a proof.

There are several possible ways of constructing a proof of this statement. Here are two common approaches – the visual proof and the direct proof.

A visual proof

A visual proof involves finding helpful pictorial representations of the problem, which, combined with some general argument, demonstrate the truth or otherwise of the statement.

For the statement 'The sum of any two odd numbers is always even', you could use discs or some similar icon to represent two general odd numbers, as shown in Figure 27.1. Notice that the three dots, . . . , in the middle of each number indicate an unknown number of pairs, showing that these could be *any* two odd numbers.

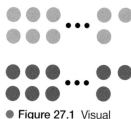

● **Figure 27.1** Visual representation of two odd numbers (any value).

Let's now turn the lower of these diagrams upside down and slide the two parts together. The result (Figure 27.2) shows how the two unpaired left-over

● **Figure 27.2** A new pair is formed.

discs add together to form a new pair.

A direct proof

In a sense, the diagrams above say it all, but figures can sometimes be deceiving. In mathematics, proofs are more commonly expressed using algebra. But before rushing into introducing an algebraic letter such as x or N into the story, it will be helpful to express the argument in words. Keeping in view the pictures above, read through the three statements below.

- Each of these odd numbers is an even number + 1.
- Adding them together gives the sum of two even numbers + 1 + 1, which is the sum of two even numbers plus 2.
- This must be even as it is divisible by 2.

Now, having clarified the story of the proof in everyday language, you should be better prepared to express it algebraically. First, note that, just as a general even number can be written as $2N$ (or using any letter other than N), so a general odd number can be written as $2N + 1$ – i.e. it is one more than a general even number.

Let the two odd numbers be $2A + 1$ and $2B + 1$, respectively (where A and B are whole numbers).

Their sum $= (2A + 1) + (2B + 1)$, which equals $2A + 2B + 2$.

Taking a common factor of 2 out, this can be rewritten as $2(A + B + 1)$. Since this result contains a factor of 2, it must be even.

You may need some practice at thinking through and writing out direct proofs, so have a go at the question below.

Something for you to try

Prove algebraically that the product of two odd numbers is always odd (an odd number $\times$ an odd number = an odd number).

Solution

Let the two odd numbers be $2A + 1$ and $2B + 1$, respectively (where A and B are whole numbers). Their product $= (2A + 1) \times (2B + 1)$, which equals $4AB + 2A + 2B + 1$.

Taking out a common factor of 2 from the first three terms, this can be rewritten as $2(2AB + A + B) + 1$. This is of the form 'even number' + 1, which is an odd number.

'For all' and 'there exists'

Proofs usually take one of two forms. The more common form is 'for all', where you are required to show that the result is true in every case. The mathematical shorthand for 'for all' is an upside-down A, written $\forall$. The other form is 'there exists', where you are required to show that there is (at least) one particular instance where the result holds true. The mathematical shorthand for 'there exists' is a backwards E, written $\exists$.

For each of these two forms, you can set about either to try to prove the result true or to try to prove it false. This makes a total of four scenarios, summarized in Figure 27.3.

	True	False
For all, $\forall$	general proof	counter example
There exists, $\exists$	example	general proof

● **Figure 27.3** Four possibilities of proof.

Chapter 27 Are you sure? Beginnings of mathematical proof

218

Proving a 'for all' statement true is hard – there may be an infinite number of possible cases and you will need some general argument that covers them all. Equally hard is proving a 'there exists' statement to be false – again, there may be an infinite number of possible cases and you will need some general argument to ensure that no one of them makes the result true.

Proving a 'for all' statement false is usually easier – although there may be many cases for which the result is true, you only need one counter example to prove the statement false. For example, to prove the statement below false, you can choose the counter example $x = 3$.

For all x, $(x - 3)^2 \neq 0$.

Finally, proving a 'there exists' statement to be true is often an easy task – again, you only need one example to prove the statement true. For example, to prove the statement below true, you can choose the example $x = 4$.

There exists a solution to the equation $x + 3 = 7$.

Proof by exhaustion

So far you have seen two ways of constructing a proof – visual proof and proof by direct argument. To end this chapter here's a brief look at a third method, known as proof by exhaustion. This approach only works if you can identify a finite number of possible cases. You then simply work through each case in turn. If you can show that the result is true for all of them, then you have proved it. Sometimes it is necessary to reduce the scope of your mathematical investigation in order to enable this method to be used. For example, suppose you want to investigate whether the following statement is true:

Between every adjacent pair of square numbers there is at least one prime number.

This is a difficult conjecture to prove, but let's change it to read:

Between every adjacent pair of square numbers less than 1000 there is at least one prime number.

With this new wording, you can now tackle the problem by going through every particular case. This will involve listing all the squares from 1 to 1000 and searching for primes between each adjacent pair of squares. Of course, in this form, your discovery will be much less interesting than if you had been able to prove it true for *all* adjacent pairs of square numbers, but occasionally you have to learn to walk before you can run!

In this chapter you have looked at three methods of mathematical proof – visual, direct argument and exhaustion. Two rather more subtle forms of proof are known as induction and contradiction, and you can read about these in Chapter 28.

The philosopher explores some simple proofs

Unlike the other five characters in this book, the philosopher conducts most of his adventures in a world inside his head. Of course, this has many advantages, not least that when he hits a problem where his solution might appear 'unrealistic', it is always possible for him to redefine his imaginary world so to accommodate the glitch.

As an aside, many years ago I was working with a professor on a problem that involved a cube shape rolling on different paths within an imaginary room. Quickly we found that we had to develop a notation to describe, efficiently, each possible move that the cube could make. At one point I pointed out to the professor that one of his moves would not be possible because the wall of the imaginary room would prevent it. He shrugged his shoulders and said, 'Move the wall!'

The word 'proof' comes from the Latin *probare*, meaning 'to test'. The testing of arguments goes back at least two and a half thousand years to ancient Greece, where both visual proofs and direct argument were used. These methods are still used by mathematicians today. One of the most famous problems, the so-called 'four-colour' theorem, was first proved by the method of exhaustion in 1976, by Kenneth Appel and Wolfgang Haken. Their method of proof caused controversy because a computer was used to test many of the 1936 cases considered. Today, using a computer to tackle proofs by the method of exhaustion is increasingly common.

1   Based on the diagram in Figure 27.4, use a visual proof to show that:
$(x + a)^2 = x^2 + 2ax + a^2$.

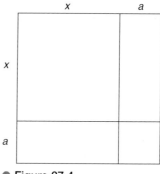

2   A quick way of squaring a 'whole number plus a half' is to multiply the whole number by the next whole number up and add a quarter to the answer.
For example:
$(6½)^2 = 6 \times 7 + ¼ = 42¼$.
Using a direct argument, prove that this rule always gives the correct answer.

● Figure 27.4

3   A computer program or calculator program or a spreadsheet can be created to prove that there are only two three-digit numbers with the property that the numbers themselves are the sum of the cubes of their digits. (In fact, the two cases are 153 and 407. So, $153 = 1^3 + 5^3 + 3^3$ and $407 = 4^3 + 0^3 + 7^3$.)
What method of proof is represented with this example?

Solutions

1   The large square in the diagram in Figure 27.5 has sides of length $x + a$, so its area is $(x + a)^2$.
The areas of each of its four components (two squares and two identical rectangles) are marked on this diagram. It follows that:
$(x + a)^2 = x^2 + ax + ax + a^2 = x^2 + 2ax + a^2$.

2   Let the whole number part be x, so the number plus a half is $(x + ½)$.
Squaring this number,
$(x + ½)^2 = x^2 + x + ¼$.
This can be rearranged as $x(x + 1) + ¼$.
This is the original whole number (x) multiplied by the next higher whole number, $(x + 1)$, plus ¼.

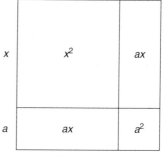

● Figure 27.5

3   Since the program will bash through every three-digit number from 000 to 999, it uses the method of proof by exhaustion.

Chapter 28
More subtle proofs

> *Do not consider it proof just because it is written in books, for a liar who will deceive with his tongue will not hesitate to do the same with his pen.*
>
> Maimonides (Spanish philosopher, 1135–1204)

Telling arguments

'One foul wind no more makes a winter, than one swallow makes a summer,' as Charles Dickens wrote in his novel *Martin Chuzzlewit*. An important working principle shared by the philosopher and the mathematician is that you can't use the evidence of one or two particular cases to prove a general case. They may refer to this disparagingly as 'arguing from the particular to the general'. In Chapter 27 you read about three well-known and fairly straightforward methods of proof – visual, direct argument and proof by exhaustion. In common with all methods of proof, they are based on showing that the result is true for all possible cases. In the first two of these, the proofs are based on a general argument rather than on the identification of particular cases.

The philosopher isn't scared of arguments that might make his brain hurt. So let's now crank it up a little and look at two more subtle forms of general argument. The first is known as *proof by induction* and the second as *proof by contradiction* (otherwise known as *reductio ad absurdum* – which translates as 'reduction to the absurd').

Proof by induction

Sometimes the evidence of a particular example can provide a good starting point for constructing a more general argument and this is the basis of a clever method of proof known as mathematical induction. Its main stages are as follows.

1   Show that the result is true for a simple particular case (usually for $n = 1$).
2   This is the tricky part! Construct an argument showing that if the result is true for any one value, then it is necessarily true for the next higher value.
3   Putting stages 1 and 2 together, we now have a starting point and then a chain that ties this first result to the next and to the next and to the next and so on. So we have a general proof for all cases.

Essentially, proof by induction is a bit like knocking down an infinitely long line of dominoes. Stage 2 above is where you stand the dominoes up in a straight line, arranged so that if one falls, it will knock over its neighbour. Stage 1 is where you knock over a first domino. In stage 3, all the dominoes fall and the result is achieved *for all* cases.

The main elements of this approach can be traced back to the ancient Greek mathematician Euclid, who used a similar method in his neat proof that there must be infinitely many primes. However, it wasn't until the 16th century CE that the method was presented in the form described above. This was when the Italian mathematician Francesco Maurolico used the method in a pair of books entitled *Arithmeticorum libri duo* (1575). Here he proved that the sum of the first n odd integers (i.e. $1 + 3 + 5 + 7 + \ldots$) is n^2.

Euclid, the 'father of geometry'

Details are sketchy about the life of this Greek mathematician, the so-called 'father of geometry'. He was born around 300 BCE but it is not known how long he lived. Of his five surviving writings, the most famous and influential on mathematics teaching over the centuries is his *Elements* – an all-time best-seller which provided the basis of geometry teaching worldwide well into the 1960s and 1970s! Starting with a few simple axioms (these are self-evident starting points that do not require proof), his work set out in thirteen separate sections a wide range of two-dimensional and three-dimensional geometric theorems. For example:

Book 1 Proposition 32 proves that the angles of a triangle add to 180°.
Book 1 Proposition 47 proves Pythagoras' Theorem.

The theorems were arranged logically so that each one was constructed using only theorems that had already been proved (and, of course, the starting axioms). Euclidean geometry is less popular today largely because there are gaps in Euclid's logical structure and in his list of axioms. Also, he occasionally assumed that if the diagram looked correct, the result was true – a piece of fallacious reasoning that can easily lead you up the mathematical garden path!

Example of proof by induction

Here is an example of proof by induction in action. Think back to the story of young Carl Gauss in the previous chapter. As you may remember, he added the first 100 counting numbers by sorting them into 50 pairs that each add up to 101 and then multiplying 50 by 101. Let's generalize this, using n instead of 100. According to Gauss's moment of classroom insight, the sum of the first n counting numbers would be $\frac{1}{2}n(n + 1)$.

Based on stages 1 to 3 above, a proof by the method of induction is as follows.

Let $S(n)$ be the sum of all the integers from 1 to n. We wish to prove that:

$$S(n) = \frac{1}{2}n(n + 1).$$

Stage 1

Test the rule for $n = 1$.
$S(1)$ is the sum of the first counting number, which is just 1. Substituting $n = 1$ into Gauss's formula:

$$\frac{1}{2}n(n + 1) = \frac{1}{2} \times 1 \times 2 = 1.$$

So our first domino is in place – the formula clearly holds true for $n = 1$.

Stage 2

At this stage we can assume the rule to be true for n; our task is to show it is true for $n + 1$, given that it is true for n. We do this in two different ways and then show that they both give the same answer. Part (a) below takes the result we assume to be true, namely that $S(n) = \frac{1}{2}n(n + 1)$, and adds on the next number, $n + 1$. In part (b), we replace the n in the formula with $n+1$ and see what answer this produces. If both parts (a) and (b) give the same result, we have completed stage 2 of the proof – i.e. we have shown that *if* the formula is true for $S(n)$, *then* it is necessarily true for $S(n+1)$.

Part (a)

We assume that $S(n) = \frac{1}{2}n(n+1)$.
Adding $n+1$ to $S(n)$:

$$S(n+1) = S(n) + n + 1 = \frac{1}{2}n(n+1) + n + 1,$$

which simplifies to $\frac{1}{2}n^2 + \frac{3}{2}n + 1$.

Part (b)

Substituting $n+1$ into the formula gives:

$$S(n+1) = \frac{1}{2}(n+1)(n+2),$$

which expands to give $\frac{1}{2}n^2 + \frac{3}{2}n + 1$.
Since the results of parts (a) and (b) are the same, we have now completed stage 2 of the proof – the dominoes are lined up so that if any one falls, the next higher domino also falls.

Stage 3

Putting stages 1 and 2 together:
- we have a starting point (the result holds true for $n = 1$); and
- we have proved that if it is true for n, it must also be true for $n+1$. Therefore, since we have shown that it is true for $n = 1$, then it must also be true for $n = 2$. And since it's true for $n = 2$, it must also be true for $n = 3$. And so on, to infinity.

Proof by contradiction

The basic idea of this form of proof is to start by assuming the opposite, or *complement*, of what you want to prove and then follow a series of logically correct consequences of this assumption. When you eventually trip up and fall into the manure, you can point to the starting point and say that this is where it must have all gone horribly wrong and so the complement of this assumption must be correct. For example, to prove that the Earth is not flat, we might start by assuming that it *is* flat. It would follow from this assumption that, if we were to travel in a straight line, we would never return to our starting position. However, experience shows that we do, so the flat-Earth assumption must be wrong. An important feature of this method of proof is that you must start by identifying only two positions – what you want to prove true and its complement, where the complement covers all other possibilities. For example, suppose you rolled a die, hoping to get a 6. It would be foolish to claim that 'I did not roll a 1, so I must have rolled a 6.' A correct form of this argument would be: 'I did not roll a 1, 2, 3, 4 or 5, so I must have rolled a 6.'

Proof by contradiction, or 'reduction to the absurd', is a form of argument often used by barristers. For example, consider the proposition that 'for whoever owns the soil, it is theirs up to Heaven and down to Hell' (this proposition is known in law as *ad coelum*, meaning 'up to heaven'). A rather overblown legal argument against the proposition might run as follows:

> Let us take this proposition to a logical extreme. This would grant a land-owner legal rights to everything contained within a cone from the centre of the Earth's core to an infinite distance out into space, including stars and planets. It is absurd that someone who purchases land on Earth should own other planets, therefore this proposition is wrong.

In fact, this refutation is itself fallacious, as it overstates the circumstances under which legal rights to land can be claimed. However, it does give an indication of the nature of proof by contradiction, as used outside mathematics.

In summary, if you wish to prove a mathematical rule true by the method of contradiction, you must adopt the following three-stage plan:

1 Start by assuming that the rule is false.
2 Make one or more logically correct steps, until …
3 … you reach a conclusion that is false.

You can now conclude that the assumption at stage 1 must have been incorrect and so deduce that the rule must indeed be true. For obvious reasons, this is known as proof by contradiction.

Example of proof by contradiction

You may remember from Chapter 4 how the Pythagoreans were in awe at the discovery of the 'unspeakable' numbers that today we refer to as irrational numbers. These include numbers like $\sqrt{2}$, $\sqrt{3}$, $\sqrt{5}$ and so on, as well as π and Euler's number, e. To illustrate the method of proof by contradiction, here is a mathematical example based on providing a convincing argument that the square root of 2, $\sqrt{2}$, is irrational. Unlike whole numbers, fractions and decimal fractions, which *can* be expressed as the ratio of two whole numbers (for example, $^3/_1$, $^{22}/_7$, $^{53}/_{100}$, and so on), irrational numbers cannot be expressed in this form.

To prove, by contradiction, that $\sqrt{2}$ is irrational:

Stage 1

We start with the assumption that $\sqrt{2}$ is rational.

Stage 2

Now follows a series of logical deductions based on this assumption.

(a) If $\sqrt{2}$ is rational, we can write: $\sqrt{2} = ^p/_q$, where p and q are whole numbers that are relatively prime – i.e. they have no factors in common.

(b) Now square both sides: $2 = p^2/q^2$
Rearranging: $p^2 = 2q^2$.

(c) If p^2 equals twice a whole number, then p^2 is even.

(d) If p^2 is even, then p must be even (more on this later).

(e) If p is even, p^2 must be divisible by 4 and can therefore be written as $4s^2$ (where s is a whole number).

(f) From step (b), $4s^2 = 2q^2$
Dividing both sides by 2 and rearranging: $q^2 = 2s^2$

(g) We can see from step (f) that q^2 is even.

(h) Using the same argument as in step (d), it follows that q must be even.

Stage 3

We have shown in steps 2(d) and 2(h) that p and q are both even, so they both have a factor of two. Since they share this same factor, p and q are clearly not relatively prime, which is a contradiction of the statement in step 2(a). The assumption that $\sqrt{2}$ is rational has had consequences that are false, so the initial assumption itself must be false. Therefore $\sqrt{2}$ is irrational.

Read through the proof again to check that you understand it. Is it completely watertight? Well, let's raise the stakes a little. Suppose you are told that if I can find two positive whole numbers, p and q, such that $p^2 = 2q^2$, then severe public humiliation will beset you (think about what happened to Galileo when he published his heliocentric theory of the planets!). This might be just the pressure you need to check the small print a little more carefully.

One possible flaw in the argument above occurs in step 2(d), where it is claimed that, if p^2 is even, then p is even. Do you really believe this to be true and, if so, can you prove it? If your very life depended on it, this is something that might need careful reflection!

The philosopher explores some harder proofs

Sometimes when tackling a tricky job, you need to dig into your tool bag and fish out the big wrench! In this chapter the philosopher discovered that not all propositions can be proved using visual proof, direct proof and proof by exhaustion. You were presented with two alternative and rather more subtle methods of proof, called *induction* and *contradiction*.

It should be stressed, however, that writing out a proof is very different from actually tackling one from scratch. Please don't be fooled into thinking that mathematicians always go through these steps strictly in sequence, working logically from one to the next until they reach their neat conclusion. In practice, constructing a mathematical proof is a much more messy business. There are many dead ends, crumpled sheets of paper and copious cups of coffee. Sometimes a long walk in the park followed by (hopefully) a creative leap of lateral thinking is required. But once the basic proof has been established, the final task for the mathematician is to present it clearly as a logical story to the reader. In this 'public' version, all the coffee stains are removed, the expletives are deleted and the stages of the story are set out in a logical sequence!

1   Using the method of mathematical induction, try to reconstruct Francesco Maurolico's proof that S(n), the sum of the first n odd integers (i.e. $1 + 3 + 5 + 7 + ...$) is n^2.

2   One of Euclid's achievements was to prove that there are infinitely many prime numbers. Try to use the method of contradiction to prove this result, based on the wording that 'there is no largest prime number'.

Solutions

1   Follow these stages:

Stage 1: When $n = 1$, $S(n) = 1^2 = 1$.

Stage 2: We assume that $S(n)$, the sum of the first n odd integers $= n^2$.

Starting with the first odd integer as 1, the value of the nth integer is $2n - 1$, so the $(n + 1)$th odd integer is $2n + 1$.

Part (a): Adding the $(n + 1)$th odd integer, $2n + 1$, to $S(n)$:

$$S(n + 1) = S(n) + (2n + 1) = n^2 + 2n + 1.$$

Part (b): Substituting $n + 1$ into the formula gives:

$$S(n + 1) = (n + 1)^2, \text{ which expands to give } n^2 + 2n + 1.$$

Since the results of steps (a) and (b) are the same, we have now completed stage 2 of the proof.

Stage 3: Putting stages 1 and 2 together: we have a starting point (the result holds true for $n = 1$), and we have proved that if the result is true for n, then it must also be true for $n + 1$. Therefore, by mathematical induction, it must be true for all n.

2   Follow these stages:

Stage 1: Start with the assumption that the statement is false, namely that there is a largest prime number; call it p.

Stage 2: Test the assumption:

(a)   Consider the number N, which is one larger than the product of all of the primes smaller than or equal to p. So, $N = 2 \times 3 \times 5 \times 7 \times 11... \times p + 1$.

(b)   Since N is the product of whole numbers that include p, N is larger than p (the largest prime) so, by the assumption in stage 1, it cannot be prime.

(c)   However, N has no prime factors between 1 and p because they would all leave a remainder of 1. So N has no prime factors and therefore must itself be prime.

(d)   There is now a contradiction: N is not prime in step (b), and N is prime in step (c).

Stage 3: We conclude that the assumption in stage 1 (that there is a largest prime) must be false and therefore have proved that there is no largest prime number.

Chapter 29
Logic

'Then you should say what you mean,'
the March Hare went on.
'I do,' Alice hastily replied; 'at least I mean what
I say, that's the same thing, you know.'
'Not the same thing a bit!' said the Hatter.
'Why, you might just as well say that
"I see what I eat" is the same thing as
"I eat what I see!"'

Lewis Carroll, from *Alice's Adventures*
in Wonderland, Chapter 7

Logic and reasoning

Logic is the glue that has held mathematics and philosophy together for centuries and it is central to the ideas of proof described in Chapters 27 and 28. We all have a tendency to think that our own arguments are logical whereas the reasoning of others around us is less so. But what does it mean to be logical? Probably the commonest error in discussions about logic is to confuse being logical with being correct.

One of the earliest proponents of logical reasoning was the Greek philosopher Aristotle (384–22 BCE). Aristotle contributed to many areas of study but is particularly remembered for his principles of deductive reasoning, sometimes referred to as *syllogisms*, which take the following form. Typically you are offered two or more initial statements, called the *premises*, and are invited to make a conclusion that follows logically from them. It is generally the case that logicians are less interested in the truth of the conclusion than in whether it follows logically from the premises. In other words, the validity of the reasoning matters more than the correctness of the final statement, and this is what often foxes people. So, you might start with a faulty premise and end up with a silly conclusion, but the process taking you from the premises to the conclusion may be valid, in which case the reasoning is valid. Conversely, if the reasoning is valid, then provided the premises are true, you can be sure that the conclusion is correct.

Logically valid?

The table in Figure 29.1 shows three statements, each consisting of two premises and a conclusion. To get a grip on what deductive reasoning is about, read through each of the three statements and try to decide if it is logically valid.

Statement	Premises	Conclusion
(a)	My spaniel is a dog. All dogs are mammals	My spaniel is a mammal
(b)	All spaniels are terriers. All terriers are Great Danes.	All spaniels are Great Danes.
(c)	All spaniels are dogs. My Great Dane is a dog.	My Great Dane is a spaniel.

● **Figure 29.1** Which of these syllogisms are logically valid?

Statement (a) is logically valid. It has the additional property that it is true, because both the premises are correct, although that was not what you were asked to consider.

Comparing statements (a) and (b), you will see that they are identical in structure, so statement (b) is also logically valid. Clearly the conclusion in this example happens to be wrong, but only because the premises are incorrect; logically, the reasoning was correct.

In statement (c), the premises are true but the conclusion does not follow from the premises. This is a logical fallacy that you often hear in everyday conversation, which can be summarized as: Set A belongs to set C and item B belongs to set C so item B belongs to set A.

Inclusion arguments like these can often be clarified and resolved by using a helpful picture such as a Venn diagram. This consists of circles (or ellipses) showing clearly which set belongs to which. In cases where sets contain common elements (for example, with the two sets 'children' and 'females'), the circles are drawn to overlap (in this case, the area of intersection represents 'girls', who are members of both sets). Figure 29.2 shows Venn diagrams for two of the dog-focused statements we have just been considering.

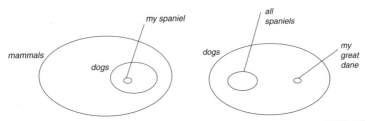

● Figure 29.2 Venn diagrams for statements (a) and (c) in Figure 29.1.

Logic and the structure of mathematics

The study of the foundations of mathematics began in earnest in the late 19th century, with attempts to develop logically coherent frameworks for geometry, arithmetic and other branches of mathematics. As Euclid had done for geometry some two thousand years earlier, British mathematician Bertrand Russell (1872–1970), the German set theorist Georg Cantor (1845–1918) and many others made a serious attempt to formalize *set theory* (the study of collections of objects such as different classifications of numbers), taking a few simple starting principles known as axioms and building on these in a systematic way.

Considerable progress was made, but unfortunately the enterprise foundered on a curve ball thrown by Russell in the form of a paradox. Before reading it in its mathematical form, have a go at it in the more tractable context of the village barber.

A close shave

A particular village has just one male barber and every man in the town keeps himself clean-shaven. If the barber shaves every man who does not shave himself, who shaves the barber?

It is clear that the barber is placed in an impossible dilemma. If he does not shave himself, he must abide by the rule and shave himself. If he does shave himself, according to the rule he should not shave himself. A more formal, mathematical version of Russell's paradox might read as follows:

> Consider the set of all sets that are not members of themselves. Such a set appears to be a member of itself if and only if it is not a member of itself – hence the paradox.

Russell's paradox was never fully resolved and this obstacle, along with a combination of other factors to do with the lack of universal acceptance of the axioms, conspired to undermine the whole enterprise. Gradually, mathematicians began to move into other areas of research as the grand plan to create a universal logical structure for mathematics was abandoned.

Russell was also interested in religious issues and came up with an entertaining analogy to challenge others' attempts to prove, by logic, that God exists. His imaginative flight of fancy was designed to demonstrate that the burden of proof in this area is on the believer, to prove God's existence, rather than on the sceptic, to disprove it (which would be impossible since logic cannot prove a negative). Known as 'Russell's celestial teapot', it reads as follows.

> If I were to suggest that between the Earth and Mars there is a china teapot revolving about the Sun in an elliptical orbit, nobody would be able to disprove my assertion provided I were careful to add that the teapot is too small to be revealed even by our most powerful telescopes. But if I were to go on to say that, since my assertion cannot be disproved, it is an intolerable presumption on the part of human reason to doubt it, I should rightly be thought to be talking nonsense. If, however, the existence of such a teapot were affirmed in ancient books, taught as the sacred truth every Sunday, and instilled into the minds of children at school, hesitation to believe in its existence would become

a mark of eccentricity and entitle the doubter to the attentions of the psychiatrist in an enlightened age or of the Inquisitor in an earlier time.

Bertrand Russell, commissioned (but never
published) by Illustrated magazine, 1952

Bertrand Russell (1872–1970)

Bertrand Russell was born in Monmouthshire, Wales, into a family of free-thinking British aristocrats. His father, Viscount Amberley, was an atheist and both parents were advocates of birth control at a time when this was considered indecent. When Bertrand was two, his mother died of diphtheria. Shortly afterwards his older sister, Rachel, died; and eighteen months later, his father died of bronchitis, following a long period of depression. Bertrand and his surviving brother Frank were placed in the care of their elderly and rather stern grandparents. As a result of these unhappy experiences, Bertrand's childhood was lonely, and in his teenage years it appears that he often contemplated suicide. It is said that it was his love of mathematics, and in particular, the works of Euclid, that got him through these difficult years.

Russell excelled across many fields, including philosophy, logic and mathematics. He was a major figure in British society and regularly appeared as a pundit on television during the 1960s, always ready to offer opinion and thoughtful comment as historian, socialist, pacifist and social commentator.

A logician has the last word

Logicians have something of a reputation for the witty one-liner. Here is a very funny joke told to me by a logician – make of it what you will.

A biologist, a mathematician and a logician were travelling together by train to attend a conference in a foreign land. Looking out of the window, the biologist noticed a sheep. 'I see the sheep here are black,' he said to his companions.

'No!' replied the mathematician quickly. 'All we can say is that at least one of the sheep here is black.'

'Not so,' said the logician, smiling. 'We can only say that at least one of the sheep here is black on at least one of its sides!'

Logic and computers

Logic has taken on a new lease of life during the 20th and 21st centuries, with the growth of computers. One area of mathematics where computers are increasingly relevant is mathematical proof. In Chapter 27 you read about a form of proof called 'exhaustion', where all possible cases are tested. Given the immense and rapid processing power of modern computers, this is increasingly the method of choice for mathematicians to construct their proofs. No matter that there might be zillions of possible cases – if it can be shown that the computer has tested them all, then the proof is valid. This was an essential component in the most famous proof of the 20th century, when Andrew Wiles finally solved the famous Fermat's Last Theorem in 1995.

If an effective computer logic system had not been invented to enable computers to perform calculations and process instructions, society in the 21st century would simply not function. Modern computers are designed to process information using what is known as Boolean logic, which was originally developed by George Boole in the mid-19th century. As mentioned in Chapter 19, all the information being processed in the deep recesses of a computer's brain, both inputs and outputs, can be represented by a series of 0s and 1s, where 0 corresponds to a low-energy pulse and 1 to a high-energy pulse. In order to transform inputs into outputs, the pulses are directed through combinations of what are galled *gates*. The beauty of this approach is its simplicity, as the range of types of gates you need to choose from in order to perform a calculation is actually very small. The three most basic gate types are named NOT, AND and OR and they work as follows.

- The NOT gate takes a single input and outputs the opposite. So, an input of 0 is output as 1 and an input of 1 is output as 0.
- The AND gate takes two inputs (let's call them A and B) and will only output 1 if both inputs (i.e. A *and* B) are 1; otherwise it outputs a 0.
- The OR gate takes two inputs and will output 1 if one or other or both of the inputs (i.e. A *or* B) are 1; otherwise it outputs a 0.

These rules are summarized below:

The NOT gate			The AND gate				The OR gate		
Input	Output		Input A	Input B	Output		Input A	Input B	Output
0	1		0	0	0		0	0	0
1	0		1	0	0		1	0	1
			0	1	0		0	1	1
			1	1	1		1	1	1

Essentially, a computer chip consists of thousands of microscopic transistors collectively opening and closing these and similar gates trillions of times every second – and all in a space smaller than a postage stamp.

The philosopher reaches for his soapbox

In 1979 the band Supertramp released an excellent single, 'The Logical Song'. Its lyrics, like those of many popular songs, raise an interesting point about the way people sometimes view logical thinking and mathematics with distrust. A world built on mathematical principles, so the argument runs, has a tendency to dehumanize us and the application of logic can lead to a stifling of creativity and a loss of passion. There may be some truth in this, but I believe it draws on a child's view of the world. From an adult's perspective, a loss of innocence is an inevitable consequence of growing up and becoming a responsible citizen. The adult world is one of uncertainty and ambiguity where you try to make the best possible choices, given the constraints that you face. I suggest that we make better, fairer decisions where they are based on evidence, clarity of thinking and the exercise of logic, rather than the alternative, which is to go with your hunch or instinct, or simply follow, uncritically, the voice of authority.

Read through the statements below and try to decide if the conclusion is logically valid.

Statement	Premises	Conclusion
1	All cups are blue. Aristotle is a cup.	Aristotle is blue.
2	Paris is the capital of France. This plane lands in Paris.	This plane lands in France.
3	All As belong to B. C belongs to B.	C must be an A.

Solutions

Statements 1 and 2 are logically valid but for statement 3 the conclusion does not follow from the premises.

Chapter 30
Under the skin of mathematics

Yes, we have to divide up our time like that,
between our politics and our equations.
But to me our equations are far more important,
for politics are only a matter of present concern.
A mathematical equation stands forever.

Albert Einstein

Well done for having reached this final chapter! In the course of the previous twenty nine, you have been invited to see the world through the eyes of six different people – explorer, artist, gambler, scientist, environmentalist and philosopher. The central conceit of the book has been that, to a greater or lesser extent, you are all of these people and may therefore be able to identify with their concerns. So these ideas are really about you. And throughout history, it has been *your* questions, both practical and philosophical, that have shaped mathematics as we know it today.

In this final chapter I ask you to come on a gentle romp through some of the big ideas in mathematics that, for me, stand out as having far-reaching effects both inside and outside the subject. But first, let's look at cargo cults.

Cargo cults and mathematics

During the Second World War, the American armed forces responded to the Japanese attack on Pearl Harbour by invading a number of islands in the South Pacific Ocean in order to limit Japan's sphere of operations. Until then, the indigenous residents of these islands had led very isolated lives – most had not seen Westerners before – and they were overwhelmed by the arrival of large naval vessels and aeroplanes. Associated with the latter were runways, microphones, radios and radio antennae, as well as the arrival of large amounts of food, weapons and furniture. The natives referred to all of these items collectively as 'cargo'.

When the war ended, the American soldiers and their ships and planes disappeared and all that remained were the remnants of their stay, including the runways, abandoned buildings and various discarded artefacts. The natives took the view that by summoning the gods, they should be able to bring back the wonderful planes that had brought the cargo. Their strategy was to copy the rituals that they had witnessed, as faithfully as they could. They erected a bamboo pole to act as an antenna; some old boxes became their radio, and they used a coconut shell as a microphone. They called repeatedly on the planes to return. But sadly, apart from the arrival of some notebook-bearing anthropological researchers a few years later, nothing came of their requests. Their ritualistic practice was subsequently described by the visiting anthropologists as a 'cargo cult'.

So what has this story to do with mathematics education? The point is that the South Pacific natives had paid attention to the *form* of their visitors' technology, but had no grasp of the substance that lay beneath. This is a helpful metaphor for one persistent view of mathematics – that it amounts to nothing more than the skills of arithmetic and being able to manipulate a few algebraic symbols. And so the thinking processes and concepts going on underneath – what might be called the big ideas of mathematics – tend to get overlooked. Practising nothing but scales on a piano, but never playing a tune, does not make you a pianist. Learning only to trap and kick a ball, while never getting to play a game, does not make you a footballer. As well as acquiring skills, you need to attend to the bigger picture of why these skills are useful and get many, many opportunities to use them purposefully.

It is sometimes suggested that the growth of calculators and computers will do away with mathematics. In fact, nothing could be further from the truth. These machines *will* do away with the mindless, number-crunching part of mathematics which they are able to perform much more rapidly and accurately than humans. It is indeed true that, today, almost all 'mechanical' calculations and manipulations can be done on a machine and for this, most mathematicians rejoice. As the Russian mathematical theorist Samuil Shchatunovsky remarked, 'It is not the job of mathematicians … to do correct arithmetical operations. It is the job of bank accountants.' (Note: for this quote to make sense today, replace 'bank accountants' with 'calculators and computers'.)

> *Computing power*
> At the time of writing, and as a rough ballpark figure, an average domestic computer can execute approximately 100 million instructions per second. In 2011, the fastest computer in the world, the IBM Sequoia computer, was designed to execute up to 20 quadrillion calculations per second – that's 20 thousand, million, million (or 20 000 000 000 000 000) calculations. It is housed in the Lawrence Livermore National Laboratory in Livermore, California, and will be used for complex tasks like weather forecasting and oil exploration. This is no pocket-sized machine – it occupies 96 refrigerator-sized racks in an area the size of a big house, with a floor space of just over 300 m².

The good news is that, provided we seize the opportunity, these machines will free us up to use our brains more constructively – to think about the big ideas of mathematics and find solutions to problems when they arise. So what are these big ideas? Clearly there can never be a single definitive list, but here are five strong contenders: counting and measuring, ratio and proportion, patterns, proof and mathematical modelling.

Counting and measuring

This is where our earliest ancestors began their mathematical journey more than 30 thousand years ago. And counting and measuring are still important today. Clearly, for society to operate effectively, there is a need for standardized measuring units and in Chapter 16 you read about the evolution of some common units of measurement. It is useful to be aware that certain measures, such as length and temperature, are measured on a continuous scale and are therefore only meaningful within a certain level of precision. It is also useful to be aware that a length of 4 metres is twice as much as 2 metres, but a temperature of 4°C is not twice as hot as a temperature of 2°C.

It was due to the desire to measure *likelihood* that the discipline of probability was born. Gradually we moved from expressing ideas of chance through language (using vocabulary such as 'likely', 'probable', 'certain', and so on) to a more precise numerical scale in the range 0 to 1 (where 0 represents impossible and 1 is certain).

Ratio and proportion

Ideas of ratio and proportion abound in mathematics and in the everyday world. In Chapter 8 and elsewhere you read about the aspect ratio of rectangular shapes like cinema and TV screens. A fraction is also a ratio – the ratio of two whole numbers. The gradient (or slope) between two points on a line on a graph is calculated as the ratio of its vertical 'rise' divided by its horizontal 'run' (rise over run). All rates of change (including velocity and acceleration) are based on ratios – velocity is change of distance divided by change of time, while acceleration is change of velocity divided by change of time. An exponential change, such as the growth of world population, is where there is a fixed proportional rate of change every unit time period. With a little investigation of exponentials, you soon discover that with, say, a regular 5% increase each time period, growth may start slowly but in absolute terms keeps getting bigger and bigger until the amounts of change each interval become vast.

Patterns

Many years ago I was in a car, driving on the motorway with a friend, Dave, whose background was engineering. At one point we were overtaken by a motorcyclist and Dave remarked, 'Amazing these solid wheels, aren't they?' I asked what he meant and he explained that he was surprised that these wheels could retain their shape without the need for spokes. 'Yes, amazing,' I replied lamely. But I realized that Dave was observing something about the world that I had never even noticed. I understood very little about the design of cars and motorcycles and so had no basis on which to be surprised when something different came along.

Our *curiosity* about the things we see motivates us to achieve a better understanding of it. You see a rainbow and think, 'how stunning!' You have the choice simply to marvel at the sight or to ask questions to attempt to uncover the mechanism of what you see. With relatively simple mathematics you can understand how, as the sunlight falls on each raindrop, the rays are reflected and bent so that the white light is split into its constituent colours, each refracted at a slightly different angle. Does discovering this mechanism 'spoil the magic' or is this attitude mere aesthetic complacency?

Being curious makes us want to solve puzzles and crack codes, just for the fun of it. It causes us to examine great works of art and architecture and consider how the artists and builders could have achieved so much without the aid of modern technology. We also look at a human face and wonder what are its features that make us think it beautiful. Again, curiosity makes us question why everyday objects are designed in their present form, and leads us to speculate about the possibility of other, better alternatives. It also extends into the abstract questions that may form in our minds – such as whether there is a pattern to prime numbers or what might be the largest number I could get on my calculator with just four key presses, or whether I can work out a way of generating the Fibonacci sequence on a spreadsheet, or whether all squares are rectangles, or why, if there are 23 people in a room, there is a greater than 50% chance that at least two of them share the same birthday, or whether simply saying that pi was equal to three would make much difference, or …

Being curious is being alive.

Proof

It is in a mathematician's nature to be sceptical and to refuse to take statements at face value. For a result to be deemed 'true', no mathematician will be satisfied with the evidence of one or three or twenty or one thousand examples, as these will be dismissed as mere 'particulars'. In order to convince the demands of rigour in mathematics, a general proof is required that demonstrates the truth of the statement 'for all' possible cases. It is sometimes said that proof is the very heartbeat of mathematics and its absoluteness is what sets mathematics apart from all other subjects. However, it should be remembered that mathematical proofs are normally applied in contexts within the narrow world where mathematical objects can be defined unambiguously – not something that is easy to achieve in other fields. As Albert Einstein wrote in his book, *Sidelights on Relativity*:

> As far as the laws of mathematics refer to reality, they are not certain; and as far as they are certain, they do not refer to reality.

A variety of methods of proof were described in Chapters 27 and 28. These included proof by direct argument, visual proof, exhaustion, mathematical induction and contradiction.

Mathematical modelling

> The essence of mathematics is not to make simple things complicated, but to make complicated things simple.
>
> S. Gudder

Tackling problems (both mathematical and everyday) by stripping them down to their bare essentials is a process known as *mathematical modelling*. With simple problems for which mathematics is used in the solution, the approach can often be reduced to the following three stages.

1 Think about the problem and decide which mathematical technique to use.
2 Apply the technique.
3 Interpret the result in the context of the problem.

Here is an illustration based on the question, 'How many first-class stamps can I buy for £5?'

1 Perform a division, remembering to ensure that the units match up. (At the time of writing, a first-class stamp costs 41p.)
2 $500 \div 41 = 12.19512195$.
3 That's 12 stamps and some change. Now, how to turn that decimal remainder into working out how much change . . .

Being aware of these sorts of simple modelling steps can help us to organize and sequence our thinking for tackling problems, both everyday and mathematical.

Is maths important?

In many everyday situations there is mathematics beneath the surface, ensuring that everything works smoothly. For example, when you stop your car at the traffic lights, you can be confident, when they show green, that the lights for traffic going the other way are showing red. You enjoy the special effects on the latest 3-D movie, surf the web on your computer and use it to book a plane or theatre ticket. And when you catch that plane, you can feel confident that it will fly because the engineers who designed it understood about aerodynamics to make sure it stays up.

A surprisingly large number of people carry around in their heart a feeling of personal failure about mathematics. In a small number of cases, this comes out as hostility to the subject. But more often I hear about the desire to conquer these fears and learn more about this intriguing subject. In my job writing courses in mathematics for the Open University, I meet many adults who, through no fault of their own, had bad experiences of mathematics at school. In every case, they have chosen to confront their demons and give mathematics a second chance. Inevitably they have moments of doubt, but my advice to them is that they are different people now and so have the confidence to say, 'I don't understand' – this would have been hard to say when they were younger and in the highly public arena of a school classroom. They also have another asset, namely their knowledge of and curiosity about the world and how it operates, both of which give them a positive attitude to learning. Compared to school experience, the learning of adults is much more learner-centred and driven by their own needs and interests.

At my Open University summer schools I have met a variety of fascinating and inspiring students over the years. One, a Galway fisherman, kept his maths books in his boat and would study them when things went quiet at sea. Another elderly gentleman, who had been a farmer for many years, said he enjoyed reading mathematics aloud, a habit he learned from his long-time love of poetry. In his youth, when ploughing, he would place a poetry book at one end of the field, memorize two lines of verse and recite them aloud as he ploughed two furrows of his field. He would learn the next two lines in the same way, and so on until he had learned the entire poem – and ploughed the entire field.

Be a philosopher
George Bernard Shaw said:

> If you have an apple and I have an apple and we exchange these apples then you and I will still each have one apple. But if you have an idea as well, and we exchange these ideas, then each of us will have two ideas.

As you will have spotted from the last five chapters, thinking as a philosopher means communicating ideas logically and clearly. Here are some simple tips to polish up your thinking and communication skills.

- Avoid being dogmatic, and instead try to make statements in the spirit of offering a conjecture.
- Share your ideas with others and be prepared to listen to criticism and counter-argument.
- Always question your assumptions and try to free yourself from the restrictions of prejudice and personal point of view when examining an issue.
- Occasionally, as an exercise, try to argue the opposite of what you believe.
- Don't be afraid to voice a radical opinion, while at the same time avoiding being arrogant.
- Look out for reasoning that is logically unsound – for example, avoid arguing from the particular to the general.
- Strike a sensible balance between passion and reason.

Appendices

Appendix to Chapter 23: A formula for exponential change

To derive the formula for exponential change, you may find it helpful to start with a recognizable everyday example. So, in this appendix, you are asked to start with the calculation of compound interest and move from this numerical example to the general case.

Calculating compound interest

Suppose that £500 is invested in a deposit account that gives a fixed 4% rate of return per annum. Assuming there are no further transactions, this is how to calculate how much the investment will be worth after 10 years.

At a rate of return of 4%, by the end of 1 year the investment will have increased in value by a factor of $^{104}/_{100}$ or 1.04.

Value at the end of 1 year = £500 × 1.04.

Value at the end of 2 years = £500 × 1.04 × 1.04
$$= £500 × 1.04^2.$$

Value at the end of 10 years
$$= £500 × 1.04 × 1.04 × 1.04 × 1.04 × 1.04 × 1.04 ×$$
$$1.04 × 1.04 × 1.04 × 1.04$$
$$= £500 × 1.04^{10}$$
$$= £740.12 \text{ (rounded to the nearest penny)}.$$

A general equation for exponential growth

We started with an initial value of £500; let's generalize this to a.

We repeatedly applied a scale factor of 1.04; let's generalize this to b.

We repeated the process over 10 years; let's generalize this to t.

We ended up with an amount, £740.12; let's call this y.

This gives the general equation describing exponential growth: $y = ab^t$.

Using the equation to predict population growth

Using the general exponential formula $y = ab^t$, it is possible to make predictions about the growth of populations over time. For example, it is estimated that world population growth is currently around 1.17% each year. This means that over one year it will have increased by a factor of $^{101.17}/_{100}$ or 1.0117. Let's see how well this value matches up with population data.

The world population in 1999 was 6.1 billion. Using the formula $y = ab^t$ and assuming a rate of population growth of 1.17%, we can estimate a world population figure for eleven years later, in 2010, as follows:

$y = 6.1 \times 1.0117^{11} = 6.82$ billion.

(In fact, this is very close to the 'true' value.)

One last thing for you to try

Based on a world population of around 7 billion in 2011, and assuming an annual rate of growth of 1.17% per year, it is estimated that world population will first reach 8 billion in 2023. Check that this is correct, using an exponential model.

Solution
This is a 12-year period so t = 12.
The estimated population (billions) in 2023, y = 7 × 1.011712 = 8.05 billion.
The estimate for 2022 (i.e. for t = 11) is just below 8 billion, so this claim seems to be correct.

Appendix to Chapter 25: Plotting the Mandelbrot set

If you are interested in pursuing the mathematics of fractals a little further, this appendix sets out a brief explanation of how fractal sets are calculated and plotted.

Of all the many beautiful, coloured pictures of fractals that have adorned books, journals and web pages in recent years, the most iconic is that of the so-called 'Mandelbrot set' shown earlier (see Figure 25.1). The picture is plotted from a sequence of many thousands of numbers, based on the following simple iterative formula:

$$Z_{n+1} = Z_n^2 + c$$

In this formula, the sub-scripted letter n acts as a counter that records which value of Z we are using. Thus, the first Z value occurs when $n = 1$ and it is labelled Z_1, the second Z

value occurs when $n = 2$ and it is labelled Z_2, and so on.

Let's start with an example by choosing a particular value of c – say, $c = 0.1$. The formula therefore becomes:

$$Z_{n+1} = Z_n^2 + 0.1$$

Conventionally, the number that is first entered into the iterative process (i.e. the value of Z_1) is taken to be zero. The first six steps in the iteration (corresponding to $n = 1, 2, 3, 4, 5$ and 6) are set out in the table below:

Z_1	0
Z_2	$0^2 + 0.1 = 0.1$
Z_3	$0.1^2 + 0.1 = 0.11$
Z_4	$0.11^2 + 0.1 = 0.1121$
Z_5	$0.1121^2 + 0.1 = 0.11256641$
Z_6	$0.11256641^2 + 0.1 = 0.112671197$

As you can see from these first few iterations, the successive values are not straying too far from a value of around 0.11 – in fact, for this particular value of c of 0.1, they will quite quickly hit the value 0.112701665 and stay there, no matter how often you repeat the iteration thereafter. It is this property of the iteration producing values that settle down, rather than shooting off to infinity, that makes $c = 0.1$ a member of the Mandelbrot set.

Now let's choose a different value for c, say $c = 1$, and observe what happens under repeated iteration. Based on setting $c = 1$, the iteration equation becomes:

$$Zn_{+1} = Z_n^2 + 1$$

You can try following through the first few iterations yourself, to complete the following table. (The first step has been entered, to get you started.)

Z_1	0
Z_2	$0^2 + 1 = 1$
Z_3	
Z_4	
Z_5	
Z_6	

What can you conclude about the results of this iteration?

You should have found that the first six values of Z for the iteration formula $Z_{n+1} = Z_n^2 + c$ when $c = 1$ are: 0, 1, 2, 5, 26 and 677. In this case, the values are clearly shooting off to infinity, and so this means that $c = 1$ is *not* a member of the Mandelbrot set.

As you might expect, there are many values of c that do belong to the Mandelbrot set and many others that don't. A fractal is a graphical picture of the numerical values of c that *do* belong to this set.

Now you may be wondering how a picture in two dimensions can be formed from a string of single one-dimensional numbers. Indeed, if you had thought this, take a pat on the back, as this was a very perceptive observation! The explanation is that these numbers represented by c are not ordinary numbers but are what is known as complex numbers. Complex numbers are of the general form $a + ib$, where a and b are real numbers and i represents, the square root of minus 1. So, just as a real number can be represented as a point plotted on a one-dimensional line, complex numbers are represented in two dimensions: the 'real' part, represented by the numerical value of a, is shown as the point's x-coordinate, while the 'imaginary' part, containing the b, forms the y-coordinate.

After repeating these iterations for many thousands of numerical values of complex numbers, c, a substantial proportion of them pass the test of settling down close to the origin and these numbers form the Mandelbrot set. When plotted in two dimensions, these numbers show the classic image of the Mandelbrot set shown in Figure 25.1. Now, as you may be aware, most published fractals are displayed in an array of gorgeous colours. So what do these colours represent in terms of the Mandelbrot set? The colours provide information about the points that failed to make it into the Mandelbrot set and disappeared off the screen. A colour code records the number of iterations that took place before each of these points first passed the 'point of no return' (defined by a numerical value known as the *magnitude* which is calculated from the value of c).

1   *A complex number can be written as a + ib. What does the i represent?*

2   *For what value of a or b does the complex number a + ib become a real number?*

Solutions

1   *i is the square root of − 1.*

2   *When b = 0, the complex number a + ib becomes a real number with value a.*

Index

Image credits

Figure 0.1 © HP_Photo – Fotolia. Figure 1.1 © Peter Endig/
dpa/Corbis. Figure 1.2 from: "Clever Hans – The horse of
Mr. Von Osten: A contribution to experimental animal and
human psychology" Author: Oskar Pfungst. EBook #33936
www.gutenberg.org. Figure 6.5 © Sergiy Guk – Fotolia.
Figure 6.10 © Scott Kim. Figure 10.2 © TopFoto. Figure 22.01
© kalafoto – Fotolia. Figure 22.05 © Dean Pennala – Fotolia.
Figure 26.01 © 2003 Topham Picturepoint / TopFoto.
Figure 26.02 © AP/Press Association Images. The explorer
opening image © James Steidl – Fotolia. The artist opening
image © Steve Young – Fotolia. The gambler opening image
© Photodisc / Getty Images. The scientist opening image
© auris – Fotolia. The environmentalist opening image
© Beboy – Fotolia. The philosopher opening image © Renáta
Sedmáková – Fotolia.